Thomas Arthur Mackenzie

Historical Records of the 79th Queen's Own Cameron Highlanders

Thomas Arthur Mackenzie

Historical Records of the 79th Queen's Own Cameron Highlanders

ISBN/EAN: 9783744764643

Printed in Europe, USA, Canada, Australia, Japan

Cover: Foto ©ninafisch / pixelio.de

More available books at **www.hansebooks.com**

General Sir John Douglas, G.C.B.
Colonel of 79th Cameron Highlanders.

Regimental Colour now in use.

HISTORICAL RECORDS

OF THE

79TH QUEEN'S OWN

CAMERON HIGHLANDERS.

Compiled and Edited by

CAPTAIN T. A. MACKENZIE,

LIEUTENANT AND ADJUTANT J. S. EWART,

AND

LIEUTENANT C. FINDLAY,

FROM THE ORDERLY ROOM RECORDS.

London:
HAMILTON, ADAMS & Co., 32 PATERNOSTER ROW.

Devonport:
A. H. SWISS, 111 & 112 FORE STREET

1887.

ILLUSTRATIONS.

THE PHOTOGRAVURES

are by the London Typographic Etching Company, from Photographs and Engravings kindly lent by the Officers' and Sergeants' Messes and various Officers of the Regiment. The Photogravure of the Uniform Levee Dress, 1835, is from a Photograph of Lieutenant Lumsden, dressed in the uniform belonging to the late Major W. A. Riach.

CONTENTS.

	PAGE
PREFACE	vii
1793—RAISING THE REGIMENT	1
1801—EGYPTIAN CAMPAIGN	16
1808—PENINSULAR CAMPAIGN	27
1815—WATERLOO CAMPAIGN	54
1840—GIBRALTAR	96
1848—CANADA	98
1854—CRIMEAN CAMPAIGN	103
1857—INDIAN MUTINY	128
1872—HOME	130
1879—GIBRALTAR	161
1882—EGYPTIAN CAMPAIGN	166
1884—NILE EXPEDITION	181
1885—SOUDAN CAMPAIGN	183
SERVICES OF THE OFFICERS	203
SERVICES OF THE WARRANT OFFICERS ETC.	291
APPENDIX	307

LIST OF ILLUSTRATIONS.

		PAGE
SIR JOHN DOUGLAS	*Frontispiece*	
REGIMENTAL COLOUR	*To face*	,,
SIR NEIL DOUGLAS	*To face*	56
LA BELLE ALLIANCE: WHERE THE REGIMENT BIVOUACKED AFTER THE BATTLE OF WATERLOO	,,	58
SIR RONALD FERGUSON	,,	86
ILLUSTRATION OF LEVEE DRESS	,,	94
SIR RICHARD TAYLOR	,,	130
COLOURS PRESENTED BY THE QUEEN	,,	152
GENERAL MILLER	,,	154
COLONEL CUMING	,,	160
COLONEL LEITH	,,	172
KOSHEH FORT	,,	186
REPRESENTATIVE GROUP OF CAMERON HIGHLANDERS	,,	196

PREFACE.

A WANT has long been felt in the Regiment for some complete history of the 79th Cameron Highlanders down to the present time, and, at the request of Lieutenant-Colonel Everett, D.S.O., and the officers of the Regiment a committee, consisting of Captain T. A. Mackenzie, Lieutenant and Adjutant J. S. Ewart, and Lieutenant C. Findlay, undertook to complete Captain Jameson's Historical Record down to the present date.

The Committee, fully sensible of their own shortcomings and unfitness for the task, have attempted very little original composition, but have merely endeavoured to string together, into a consecutive narrative, the various books and manuscripts in possession of the Orderly Room.

The Records, as far as the close of the Crimean War, are, with a few slight additions, copied entirely from Captain Jameson's book, which is the foundation of the present work.

The Officers of the Regiment are much indebted to Mr. Mackenzie for his kindness in permitting them to use the valuable information contained in his "*History of the Camerons*," from which most of the details of the early life of Sir Alan Cameron are taken.

The List of Officers, Non-commissioned Officers, and Men who fought at the battle of Waterloo is taken from the old Waterloo Medal Roll, which is still in possession of the Regiment.

The manuscript Records kept during the Indian Mutiny are extremely meagre, and the Committee have to thank Quarter-Master Sergeant Mackenzie, late paymaster-sergeant of the regiment, for the details which they have been able to publish.

The account of the Campaign in Egpyt in 1882 is copied from Major Baynes' "*Narrative of the part taken by the 79th in the Egyptian Campaign of 1882.*"

The Services of the Officers are taken from the record of service books in the Orderly Room, "*Hart's Army Lists,*" and from "*Smith's List of Officers of the 79th,*" and are probably nearly complete, but it is a subject of great regret that the services of so few of the many distinguished non-commissioned officers who have been in the regiment are procurable.

The Committee are well aware that in a work of this description there must be many errors and inaccuracies, but they feel sure that all members of the regiment, past and present, will regard their efforts leniently.

The publication of the book has been undertaken by Mr. A. H. Swiss, of Devonport, who has spared no pains to meet the wishes of the officers and to produce a book worthy of the regiment.

HISTORICAL RECORDS

OF THE

79th CAMERON HIGHLANDERS.

1793.

THE 79th Regiment of Foot (or Cameron Highlanders) bears on its colours the following inscriptions and device in commemoration of its services:—" Egmont-op-Zee," " Egypt," with the Sphinx, " Fuentes d'Onor," " Salamanca," " Pyrenees," " Nivelle," " Nive," " Toulouse," " Peninsula," " Waterloo," " Alma," " Sevastopol," " Lucknow," " Egypt, 1882," " Tel-el-Kebir," " Nile, 1884-5."

At a time so highly fraught with momentous events as the early part of the long and sanguinary wars of the French Revolution, the British Ministry found itself imperatively called upon to make a large increase to the standing army of the country with the view of repelling the aggressions of revolutionised and republican France. Along with many other levies made about the same time, a letter of service, dated 17th August, 1793, was granted to Alan Cameron, Esq., of Erracht, in the county of Inverness, for the purpose of raising a Highland regiment of foot, to be numbered 79, and designated the " Cameronian Volunteers." This designation was subsequently changed to " Cameron Highlanders," " Cameronian " being a name applied to a religious sect of Lowlanders. Mr. Cameron received the commission of major in the corps about to be raised, together with the local rank of commandant thereof; and from repeal of the statute prohibiting the wearing of the Highland dress, which had been in force since 1745.

On the 17th August, 1793, in answer to several applications he had made, he received the following letter of service to raise a Highland regiment—

"Letter of service for raising the Seventy-Ninth Regiment.

"War Office, 17th August, 1793.

"SIR,

"I am commanded to acquaint you that His Majesty approves of your raising a Highland Regiment of foot, without any allowance of levy money, to be completed within three months, upon the following terms, viz :—

"The corps is to consist of one company of Grenadiers, one of light infantry, and eight battalion companies.

"The Grenadier company is to consist of one captain, two lieutenants, three sergeants, three corporals, two drummers, two pipers, and fifty-seven private men; the light infantry company of one captain, two lieutenants, three sergeants, three corporals, two drummers, and fifty-seven private men; and each battalion company of one captain, one lieutenant, one ensign, three sergeants, three corporals, two drummers, and fifty-seven private men, together with the usual staff officers, and with a sergeant-major and quarter-master-sergeant, exclusive of the sergeants above specified.

"The captain-lieutenant is, as usual, included in the number of lieutenants above mentioned.

"The corps is to have one major with a company, and is to be under your command as major with a company.

"The pay of the officers is to commence from the dates of their commissions, and that of the non-commissioned officers from the dates of their attestations.

"All the officers, the ensigns and staff officers excepted, are to be appointed from the half pay, according to their present ranks; and you will be pleased to transmit to Lord Amherst the names of the gentlemen whose appointment to your regiment you conceive will essentially conduce to the more speedy completion of the corps, taking care, however, to recommend such officers only as have not taken any difference on their being placed on half pay, and that the gentlemen recommended for ensigncies are upwards of sixteen years of age.

"In case the corps should be reduced after it has been once established, the officers will be entitled to half pay.

"No man is to be enlisted above thirty-five years of age, nor under five feet five inches high. Well made growing lads between sixteen and eighteen years of age may be taken at five feet four inches.

"The recruits are to be engaged without limitation as to the period or place of their service, but they are not to be drafted into any other regiment, and whenever the reduction is to take place they shall be marched into their own country in a corps, and disembodied therein.

"The non-commissioned officers and privates are to be inspected by a general officer, who will reject all such as are unfit for service or not enlisted in conformity to the terms of this letter.

"When established the regiment is to be called the Seventy-Ninth, or Cameronian Volunteers.

"In the execution of this service I take leave to assure you of every assistance which my office can afford.

"I have the honour to be,

"Sir,

"Your most obedient servant,

(*Signed*) "GEORGE YONGE."

"To Alan Cameron, Esq."

On receipt of this communication Major Cameron at once wrote to his father-in-law, Mr. Phillips, and was assured by him that the necessary funds could be placed at his disposal. This relieved him from his principal difficulty. The next consideration was how far it would be prudent to make the recruiting ground his own native district of Lochaber, remembering how he had left it as a fugitive from the vengeance of a considerable portion of its inhabitants. He decided to send several copies of the *London Gazette*, containing his authority to raise a Highland Regiment, to his brother Ewen, who was living in Lochaber, stating in a letter to him, "having been favoured with the honour of embodying a Highland Regiment for His Majesty's service, where could I go but to my own native Lochaber, and with that desire I have decided on appealing to their forgiveness of byegone events, and their loyalty to the Sovereign in his present exigencies. The few commissions at my disposal shall be offered to the relatives of the gentleman whose life was unfortunately sacrificed by my hand."

His brother Ewen circulated copies of the Gazette and this letter as best he could, but with such effect that, when Major Cameron arrived in Lochaber, he had already enlisted a company.

Thus the credit of raising the nucleus of the Cameron Highlanders rests with Ewen Cameron. For this service his brother obtained for him a commission as captain and recruiting officer of the regiment in Lochaber.

Major Cameron's first duty, imposed upon him by his letter of service, was to select and recommend the officers from the half pay list to be associated with him in raising the regiment. In the disposition of these he was to a certain extent under the guidance of his own inclination to have as many as he could of his old American brother officers with him. The following list of officers selected was duly submitted to the War office and approved:—

Rank.	Name.	Date of Appointment.
Major Commandant	Alan Cameron	August 17th, 1793
Major	George Rowley	April 16th, 1794
Captain	Neil Campbell	August 17th, 1793
,,	Patrick McDowall	,, 18th, 1793
,,	Donald Cameron	,, 19th, 1793
,,	George Carnegie	,, 20th, 1793
Captain-Lieutenant and Captain	Archibald McLean	,, 17th, 1793
Lieutenant	Archibald McLean	,, 17th, 1793
,,	Alexander McDonnell	,, 18th, 1793
,,	Duncan Stewart	,, 19th, 1793
,,	John Urquhart	,, 20th, 1793

Rank.	Name.	Date of Appointment.
Lieutenant	Colin McLean	January 29th, 1794
,,	Joseph Dover	March 26th, 1794
,,	Charles McVicar	,, 27th, 1794
Ensign	Neil Campbell	August 17th, 1793
,,	Gordon Cameron	,, 18th, 1793
,,	Archibald McDonnell	,, 19th, 1793
,,	Archibald Campbell	,, 20th, 1793
,,	Donald McLean	,, 21st, 1793
,,	Archibald Cameron	,, 22nd, 1793
,,	Alexander Grant	,, 23rd, 1793
,,	William Graham	,, 24th, 1793
Chaplain	Thomas Thompson	,, 17th, 1793
Adjutant	Archibald McLean	,, ,,
Quarter-Master	Duncan Stewart	,, ,,
Surgeon	John McLean	,, ,,

Reference to this list shows that Major Cameron was not unmindful of his old brother officers of the Highland Emigrant Corps, as he selected five officers of the Clan Maclean. When the half pay lists were exhausted, and he was released from the War office regulations, commissions in the regiment were always given to his Lochaber relations, as reference to the Army list in subsequent years will fully testify.

The business of raising the regiment, which was done without bounty at Major Cameron's own expense, was carried on in real earnest during the closing months of 1793, and, as it was Major Cameron's desire that the complement should be made up of as many men from his own district as possible, he and his officers visited every part round about, so that between Lochaber, Appin, Morvern, and Mull 750 men were collected at Fort William in less than two months.

The Earl of Breadalbane kindly permitted 70 or 80 men of the Breadalbane Fencibles to volunteer to the Cameron Highlanders, but, having omitted the perhaps necessary formality of asking the permission of Lord Adam Gordon (then commanding the forces in

Scotland) before doing so, Major Cameron received a peremptory order to return them to their corps.

In December, 1793, the regiment was assembled at Fort William, where it paraded for the first time, the roll being called by its first Adjutant, Archibald McLean: the ranks of the regiment were filled for the most part with men of the names of Cameron, Gunn, Maclean, and Mackay.

A few days later Major Cameron and his regiment marched out of Fort William, the pipers playing the well known air—" *Gabhaidh sinn an rathad mor*," * and proceeded to Stirling, a large crowd of the inhabitants accompanying the regiment for a considerable distance.

1794.

The regiment reached Stirling on the third day of the march at noon.

On the 3rd of January, 1794, it was inspected by Lieutenant-General Leslie, in the King's Park, at Stirling, and was passed by him as an effective corps, receiving the designation of the "79th Cameron Highlanders:" no less than 100 supernumeraries were present on parade.

On the 10th of January Major Cameron received the following letter from Lord Amherst, directing him to augment the regiment to 1,000 rank and file.

" St. James's Square,
" 10th January, 1794.

" SIR,

"I have the honour to acknowledge the receipt of your letter of the 29th, and to acquaint you that the order for augmenting your regiment to the same establishment as regiments in Ireland has received the king's approbation, and the particular directions will be transmitted to you soon.

" I am to acknowledge also your favour of the 4th instant, and a state of your regiment and a list of officers therewith enclosed, which have come to my hands this day.

" Your supernumerary men will of course make a part of your

* ' We will keep the high road."

augmentation, and you will leave such officers and parties for carrying out the recruiting service as you shall think necessary.

"I have the honour to be, etc.,

(*Signed*) "AMHERST."

"To Major Alan Cameron."

Major Cameron and some of his officers at once repaired to Lochaber, and in five-and-twenty days had raised the required number of men. When the establishment of 1,000 was completed, Major Cameron was advanced to the lieutenant-colonelcy of the regiment.

In the month of February the regiment received its colours, and shortly afterwards marched from Stirling to Portpatrick, where it embarked for Ireland and was stationed in Belfast until the month of June.

Whilst at Belfast the regiment was first issued with its uniform, which was very similar to that worn by other Highland corps, except that the facings were green. Lieutenant-Colonel Cameron however did not adopt the Cameron tartan proper as the dress of the regiment, considering that its prevailing colour red would not be suitable for wear with a scarlet tunic. He therefore introduced a tartan designed by his mother, now known as the "Cameron Erracht," which has been worn by the 79th ever since.

In June, 1794, the Cameron Highlanders were ordered to England, and, landing at Southampton, were quartered at Frome.

The new regiment was not destined to remain long in a state of inactivity, for, on the 14th August, 1794, it formed part of an expedition which embarked at Southampton under the command of Major-General Lord Mulgrave, proceeding to reinforce the combined English and Austrian army then acting against the French in Flanders, under the command of His Royal Highness the Duke of York.

The troops composing this reinforcement landed at Gorcum, near Flushing, on the 26th of August, and marched to Arnheim, then the head-quarters of the army, from whence the Cameron Highlanders were immediately despatched with other troops to reinforce the garrison of Nimeguen, then in possession of the allies. Nimeguen, however, being soon afterwards evacuated by the allied troops, the regiment shared in the subsequent disasters which attended the retreat of the army through Westphalia till its arrival at Bremen.

1795-6-7.

In the spring of 1795 the regiment embarked at Bremen, and landed in the Isle of Wight on the 12th of May, having lost in this short and inglorious campaign no less than 200 men from privation and severity of the climate.

The regiment was quartered at Newport until June, when orders were received by Colonel Cameron for its immediate completion to 1,000 rank and file, preparatory to its embarkation for India; but, whilst making every endeavour to recruit the regiment to the requisite strength, he received a private intimation that directions had been forwarded to Major-General Hunter, then commanding the troops in the Isle of Wight, to draft the Cameron Highlanders into four other regiments. Fortunately His Royal Highness the commander-in-chief happened to be at this time on a tour of inspection at Portsmouth, and Colonel Cameron lost no time in obtaining an interview with him, and respectfully but firmly remonstrated on the extreme hardship and injustice of the proposed measure, which, besides being a direct breach of faith to him personally, was also in open violation of a specific clause in His Majesty's "Letter of Service" for raising the regiment.

It is related that at this interview Colonel Cameron plainly told the Duke that "to draft the 79th is more than you or your Royal father dare do." The Duke then said: "The King, my father, will certainly send the regiment to the West Indies." Colonel Cameron, losing his temper, replied: "You may tell the King, your father, from me, that he may send us to h—— if he likes, and I'll go at the head of them, but he daurna draft us:"—a line of argument which, it is unnecessary to add, proved to the Royal Duke perfectly irresistible.

The vexatious order for drafting was rescinded, and the intended destination of the regiment changed, directions being given for it to be held in readiness to embark for the Island of Martinique in the West Indies, which had, during the previous year, been captured from the French. The regiment accordingly sailed from Cowes on this service on the 10th of July, 1795, and landed at Fort Royal on the 20th of September. It was stationed in this island, performing the most laborious duties on board infectious prison ships and in sickly quarters, until June, 1797, by which time it had become so much reduced in strength from the diseases incidental to such an unhealthy climate, that it was proposed by Sir Ralph Abercromby, the general commanding the station, who, if the manuscript records in possession of the regiment may be believed, was actuated by great personal animosity against Colonel Cameron, to send home the skeleton of the corps, consisting of the officers, sergeants, and drummers, and to draft the remaining rank and file—229 in number—to other regiments on the station. This proposition of Sir Ralph Abercromby, which Colonel Cameron strongly opposed as being most harsh and unfair, after much correspondence was peremptorily insisted upon and carried into effect as follows :—

        To 42nd Royal Highlanders - - - 217 men.
        ,, 38th Foot - - - - - 1 man.
        ,, 53rd Foot - - - - - 8 men.
        ,, 57th Foot - - - - - 2 men.
        ,, 60th Foot - - - - - 1 man.

The skeleton of the regiment accordingly embarked on board the *Coromandel*, an armed East Indiaman, commanded by Lieutenant Harrison, R.N., and sailed for England. In passing the island of Nevis the ship struck on a sunken rock, where she remained fast without any assistance for several hours. Some lighters from the island being procured, large quantities of her stores were transhipped, by which she was enabled to float off, and on arrival soon after at St. Kitts she was inspected and declared by her commander fit to proceed on her voyage. The ship arrived at Gravesend in the middle of August, 1797, when the remnant of the 79th landed and marched into Chatham Barracks. Colonel Cameron at once hastened to report his arrival to the commander-in-chief, forwarding a complaint of the manner he and his regiment had been treated. As a result, immediate orders were issued to complete the 79th, and, with a view to facilitate the recruiting in the Highlands, the regiment was removed to Inverness. So indefatigable were Colonel Cameron and his officers in their exertions during the winter of 1797, that, by the month of June, 1798, when the corps marched to Stirling, it mustered 780 men on parade exclusive of officers.

1798.

In July the Cameron Highlanders marched to Leith, where they embarked for Guernsey, and landing on the 10th of August occupied Vale Castle Barracks.

1799.

The regiment remained at Guernsey until the 23rd of June, 1799, when it embarked for England in order to form part of a second expedition to Holland under the command of His Royal Highness the Duke of York. Early in August it sailed with the first division of troops from Ramsgate, and landed on the 27th without opposition at the Helder, in North Holland, at the entrance of the Zuyder Zee. The 79th was brigaded with the 2nd Battalion Royals, 25th, 49th, and 92nd regiments, under the command of Major-General Moore. A portion of the Brigade, including the 79th, was selected to garrison the forts and batteries at Helder Point, which had been evacuated by the enemy. On the 10th of September the regiment marched to Schagen and encamped, and on the 18th joined the army near Hoorn.

At half-past six a.m. on the 2nd of October, (in pursuance of a plan of attack on the whole of the enemy's line), the 4th Division of the army, commanded by Sir Ralph Abercromby, advanced in column along the beach, for the purpose of turning his left flank, protected by a wide and broken range of sand hills, amongst which, after a march of some hours, and when within a mile of the village of Egmont-op-Zee, the enemy was found posted. Major-General Moore's brigade formed line to the left of the division, and advanced to the attack; but the hills, consisting of detached knolls of loose sand, in proportion as they favoured the enemy, by enabling him to conceal his numbers and exact position, were, by the difficulties which they opposed to the regular formation and advance of the brigade, highly unfavourable to the attacking line. A charge with the bayonet was therefore ordered, and this bold attack was executed with the greatest gallantry and success by the 79th, 92nd, 1st Royals, and 25th. The enemy was quickly driven from all parts of his position, pursued closely by the brigade to a considerable distance over the sand-hills, until darkness intervening put an end to the conflict, and the troops bivouacked for the night on the ground from which the enemy had been dislodged. The second brigade of the division and the columns of Generals Dundas and Pulteney, together with the Russian contingent under the command of Count D'Essen, were in the meantime enabled to continue corresponding movements on the enemy's centre and right, and his line being forced at every point of attack, he was compelled to retire and take up a new position between Beverwyck and Wyck-op-Zee. A complete victory was thus obtained, but, owing to the exhausted state of the troops and the difficult nature of the country, the army was prevented from following up its success by pursuit.

The loss of the regiment in this, the maiden-field of the newly raised battalion, was Captain James Campbell of the Grenadier company, Lieutenant Stair Rose, and 13 rank and file killed; Lieutenant-Colonel Alan Cameron, Lieutenants Donald McNeil and Colin McDonald, 4 sergeants, and 54 rank and file wounded; 2 rank and file missing. Colonel Cameron was shot through the arm early in the action, and later in the day was very severely wounded in the wrist, which latter wound deprived him of the use of his arm for the rest of his life.

In General Orders, dated 5th October, 1799, "Head-quarters, Alkmaar," the brigade received the thanks of His Royal Highness the commander-in-chief, who, in passing it the day after the battle, approached the 79th, and addressing Major McLean enquired for Colonel Cameron, and expressed a hope that his wound was not severe; then, turning to the officers and men of the corps, he said, "Major McLean, nothing could do the regiment more credit than its conduct yesterday!"

Some days after the thanks of Major-General Moore (who was confined from the effects of a severe wound) were communicated to the regiment—paraded for that purpose—accompanied by an expression of the general's regret that he was unable to convey them to the corps in person.

For its distinguished conduct in this action the regiment received the royal authority to have the word "Egmont-op-Zee" inscribed on its colours and appointments.

In the severe action which followed on the 6th of October in the vicinity of Alkmaar, the 79th was not engaged; and the army having retired towards Petten on the 7th, an armistice was concluded between His Royal Highness and the French General Brune, by which it was stipulated that the allied English and Russian armies should evacuate Holland.

The regiment accordingly embarked at the Texel on the 29th of October, and having landed at Yarmouth on the 1st of November, marched first to Norwich and afterwards to Chelmsford barracks.

1800.

In the month of April, 1800, the regiment was removed from Chelmsford to the Isle of Wight, where it occupied Sandown barracks until the following June, when it was removed to Southampton and encamped with other troops on Netley Common, preparatory to joining a combined naval and military expedition, then assembling under the command of Rear-Admiral Sir John Borlase-Warren, and Lieutenant-General Sir James Pulteney, with the design of destroying the Spanish arsenals and shipping in the harbours of Ferrol and Cadiz. The fleet, with the troops on board, sailed from Southampton on the 16th of August, and on the 25th of the same month arrived before Ferrol on the coast of Galicia. A debarkation was effected the same evening in a small opening near Cape Prior, a few miles north of Ferrol, whilst the men-of-war proceeded off and blockaded the mouth of the harbour.

The Rifle corps, then newly-formed by detachments from different regiments, under command of Lieutenant-Colonel Stewart, acted as an advance guard of the army, which was put in motion towards Ferrol, and ascending a ridge of hills immediately dislodged a strong body of the enemy which was favourably posted to resist its advance. The troops were occupied in gaining this position till 1 a.m. on the 26th, when, having reached the summit of the ridge, they bivouacked for the remainder of the night.

At daybreak on the following morning Major-General Morshead's brigade, consisting of the 1st and 2nd battalions of the 2nd Foot, 27th Foot, and 79th Highlanders, moved forward to support an attack made by the 52nd regiment, under Lieutenant-Colonel Kirkman, upon a considerable body of the enemy, and were assailed by a brisk fire from the Spanish troops, who, however, immediately commenced to retreat, and were pursued along the ridge to the mouth of the harbour, where, under the protection of the guns of Fort St. Philip, they were conveyed in boats to the town. The army was now in undisputed possession of the heights of Brian and Balon, which completely commanded the town of Ferrol and the shipping in its harbour; but, to the surprise of all, when complete success appeared to be within his grasp, Sir James Pulteney ordered a retreat and the troops re-embarked again on the 29th. The fleet then weighed and anchored again in Vigo Bay.

In this indecisive affair the regiment had Captain Robert Travers, two sergeants, and two rank and file wounded; and the staff of the regimental colour, carried by Ensign Cooksey, was pierced by a musket ball.

The fleet whilst anchored in Vigo Bay encountered a heavy gale, and the *Minerva* transport, with three companies of the 79th on board, narrowly escaped destruction.

On the 6th of September the fleet left Vigo, and arrived in the Bay of Gibraltar on the 19th. Here a combined naval and military expedition was organised under Admiral Lord Keith and Lieutenant-General Sir Ralph Abercromby, the latter superseding Sir James Pulteney in command of the troops, with a view to destroying the town and arsenal at Cadiz. The whole fleet then proceeded to Tetuan Bay, on the Barbary coast, where it was delayed for some time by bad weather; it eventually appeared before Cadiz on the 4th of October.

As a summons to surrender met with a prompt refusal from the governor of the city—Don Thomas de Morla—hostilities were resolved upon, and the Cameron Highlanders amongst other troops were actually in the boats ready to land and assault the town, when the enterprise was suddenly abandoned owing to threatening weather and a fear that the troops might be infected with the plague which was then raging in Cadiz.

The fleet then put to sea and arrived in Gibraltar bay on the 23rd of October, from whence it again sailed on the 4th of November, with the troops still on board, on an expedition for the expulsion of the French army in Egypt. The fleet stopped for about twenty days at Malta, during which time the 79th was encamped on shore. Whilst at Malta 279 volunteers from Highland Fencible Corps joined the regiment.

1801.

In January, 1801, the fleet rendezvoused in Marmorice Bay on the coast of Caramania, in Asia Minor, where it remained until the 23rd of February. During its stay there the Cameron Highlanders were on shore collecting wood and water. When all preparations for the descent upon Egypt were made, the fleet sailed, and dropped anchor in Aboukir Bay on the 1st of March; but from the unfavourable state of the weather it was found necessary to delay the debarkation until the 8th. At 9 o'clock on the morning of that date the troops disembarked under a severe fire from the French batteries; but the enemy being quickly repulsed and driven in the direction of Alexandria, a position was selected for the army across the peninsula of that name, at some distance in advance of the place of landing.

The period from this date until the 12th was occupied in making the necessary dispositions for an attack and in landing artillery and stores from the fleet. On the 12th the whole army moved forward in a long line extending from the Mediterranean to Lake Mareotis, driving in the French picquets, and arrived within sight of the enemy, who was occupying an advantageous ridge of sand-hills, with his right on Lake Maadie and his left on the sea, and barring the approach to Alexandria.

The 79th was brigaded with the 2nd and 50th regiments, under the command of Major-General Lord Cavan. On the morning of the 13th of March this brigade, with Major-General Craddocks' brigade on its right, was directed to attack the enemy's right flank, supported by a corresponding movement on his left and centre by the remainder of the army. The 90th and 92nd Highlanders, forming the advanced guards of the two left columns of attack, met at a short distance from the encampment with the enemy's first line, which offered a spirited resistance, causing a severe loss, and at the same time the enemy's cavalry charged the 90th, which received and repulsed this charge in line with the greatest steadiness. The British then pushed forward and charged the enemy, who was posted behind an elevated ridge of sand, and drove him from his position with the bayonet. The enemy was compelled to retreat, and withdrew, pursued by the British line, for several miles over plains of sand; ultimately he took refuge under the walls of Alexandria.

The loss of the regiment in this action was 5 rank and file killed; Lieutenant-Colonel Patrick McDowall, Lieutenants George Sutherland and John Stewart, Volunteer Allan Cameron, Surgeon Egan, 2 sergeants, and 56 rank and file wounded.

The idea of a renewed attack on the enemy being for the present relinquished, the army retired two miles, and took up a position on some high ground with its right on the sea at an old ruin called Cleopatra's Palace and its left on the Canal of Alexandria and Lake Mareotis. The time between this and the 20th was occupied in strengthening this position by redoubts and entrenchments.

During the night of the 20th a false alarm caused most of the troops to stand to their arms, and Colonel Cameron decided, as it was getting near morning, to remain under arms until daylight. Fortunate, perhaps, it was he did so, for in the grey dawn a body of the enemy suddenly surprised our advanced battery on the left. The report of the firing at once brought Lord Hopetoun, the Adjutant-General, to where the Cameron Highlanders were drawn up, and in answer to his enquiries Colonel Cameron replied, that, from the nature of the ground, it must be a false attack to favour a real one elsewhere.

Almost immediately the firing ceased suddenly on the left, and gave place to a general and uninterrupted fire on the right, thus revealing the real object of the enemy's attack. The approach of day discovered the French columns of cavalry and a numerous artillery drawn up in the plain at a short distance, when a mutual cannonade began. The light companies of the 2nd, 50th, and 79th regiments, and some dismounted dragoons were thrown out in front to hold the enemy's riflemen in check, and the contest on the right raged with

c

the greatest fury, but without any apparent result, until a sudden and formidable attack was made on the British centre by the advance of a large body of infantry in close column. This attack was most gallantly repulsed by the foot guards, under Major-General Ludlow, and the enemy, despairing of success, collected his broken and dispersed columns and withdrew to his original position.

In this engagement His Majesty's service sustained a severe loss in Lieutenant-General Sir Ralph Abercromby, who was mortally wounded towards its close. The loss of the 79th was 1 sergeant killed; Lieutenant Patrick Ross,* 2 sergeants, and 18 rank and file wounded.

The Cameron Highlanders having been transferred to Major-General Craddock's brigade, that portion of the army and a division

---

* Lieutenant Patrick Ross was a most gallant officer. His wound necessitated the amputation of his arm, but so great was his zeal and determination that within three weeks he returned to regimental duty and went on outlying picquet.

His father, Mr. William Ross, late tacksman of Brae, in Ross-shire, evinced similar qualities early in life. In the summer of 1746, when so many gentlemen who had been engaged in the rebellion were forced to take refuge in the woods and mountains, and when the troops were quartered on their estates, Ross of Pitcalney, a chieftain of the clan, was an object of more than ordinary search, having joined Prince Charlie in opposition to the remonstrances and threats of his uncle, the Lord President Forbes. As no concealment from the people was necessary, Pitcalney was in the habit of sleeping in bad weather in his tenants' houses, but always going to one or other of his hiding places before daylight in case of a search of the house by the troops. One night he slept in the farm house at Brae, and, remaining later in the morning than ordinarily, Mr. Ross, then a lad of fifteen, was directed by his father to accompany Pitcalney through the most unfrequented parts of the woods in case the troops should be stirring at that late hour of the day. The lad had performed his task, and was returning home, when he met a party of soldiers who knew him, and, suspecting where he had been, questioned him very sharply about Pitcalney's retreat. He pleaded total ignorance, and, persisting in doing so, they threatened to shoot him or hang him on the next tree—a menace which, in those times, was the usual mode of extorting confession. But this having no effect they proceeded to action, and tied him up to a tree, placing four men before him with their pieces ready to fire if he still denied what they were sensible he knew. But all in vain, neither the fear of death nor the previous preparation, which, to a boy of his age, must have been sufficiently trying, could induce him to betray the friend and landlord of his father, so strong were the principles instilled thus early by the instruction of his parents and the example of his countrymen. The party either respecting the boy's firmness, or not wishing to carry matters to extremity, released him and allowed him to go home. When he told the story, he always concluded—" When I shut my eyes, waiting to be shot, I expected to open them again in heaven." Such was the father of the brave Lieutenant Patrick Ross.

General Stewart's Book, "*History of the Highland Regiments.*"

of Turks under the Capitan-Pasha were selected to proceed to Cairo, and, after a toilsome march of many days up the left bank of the Nile, they were encountered on the evening of the 9th of May by a French force under General le Grange, near the village and fort of Rhamanieh. In this affair the light companies only were engaged, and the enemy retired towards Cairo during the night, leaving a small garrison in the fort, which surrendered at discretion the following morning. In this skirmish the regiment had Captain Samuel McDowall and 1 rank and file wounded. The division then proceeded to Cairo, where the French capitulated under a convention signed by the French General Belliard and Lord Hutchinson, and the Cameron Highlanders had the honour of being selected to take possession of the advanced gate, termed the Gate of the Pyramids, in the fortress of Ghizeh.

The army of Sir David Baird, which had arrived from India by way of the Red Sea, having been left to occupy Cairo, the Cameron Highlanders then proceeded to join the army then laying siege to Alexandria, which city, being closely invested on all sides, in a few days surrendered, and with its fall closed this short but arduous and glorious campaign, whereby a second convention was obtained resulting in the total expulsion of the French from Egypt.

For its distinguished services during the campaign, the 79th received, in conjunction with other corps, the thanks of His Majesty George III., of both Houses of Parliament, as well as of Lieutenant-General Hely Hutchinson, afterwards Lord Hutchinson and Earl of Donoughmore, who, after the death of Sir Ralph Abercromby, assumed the chief command. The regiment also received the royal authority to bear the figure of a sphinx with the word "Egypt" on its colours and appointments, in commemoration of its services. The French troops having been shipped off to Europe, the army prepared to return to England; and on the 21st October, one wing of the regiment, with many other corps, embarked and had actually sailed, when it became known to General Hutchinson that several Mameluke Beys had been perfidiously murdered by order of the Capitan-Pasha. The remaining part of the army which had also embarked, including the second wing of the 79th, was instantly re-landed, and forthwith marched to the front of the Turkish encampment near Alexandria. The Capitan-

Pasha was seized and made a prisoner in his tent, while reparation was demanded for this atrocious act committed in presence of and under the protection of the British flag. Every submission was of course tendered, and a justification attempted by alleging that he had acted in accordance with orders from his Government. The troops then finally re-embarked, and the left wing of the Cameron Highlanders proceeded to the island of Minorca, where it landed in the month of December, and joined the head-quarters of the regiment, which had in the meantime been ordered into garrison there.

1802.

The regiment was stationed in Minorca till June, 1802, when it sailed for England, and landed at Kirkcaldy, in Fifeshire, on the 2nd of August. Detachments were forthwith sent to Cupar and Dundee, and various recruiting parties despatched to the north to make up deficiences, all of which were filled up by the end of the year.

1803.

In February, 1803, the regiment moved to Ireland, where it remained performing garrison duty in different parts of the country till 1805.

1804.

In the month of April, 1804, a letter of service was granted to Colonel Cameron, at the special request of His Majesty the King, to raise a second battalion to the regiment, which was to consist of 1,000 Highlanders.

"Letter of Service to raise the second battalion 79th Regiment.

"War Office, 19th April, 1804.

"SIR,

"I have the honour to acquaint you that His Majesty has been pleased to approve of a 2nd battalion being added to the 79th regiment of foot under your command, to consist of the numbers mentioned below, and to be raised upon the following conditions, viz.—

TEN COMPANIES.

1 Lieutenant-Colonel	1 Quartermaster	1 Armourer-Sergeant
2 Majors	1 Surgeon	50 Sergeants
10 Captains	2 Assistant-Surgeons	50 Corporals
12 Lieutenants	1 Sergeant-Major	20 Drummers
8 Ensigns	1 Quartermaster-Sergt.	2 Pipers
1 Paymaster	1 Paymaster-Sergeant	950 Privates.
1 Adjutant		

"The recruiting is to be undertaken by such officers of the line as shall be selected by His Royal Highness the commander-in-chief, who are respectively to raise for their promotion the undermentioned number of recruits:—

Major, for Lieutenant-Colonel	82 men	-	82
2 Captains for majorities, each	90 „	-	180
10 Lieutenants for companies, each	45 „	-	450
12 Ensigns for Lieutenancies, each	10 „	-	120
8 Gentlemen for Ensigncies, each	21 „	-	168
Total			1000

"It is to be clearly understood that no pecuniary consideration is to be given by the officers concerned in the levy for their promotion, their personal exertions being all that is required. The men are to be enlisted without limitation as to time and place of service.

"The levy is to be completed within six months of the date of this letter.

"The officers who raise their respective quotas within the said period, and whose recruits shall have been finally approved of at the headquarters of the regiment or battalion by the general officer by whom the men will be inspected, will be recommended to His Majesty for commissions of an equal date with this letter of service.

"The officers who fail to complete their quotas within the period above specified will have no claim to promotion on this occasion, but must remain in their former ranks. Whatever recruits they may have raised are to be attached to your regiment, and for such recruits the charge of levy money as undermentioned will be admitted.

"The levy money allowed by the public to the officers raising men for promotion on this occasion will be as follows :—

Bounty for each approved recruit, including necessaries according to regulation	£10 10
Allowance to the recruiting officer for each approved recruit	£2 2
Allowance to the recruiting party for each approved recruit	£1 1

"The bounty above mentioned for the recruit is not, on any occasion, or under any pretence, to be exceeded; any officer disobeying this injunction, or deviating from the instructions under which he is raising men, will, from that circumstance, be considered absolutely to have forfeited his claim to promotion.

"Men enlisted are not to be taken above 35 years of age, nor under 5 feet 4 inches high. Growing lads under 18 years of age may be taken at 5 feet 3 inches. The greatest care is to be taken that no man be enlisted who is not stout and well made, and that the lads are perfectly well limbed and open chested.

"The greatest caution is to be taken in ascertaining that the lads who offer themselves are not apprentices; and every enquiry is to be made on this head both by the recruiting officer and by the inspecting field officer.

"It will be advisable in all cases where it is practicable to procure a certificate from the parish officer, to be annexed to the attestation, setting forth that the lad so enlisted is not, to their knowledge and belief, an apprentice; likewise specifying his age.

"In all points, not specially adverted to in this letter, you are to be guided by the established recruiting instructions of the army.

"In the execution of this service I have leave to assure you of every assistance that this office can afford.

"I have the honour to be,
"Sir,
"Your most obedient humble servant,
(Signed) "C. Bragge."

"To Colonel Cameron,
"79th Regiment of Foot."

No greater proof of Colonel Cameron's great popularity and local influence in the Highlands is needed than the fact that he raised this second battalion in a very few months.

It was never employed on active service, and merely served annually to supply the numerous vacancies occurring in the first battalion from the casualties of war. It was inspected and passed as an effective corps at Stirling on the 3rd of April, 1805, and was reduced at Dundee barracks on the 25th of December, 1815.

Whilst engaged in recruiting for this battalion, Colonel Cameron received the following letter from Henry Thorpe, Esq., then secretary to His Royal Highness the commander-in-chief, relative to a proposal to abolish the kilt as the dress of the Highland regiments:—

"Horse Guards, 13th October, 1804.

"DEAR COLONEL,

"I am directed to request that you will state for the information of the Adjutant-General, your private opinion as to the expediency of abolishing the kilt in Highland regiments, and substituting in lieu thereof the tartan trews, which have been represented to the Commander-in-Chief, from respectable authority, as an article now become acceptable to your countrymen, easier to be provided, and better calculated to preserve the health and promote the comfort of the men on service.

"I take this opportunity, by General Calvert's directions, to inform you that His Royal Highness the commander-in-chief cannot approve of any distinction in the buttons of the two battalions of the 79th regiment. Your request, in regard to the title of your regiment, His Royal Highness will submit to the King.

"I have the honour to be,

"Sir, &c.,

(Signed) "HENRY THORPE."

"To Colonel Alan Cameron."

To this letter Colonel Cameron sent the following characteristic reply:—

"Glasgow, 27th October, 1804.

"SIR,

"On my return hither some days ago from Stirling, I received your letter of the 13th inst. (by General Calvert's orders), respecting the propriety of an alteration of the mode in clothing Highland regiments, in reply to which I beg to state, freely and fully, my sentiments upon that subject, without a particle of prejudice in either way, but merely founded on facts as applicable to these corps—at least as far as I am capable, from thirty years' experience, twenty years of which have been upon actual service in all climates, with the description of men in question, which, independent of being myself a Highlander, and well knowing all the convenience and inconvenience of our native garb in the field and otherwise, and perhaps, also, aware of the probable source and clashing motives from which the suggestion now under consideration originally arose. I have to observe progressively, that in course of the late war, several gentlemen proposed to raise Highland regiments—some for general service, but chiefly for home defence; but most of these corps were called upon from all quarters, and thereby adulterated by every description of men, that rendered them anything but real Highlanders, or even Scotchmen (which is not strictly synonymous); and the colonels themselves being generally unacquainted with the language and habits of Highlanders, while prejudiced in favour of, and accustomed to wear, breeches, consequently averse to that free congenial circulation of that pure wholesome air (as an exhilarating native bracer), which has hitherto so peculiarly benefitted the Highlander for activity and all the other necessary qualities of a soldier, whether for hardship upon scanty fare, readiness in accoutring, or making forced marches,—besides the exclusive advantage, when halted, of drenching his kilt in the next brook, as well as washing his limbs, and drying both, as it were, by constant fanning, without injury to either, but, on the contrary, feeling clean and comfortable; whilst the buffoon tartan pantaloon, with its fringed frippery (as some mongrel Highlanders would have it), sticking wet and dirty to the skin, is not very easily pulled off, and less so to get on again in case of alarm or any other hurry, and all this time absorbing both wet and dirt, followed by rheumatism and fevers, which alternately make great havoc in hot and cold climates; while it consists with knowledge, that the Highlander in his native garb always appeared more cleanly, and maintained better health in both climates than those who wore even the thick cloth pantaloon.—

Independent of these circumstances, I feel no hesitation in saying that the proposed alteration must have proceeded from a whimsical idea, more than from the real comfort of the Highland soldier, and a wish to lay aside that national martial garb, the very sight of which has, upon many occasions, struck the enemy with terror and confusion, and now metamorphose the Highlander from his real characteristic appearance and comfort in an odious incompatible dress, to which it will, in my opinion, be difficult to reconcile him, as a poignant grievance to and a galling reflection upon Highland corps, as levelling that martial distinction by which they have been hitherto noticed and respected,—and from my own experience, I feel well founded in saying that if anything was wanted to aid the rack-renting Highland landlord in destroying that source which has hitherto proved so fruitful in keeping up Highland corps, it will be that of abolishing their native garb, which His Royal Highness the commander-in-chief and the Adjutant-General may rest assured will prove a complete death-warrant to the recruiting service in that respect; but I sincerely hope His Royal Highness will never acquiesce in so painful and degrading an idea (come from whatever quarter it may) as to strip us of our native garb, (admitted hitherto our regimental uniform,) and stuff us in a harlequin tartan pantaloon, which, composed of the usual quality that continues as at present worn, useful and becoming for twelve months, will not endure six weeks' fair wear as a pantaloon, and when patched makes a horrible appearance; besides that, the necessary quantity to serve decently throughout the year would become extremely expensive, but, above all, take away completely the appearance and conceit of a Highland soldier, in which case I would rather see him stuffed in breeches and abolish the distinction altogether.

"I have the honour to be, Sir, &c.,

(Signed)   "ALAN CAMERON."

"To Henry Thorpe, Esq."

This ridiculous proposal to abolish the kilt was then dropped.

1805.

The first battalion performed garrison duty in various stations in Ireland, until the month of November, when it sailed from Monkstown for England, and, landing at Ramsgate, marched to Ospringe barracks.

1806.

In the month of January, 1806, the regiment marched from Ospringe barracks to London, where it formed part of the procession attending the funeral of Vice-Admiral Lord Nelson. After the funeral the regiment marched to Colchester barracks, which it occupied till May following, when it marched to Weeley barracks.

1807.

In February the regiment moved from Weeley to Harwich barracks, when, on the 8th of April, it had the great misfortune to lose Captain Dawson, 3 Sergeants, and 56 rank and file, in crossing from Landguard Fort to Harwich, the vessel conveying them having been upset in a sudden squall.

The regiment having been completed to 1,000 rank and file by a draft from the 2nd battalion, which remained in Scotland, embarked at Harwich on the 26th of July on an expedition to be employed against Denmark, under Lieutenant-General the Earl Cathcart, and arrived in Elsinore roads on he 3rd of August. The Cameron Highlanders landed at Zealand on the 16th, and marched with other troops to Frederickswerk, in the vicinity of Copenhagen. All attempts at negotiation having failed, the trenches were opened against the City of Copenhagen on the 2nd of September, and a vigorous bombardment continued without intermission both by sea and land until the 7th, when the proposed terms were acceded to and the city capitulated. On the surrender, Colonel Cameron of the 79th was directed to take possession of the citadel with the flank companies of the army; and the objects of the expedition being fully accomplished, the troops embarked for England in the month of October. The regiment sailed in three Danish prizes, the "*Mars*," the "*Fuen*," and "*Frega*," and landed at Deal and Yarmouth in November following, proceeding to Weeley barracks.

The only casualties in the regiment during the bombardment of Copenhagen were 4 rank and file wounded.

The thanks of both Houses of Parliament were unanimously voted to the army for the manner in which this service was performed, and the following letter was received by Colonel Cameron from Lieutenant-General Lord Cathcart :—

"Gloucester Place,
"1st February, 1808.

"SIR,

"I take the earliest opportunity of transmitting to you a copy of the resolutions of the House of Lords, and those of the House of Commons, dated 28th January, 1808, which contain the thanks of both Houses of Parliament to the army lately employed in Zealand. In communicating to you this most signal mark of the approbation of the Parliament of the United Kingdom of Great Britain and Ireland, allow me to add my warmest congratulations upon a distinction which the battalion under your command had so great a share in obtaining for His Majesty's Service, together with the assurance of the truth and regard with which I have the honour to be, etc.,

(Signed)   "CATHCART,
"Lieutenant-General."

"To Colonel Cameron,
    "79th Highlanders."

1808.

In the month of May, 1808, the regiment embarked at Harwich on an expedition to Sweden, consisting of ten thousand troops, under the command of Lieutenant-General Sir John Moore, in virtue of a stipulation of the subsidiary treaty existing between Great Britain and that country. On the 17th the fleet with the troops on board dropped anchor in Gottenburgh roads, and Sir John Moore proceeded to Stockholm; but finding from the views of His Majesty, the King of Sweden, that the required service was unsuited to the limited army under his command, he refused to debark the troops, and returned to Gottenburgh, after narrowly escaping being made a prisoner by the eccentric and enraged monarch. The fleet thereupon sailed for England, and arrived at Spithead early in July, where, without being permitted to land, the Cameron Highlanders were ordered to proceed, with other reinforcements then assembling at Portsmouth under the command of Sir Harry Burrard, to join the army in Portugal operating against the French in that country. After a delay of several weeks occupied in taking in provisions and water, the fleet sailed from Spithead on the 31st of July, and on the 26th of August the regiment landed at Maceira Bay, and proceeded to join the army then encamped in the neighbourhood of Lisbon. The convention of Cintra immediately followed, producing a complete cessation of hostilities in that quarter; and the 79th, as part of Major-General Fane's brigade, was incorporated in the army, under the command of Lieutenant-General Sir John Moore, destined to co-operate with the Spanish army of the Marquis de Romana, with a view of rescuing the country from French domination.

This closed the services of Colonel Alan Cameron as a regimental officer,—the appointment of Commandant of Lisbon, together with the rank of Brigadier-General, having been conferred upon him. His personal command of the regiment therefore ceased after fifteen years of unremitting and unwearied zeal in the public service, sharing its every privation, and his almost paternal anxiety for his native Highlanders had never permitted him to be absent from their head. He finally resigned the command of the regiment into the hands of his eldest son, Lieutenant-Colonel Philips Cameron, who henceforth assumed command of the corps.

The army of Sir John Moore having advanced by rapid marches into Spain, and being joined at Mayorga by the division of Sir David Baird from Corunna, the whole proceeded as far as Sahagun; but here Sir John Moore received reliable information that three several French Corps d'Armée, one of them commanded by Napoleon in person, and each exceeding his own army in numerical strength, were advancing from different points to attack him. This information, together with the total dispersion of Romana's army, and the apathy of the Spanish authorities, determined Sir John Moore to make a retrograde movement through Gallicia, and the ever memorable although disastrous retreat to Corunna ensued, throughout which severe service the Cameron Highlanders were not exceeded in discipline and efficiency by any other corps.

1809.

In the brilliant action of Corunna on the 16th of January, 1809, the regiment had not the honour to be engaged. It belonged to the Division of Lieutenant-General Fraser, which held the heights immediately in front of the gates of Corunna, to repel any attack in that quarter; consequently it was not brought into action. The light company, however, with the other light troops of the division, was engaged in skirmishing with the enemy, near the village of Elvina, but suffered no loss.

The troops embarked successfully after the battle, and the fleet sailed that evening for England.

The gallant Sir John Moore, who was mortally wounded in the action, was buried on shore before the troops left.

When information reached Lisbon that Sir John Moore's army in Spain was being hard pressed by an overwhelming force of the enemy, Major-General Alan Cameron was ordered to advance with all the troops that could be collected to effect a junction with him. General Cameron marched on the 27th December, 1808, to Almeida, and thence for a considerable distance into Spain, when the news of Sir John Moore's retreat on Corunna placed him and his force in a most critical position. However, he successfully conducted his force back to Lisbon, although it underwent the greatest hardships and privations during the retreat. On his return to Lisbon General Cameron was confined to hospital for two months by a severe fever, induced, no doubt, by exposure.

The Cameron Highlanders landed in England in February, 1809, at Portsmouth, and marched to Weeley barracks. Here fever, probably owing its origin to causes connected with the fatigues and sufferings undergone in the recent retreat, immediately attacked the regiment, and many men fell victims to its ravages. In a few weeks, however, after its outbreak it began to decline, and in about a month entirely disappeared.

In June following, the regiment was completed to 1,000 rank and file by a draft of 258 men from the 2nd battalion; and being again in the highest order, it embarked at Harwich on the 15th of July on a combined naval and military expedition then fitting out under Admiral

Sir Richard Strachan and Lieutenant-General the Earl of Chatham, having for its object the destruction of the French arsenals and shipping on the Scheldt. During this service it was brigaded with the 11th and 50th regiments, under the command of Major-General Leith.

Having landed at Veer (which had just surrendered) on the 2nd of August, it marched through Middleburgh to the lines before Flushing, where it bivouacked in the open fields.

After an incessant bombardment from the 13th till the 15th of August, the French garrison capitulated, and marched out and laid down its arms on the 19th. In the service in the trenches the regiment suffered no loss, and on the 19th it proceeded with other troops up the Scheldt, with the design of attacking Antwerp and the fleet there; but this having been found from various causes impracticable, and the army suffering dreadfully from fever, the expedition returned to England.

During these operations in the Low Countries, a detachment of the 79th, consisting of the sick left at Lisbon when the army of Sir John Moore marched into Spain, and those left behind on the retreat to Corunna, amounting to 5 officers, 4 sergeants, and 45 rank and file—had, together with officers and men of other corps similarly situated, been formed into a corps designated the first battalion of detachments. This was placed under the command of Lieutenant-Colonel Bunbury, and was warmly engaged at the battle of Talavera on the 27th and 28th of July, 1809. The loss of the contingent of the Cameron Highlanders was very severe, being 14 rank and file killed; 1 sergeant and 27 rank and file wounded, and Lieutenant John Campbell Cameron missing,—a clear proof that it bore its full share in the brunt of battle on that hard-fought field.

Lieutenant Cameron was taken prisoner by the French, but made his escape during the night and returned to his detachment. During these operations, Major-General Alan Cameron, who commanded a brigade at the battle of Talavera, had the sad misfortune to lose the youngest of his three sons—Lieutenant Ewen Cameron of the 79th—who was acting as his aide-de-camp. He died of fever at Lisbon, brought on by hardship and exposure.

The 79th, returning from the Scheldt, disembarked at Harwich in the month of September, 1809, and marched to Weeley barracks. Notwithstanding the great mortality that prevailed in the army during the occupation of the Island of Walcheren, the regiment lost only Paymaster Baldock and one private from the effects of the climate; but, upon its return to Weeley, it is remarkable that, for the second time in the same year under nearly similar circumstances, the regiment was again attacked with fever, which occasioned several deaths; and 2 officers and 42 men not being sufficiently recovered, were left behind and transferred to the 2nd battalion when the regiment marched to Portsmouth to embark for Portugal in December following.*

1810.

The regiment, reinforced by a draft of 60 men from the 2nd battalion, was ordered to join the army acting in Portugal under the command of Sir Arthur Wellesley, and having accordingly embarked at Portsmouth in January, it arrived at Lisbon on the 31st of the same month, but had scarcely landed when it was again ordered to re-embark for Cadiz to assist in the defence of that city, which was closely blockaded on the land side by the French, under Marshal Victor.

The regiment landed at Cadiz on the 12th of February, and was quartered in the convent of "Del Carmen," in the town of La Isla de Leon, the most advanced position occupied by the British troops.

* In 1809 the 79th accomplished what no other regiment did. In January of that year they were in Spain at the battle of Corunna, and returned to England in February, when 700 men and several officers suffered from a dangerous typhus fever, yet not a man died. In July they embarked 1,002 bayonets for Walcheren, were engaged during the whole seige of Flushing in the trenches, yet had not a man wounded, and whilst there lost only one individual of fever—Paymaster Baldock, the least expected of any one.

"During the three months after their return to England, only ten men died, and in December of the same year again embarked for the Peninsula 1,032 strong."— *Vide Smith's list of officers of the 79th.*

It should, however, be stated that during the disastrous retreat to Corunna the 79th lost 90 officers, N.C. officers, and men by death or as prisoners of war.

On the 16th of March Sir Thomas Graham, intending to attack the advanced French position of the Trocadero, with a view of dislodging them from the isthmus of that name, ordered a company of the 79th, under Captain Donald Cameron, across a small river called the Sancti Pietri to effect a diversion in favour of his main attack; but this having been abandoned in consequence of the General's design being betrayed to the enemy, the company was recalled, after having Lieutenants Patrick McCrummen and Donald Cameron and 25 rank and file wounded.

The 79th continued in garrison at Cadiz until the 16th of August, when, the city being considered safe from further attack and the services of the regiment being required in Portugal, it embarked on that date and landed at Lisbon on the 29th. Having been supplied with all necessary field equipment, it was despatched up the country on the 8th of September, and joined the army, under Lord Wellington, at Busaco on the 25th, when it was brigaded with the 7th and 61st regiments under the command of Major-General Alan Cameron.

The French Army commanded by Marshal Massena having possessed itself of Ciudad Rodrigo and Almeida, had penetrated to the Sierra de Busaco, where, in order to resist his further advance, Lord Wellington had chosen a favourable position. The 79th with its division was posted on the extreme right of the line, which extended along the Sierra de Busaco. Picquets from the division forming an advanced communicating chain were thrown out in front, down the steep and rugged declivity on the crest of which the army was posted.

At daybreak on the 27th of September the French columns of attack advanced against the right of the English line with great impetuosity, headed by a swarm of skirmishers who quickly drove in the advanced posts, and from their numerical superiority had nearly surrounded and cut off the picquet of the 79th, when Captain Neil Douglas gallantly volunteered with his company to go to its support, and opening fire from a favourable position checked the enemy's advance and enabled the picquet to retire in good order. Unfortunately, however, Captain Alexander Cameron, who commanded the picquet, was killed. This gallant officer would not withdraw. He was last seen by Captain (afterwards the late Lieutenant-General Sir Neil) Douglas, fighting hand to hand with several French soldiers, to whom he refused to deliver his sword. His body was found pierced with seven bayonet wounds.

The attack in this quarter was however soon abandoned and directed chiefly upon the centre and left of the army. The regiment therefore had no further share in the subsequent operations of this victorious day. Its loss was, nevertheless, very severe in proportion to the small number engaged, being Captain Alexander Cameron and 7 rank and file killed, Captain Neil Douglas and 41 rank and file wounded, and 6 rank and file missing. Captain Neil Douglas was wounded in his shoulder, the ball being extracted on the field.

The day after the battle, Massena having made a flank march to Boyalöa to turn Lord Wellington's left, the army retreated in perfect order upon the celebrated lines of Torres Vedras, which it reached on the 8th of October, followed by the enemy, who found in them a barrier to his further advance.

This closed the long and honourable military career of that most distinguished soldier Major-General Alan Cameron after nearly forty years' service—twenty-two of which had been spent on active service in the field. Finding that his health was utterly shattered, he reluctantly resigned the command of his brigade, and proceeded to England, consoling himself with the thought that he left his devoted Highlanders under the care and guidance of his eldest son, Lieutenant-Colonel Philips Cameron.

The army remained inactive and unmolested in camp till the 14th of November, when the French army being excessively straitened for provisions, its ranks becoming constantly thinned by disease and desertion, and being wholly foiled in his project of turning the position of Torres Vedras, Massena broke up his camp silently at night and began to retire upon Santarem.

The British army followed rapidly in pursuit, by divisions, upon Alemquer, Cartaxo, and Elvalle. At Cartaxo the Cameron Highlanders were joined by a draft from the 2nd battalion of 2 sergeants and 83 rank and file, under Captain Andrew Brown.

The pursuit of the French army was continued with great activity until its arrival at Santarem, where Lord Wellington judged it inexpedient to attack it in that precipitous and formidable position.

1811.

On the 5th of March, 1811, the enemy broke up his camp at Santarem and resumed his retreat, when the army again moved forward in close and rapid pursuit. Several partial actions occurred with the French rear-guard; and in a severe skirmish at Foz d'Aronce, on the 15th of March, the light company of the 79th attached to the light division of the army was engaged from 4 p.m. until dark, when the enemy was driven across the river Ceira with great loss. In this affair, Lieutenant Kenneth Cameron of the 79th captured the lieutenant-colonel of the 39th French infantry, and conveyed him a prisoner to head-quarters. The light company had 2 rank and file killed and 7 rank and file wounded.

The enemy finally re-entered Spain on the 4th of April, and on the 2nd of May, Massena, desirous of relieving Almeida, which Lord Wellington had invested, advanced his army to a position in front of the Duas Casas and Fuentes D'Onor. The English position was a line whose left extended beyond the brook of Onoro, resting on a hill supported by fort Conception; the right, which was more accessible, was at Nave d'Aver, and the centre at Villa Formosa.

On the afternoon of the 3rd of May, Massena made various attacks upon several parts of the English position; but it soon became apparent that his grand object was to carry the village of Fuentes D'Onor, and thereby turn the British right flank. This village, which is situated in a valley, with several detached buildings on high ground at its upper extremity, was entrusted to the 71st and 79th Highlanders, with the 24th regiment and several light companies in support, the whole commanded by Lieutenant-Colonel Philips Cameron of the 79th. The enemy having advanced in great force, succeeded, from his numerical superiority, in gaining a temporary possession of several parts of the village; but after a succession of most bloody hand-to-hand encounters, he was completely driven from it at nightfall, when darkness put an end to the conflict. The various light companies were then withdrawn, leaving it occupied by the 24th, 71st, and 79th regiments.

The whole of the following day was occupied by Massena in making dispositions for a renewal of the attack, and early on the morning of the 5th the enemy again advanced in great force on several parts of the British position; but his most strenuous efforts were directed again on Fuentes D'Onor; however, notwithstanding that the whole sixth French Corps d'Armée was at different periods engaged in the attack, the enemy never succeeded in gaining more than a temporary possession of the village. Its lower portion was however completely carried, and two companies of the 79th, which had become separated from the main body in the struggle, were surrounded and made prisoners; but the troops still held the upper and much larger portion, where a fierce and bloody hand-to-hand combat was maintained with the French Imperial Guard, part of the Corps d'Elite of Napoleon Buonaparte, the Highlanders in numerous instances clubbing their muskets and using the butts instead of their bayonets, so close and deadly was the nature of the strife maintained. About this period of the action a French soldier was observed to step aside into a doorway and take deliberate aim at Colonel Cameron, who fell from his horse mortally wounded. A cry of grief and revenge arose from the Highlanders, who called in Gaelic to their comrades of the 71st, "*Thuit an Camshronach,*"* and the two Highland regiments, supported by the 88th Connaught Rangers and 74th Highlanders, hurled themselves upon the French. The excitement amongst the 88th and 74th men, who also spoke Gaelic, was intense when they heard that it was "*Cia Mar tha's*" son,† who was being carried to the rear. The French were driven with great slaughter out of the village, and the Highlanders being then withdrawn were replaced by a brigade of the light division.

During these two sanguinary days, besides Lieutenant-Colonel

* "Cameron has fallen."

† Sir Alan Cameron was known amongst the men of the Highland regiments by the soubriquet of "*Old Cia Mar tha,*" in consequence of almost invariable habit of addressing them with the Gaelic salute of "*Cia Mar tha thu*" ("How are you?")—

Mackenzie's "History of the Camerons."

Philips Cameron, mortally wounded, the Cameron Highlanders had Captain William **Imlach**, 1 sergeant, and 30 rank and file killed; Captains Malcolm Fraser and Sinclair Davidson; Lieutenants James Sinclair, John Calder, Archibald Fraser, Alexander Cameron, John Webb, and Fulton Robertson; Ensigns Charles Brown and Duncan Cameron; 6 sergeants and 138 rank and file wounded; 2 sergeants and 92 rank and file missing. After this return it was found that most of those returned as missing had been killed in the village. Captain Sinclair Davidson and 13 rank and file died of their wounds the following day.

The brevet rank of lieutenant-colonel and the distinction of a gold medal was conferred upon Major Alexander Petrie, who succeeded to the command of the regiment after Colonel Cameron was wounded; the senior captain (Andrew Brown) was promoted to the brevet rank of major in the army; and the regiment received the royal authority to bears on its colours and appointments the words "*Fuentes d'Onor*" in addition to its other distinctions. For its distinguished services the regiment likewise received the particular commendation of Lord Wellington, as proved by the following letter from the military secretary to the officer commanding :—

"Villa Formosa, 8th May, 1811.

"SIR,

"I am directed by Lord Wellington to acquaint you that he will have great pleasure in submitting to the Commander-in-Chief, for a commission, the name of any non-commissioned officer of the 79th regiment whom you may recommend, as his lordship is anxious to mark his sense of the conduct of the 79th during the late engagement with the enemy.

"I have the honour to be, etc.,

(*Signed*) "FITZROY SOMERSET."

"Major Petrie, commanding
 "79th Highlanders."

In consequence of the above communication, sergeant Donald McIntosh was recommended for a commission, and was appointed ensign in the 88th regiment on the 4th of June, 1811.

In Massena's despatch to the French war minister, giving an account of the battle, the following singular passage occurs, evincing his sense of the share borne by the Scotch regiments in his defeat on both days of the battle :—

"They (the British) lost 500 prisoners, and had more than 800 killed, among whom are many officers and Scots."

The gallant Colonel Cameron, as previously stated, was the eldest son of Major-General Alan Cameron, the founder of the corps, and an officer of much professional talent and promise. So highly was he esteemed by Lord Wellington, that his lordship, with his whole staff, and also all the generals within reach, attended his funeral, which was conducted with military honours.

Sir Walter Scott, in his "*Vision of Don Roderick*," alludes to the circumstances of Colonel Cameron's death in the following lines :—

> "And what avails thee that, for Cameron slain,
>   Wild from the plaided ranks the yell was given?
> Vengeance and grief gave mountain rage the rein,
>   And, at the bloody spear-point headlong driven,
> Thy despot's giant guards fled like the rack of heaven."

The following note to the above lines, by Sir Walter Scott, is also interesting :—

"The gallant Colonel Cameron was wounded mortally during the desperate contest in the streets of the village called Fuentes d'Onor. He fell at the head of his native Highlanders, the 71st and 79th, who raised a dreadful shriek of grief and rage. They charged with irresistible fury the finest body of French Grenadiers ever seen, being a part of Buonaparte's selected guard. The officer who led the French, a man remarkable for stature and symmetry, was killed on the spot. The Frenchman who stepped out of his rank to take aim at Colonel Cameron was also bayonetted, pierced with a thousand wounds, and almost torn to pieces by the furious Highlanders, who, under the command of Colonel Cadogan, bore the enemy out of the contested ground at the point of the bayonet."—*Note by Sir Walter Scott.*

As Colonel Cameron was much and deeply lamented, and as his character and conduct were intimately identified with that of the regiment, the following copies of letters to his father, Major-General Alan Cameron, are selected from amongst the many sent to him at that time by officers of distinction :—

"Villa Formosa,
"15th May, 1811.

"MY DEAR GENERAL,

"When I wrote to you last week, I felt that I conveyed to you information which would give you great pain; but I hoped that I made you acquainted with the fullest extent of the misfortune which had befallen you. Unfortunately, however, those upon whose judgment I relied were deceived; your son's wound was worse than it was supposed to be—it was mortal, and he died the day before yesterday at two in the morning.

"I am convinced that you will credit the assurance which I give you that I condole with you most sincerely upon this misfortune, of the extent of which no man is more capable than myself of forming an estimate, from the knowledge which I had, and the just estimate which I had formed in my own opinion, of the merits of your son.

"You will, I am convinced, always regret and lament his loss; but I hope you will derive some consolation from the reflection that he fell in the performance of his duty, at the head of your brave regiment, loved and respected by all who knew him, in an action in which, if possible, the British troops surpassed anything they had ever done before, and of which the result was most honourable to his Majesty's arms.

"At all events, if Providence had decreed to deprive you of your son, I cannot conceive a string of circumstances more honourable and glorious than those under which he lost his life in the cause of his country.

"Believe me, however, that although I am fully alive to all the honourable circumstances attending his death, I most sincerely condole with you upon your loss, and that I ever am,

"Yours most sincerely,
(*Signed*) "WELLINGTON."

"Major-General Alan Cameron, etc."

"Villa Formosa,
"15th May, 1811.

"My Dear Sir,

"If anything can alleviate the distress of mind you must now labour under, it must be the concurrent sentiments of regret and approbation of the gallant conduct of your ever-to-be-lamented son which reign throughout the whole of this army. I should forbear to have intruded upon you at this moment, if I did not believe that the expressions of these feelings would afford you a ray of consolation, and, in addition to my situation, which affords me an opportunity of knowing and detailing to you what we all experience of grief mixed with admiration, my personal regard towards you prompts me to trouble you even at such a crisis.

"Your own heroism and fortitude, my dear Sir, is now more than ever put to the test, and I fervently hope that they will carry you through your severe trial.

"I was by the side of your intrepid son, and by his equally intrepid 79th, on the evening of the 3rd, in the gallant defence of Fuentes. I witnessed him there in the hottest fire only adding to his men's excellent conduct by his coolness, foresight, and bravery. I estimated him still higher than I did before; and when I heard on the 5th of his fall at his fatal post, being myself then in another part of the field, I hardly know an event that could have occurred to have given more pain.

"We endeavoured, and Lord Wellington was the foremost, to pay him those last honours which his heroic life and conduct deserved, in the manner that could best mark the opinions we entertained of him as a brother soldier, and the loss his country had sustained by his fall.

(Signed) "Charles Stewart,
Major-General and Adjutant-General."

Mr. Mackenzie in his "*History of the Camerons*" states that the following letter from his father was found in Colonel Cameron's pocket after his death.

"London,
"20th February, 1811.

"I arrived home some few days ago after rather a rough passage to Falmouth. Captain Stanhope favoured me with his best cabin, for which I was thankful. I am glad to say that I found your sister quite well; and, now my own health has so much improved, I begin to regret having resigned my command in the army.

"Let me, however, charge you to appreciate your own position at the head of a fine regiment: be careful of the lives of the gallant fellows, at the same time that you will also hold sacred their honour, for I am sure they would not hesitate to sacrifice the one in helping you to maintain the other. I will not trouble you with more at present; but write when you can."

Massena being thus baffled in every attempt to relieve Almeida, and failing to turn the position of Lord Wellington, withdrew his army across the Agueda, leaving that fortress to inevitable capture or surrender.

The army was now put into cantonments, and the regiment occupied the village of Aldea de Ponte from the 14th of May to the 6th of June, when it marched for the camp at St. O'Laya, where it remained till the 21st of July; from thence it marched and again went into cantonments at Bemquerenca from the 11th to the 22nd of August. Here it was so severely attacked by intermittent fever and dysentery that upwards of 300 men were sent into general hospital.

On the 2nd of September the regiment moved to Mealhada de Sorda, and on the 11th to Muizella, whence it proceeded to Vellades, where it remained till the 3rd of October. It was here joined by a draft of 5 sergeants and 231 rank and file from the 2nd battalion, under command of Lieutenant-Colonel Robert Fulton, who now assumed command of the regiment.

During this month Lieutenant-Colonel Nathaniel Cameron succeeded to the command of the 2nd battalion at home. He was the only surviving son of Major-General Alan Cameron.

On the 4th of October the regiment removed to Trecas, where it continued till the 24th of November, when the troops were advanced to quarters more contiguous to the Spanish frontier, to assist in the preparations for the siege of Ciudad Rodrigo.

On the 3rd of December the regiment went into quarters at Alma Fala, within **four leagues of Ciudad Rodrigo**; but sickness still prevailing to a great extent, on account of its weak state, it was removed on the 1st of January, 1812, to Vizen, a healthier locality, where it was stationed till the 19th of February, 1812.

1812.

On the 19th of February, 1812, as the men were to a great degree recovered, the regiment was ordered into the Alemtejo to assist in covering the siege of Badajoz, and on the 14th of March it arrived in camp before Elvas. On the 16th of March the 79th, with the first division of the army, commanded by Sir Thomas Graham, crossed the Guadiana in order to check Marshal Soult, then advancing from Seville to the relief of Badajoz. On the morning of the 20th, after a forced march of twelve leagues undertaken to surprise a division of the enemy, Llerena was entered just as the French were quitting it in all haste. The troops being jaded by so long a march were incapable of successfully following them up; notwithstanding, the 42nd and 79th, with some cavalry and light guns, continued a spirited pursuit until the enemy had gained a ridge of hills running in the direction of his main body.

Badajoz having been taken by storm on the 6th of April, the regiment returned into the Alemtejo, where it continued till the 20th, when it joined the army directed against Marshal Marmont, who had made an incursion into Portugal during the siege; but upon the approach of the British to Castello Branco he retired precipitately, plundering the district through which he passed.

On the 2nd of May the 79th went into quarters at Alpalhao, where, on the 11th, it was joined by a draft of 5 sergeants and 113 rank and file from the 2nd battalion, under the command of Captain Peter Innes. On the 19th it moved to Castello de Vide, thence to Sardoal, which it left on the 1st of June to advance with the army towards the Portuguese frontier.

On the 13th the army crossed the Agueda, and on the 16th of July arrived before Salamanca. In the memorable victory achieved by the British army at the battle of Salamanca, on the 22nd of July, the Cameron Highlanders can scarcely be said to have participated. They were stationed in reserve with Major-General Campbell's division on the extreme left of the line, and were not brought into action till the close of the day. The loss of the regiment was only 2 rank and file wounded, nevertheless the services of the regiment were considered of sufficient importance to obtain the royal authority for the word "Salamanca" to be inscribed on their colours and appointments, and a gold medal was conferred on the commanding officer, Lieutenant-Colonel Robert Fulton.

On the 12th of August the allied army entered Madrid; the 79th following on the 14th with Major-General Campbell's division, when it was quartered in the Escurial. Lord Wellington having now determined to lay siege to Burgos, the army left Madrid on the 1st of September, and on the 18th arrived before that city, when preparations were at once commenced for the investment of the castle, held by a strong French garrison commanded by General Dubrêton.

On the morning of the 19th, the light battalion, formed by the several light companies of the 24th, 42nd, 58th, 60th, and 79th, commanded by Major the Honourable E. C. Cocks of the 79th, was selected for the purpose of driving the enemy from his defences on the heights of St. Michael's, consisting of a horn-work and flêches commanding the approach to the castle on the right side.

The attack was made by a simultaneous movement on the two advanced flêches, which were carried in a most gallant manner by the light companies of the 42nd and 79th; but a small post close to and on the left of the horn-work was still occupied by the enemy, from which he opened a fire upon the attacking party. Lieutenant Hugh Grant, with a detachment of the light company, was sent to dislodge him, but finding himself opposed by ever-increasing numbers, he found it impossible to advance, but equally resolved not to retire, he drew up his small party under cover of an embankment, and, possessing himself of a wounded soldier's musket, fired together with his men, and gallantly maintained the position. The remainder of the company now came up and the enemy was driven within the works;

but this brave young officer was unfortunately mortally wounded, and died a few days afterwards, sincerely and deeply regretted.

The two light companies maintained their position until night-fall, when the light battalion was assembled at this point with orders to storm the "Horn-work" at 11 p.m. A detachment of the 42nd and a Portuguese regiment were directed to enter the ditch on the left of the work, and to attempt the escalade of both demi bastions, the fire from which was to be kept in check by a direct attack in front by the remainder of the 42nd. The light battalion was to advance along the slope of the hill, parallel to the left flank of the work, which it was to endeavour to enter by the gorge. The attack by the 42nd was to be the signal for the advance of the light battalion; the command of the whole was entrusted to Major-General Sir Denis Pack.

At the appointed hour the troops moved to the assault. The light companies, on arriving at the gorge of the work, were received by a heavy musketry fire through the loop holes in the palisading, which caused severe loss; they pressed on however, and without waiting to use their felling axes and ladders, lifted the foremost men over the palisades. The first man to enter the "Horn-work" was Sergeant John McKenzie of the 79th. He was lifted over the palisades by Sergeant Masterton McIntosh of the regiment, receiving a bayonet thrust through his left arm as he reached the ground inside. He was closely followed by Major Cocks and Sergeant Masterton McIntosh and others of the storming party. In this manner, and by means of the scaling ladders, the light battalion was, in a few minutes, inside the work, and a guard of 12 men under Sergeant Donald McKenzie of the 79th having been placed at the gate leading to the castle, a charge was made upon the garrison, and a fierce struggle ensued. The French overpowered by the light battalion, rushed to the gate occupied by the small guard of the 79th. Sergeant McKenzie and his party behaved with the greatest bravery in their endeavours to prevent the escape of the French garrison. Sergeant McKenzie was very severely wounded, and Bugler Charles Bogle of the 79th was afterwards found dead at the gate near to a French soldier, the sword of the former and the bayonet of the latter through each other's bodies!

The front attack had in the meantime completely failed, and a severe loss was sustained.

The enemy now opened fire from the castle on to the "Horn-work" with showers of grape, and, as this proved most destructive, the light battalion was withdrawn to the ditch of the curtain. The storming party was then relieved by other troops, who were employed during the night in forming a parapet in the gorge.

Sergeant Donald McKenzie, who was so severely wounded, had also, it should be stated, volunteered to command the party carrying the scaling ladders, and had himself placed some of them against the palisades. He and Sergeant Masterton McIntosh were brought to the notice of Lord Wellington, and recommended for commissions. Sergeant McKenzie had previously applied to Major Cocks for the use of his dress sabre, which the major readily granted, and he related with satisfaction that the sergeant had returned it to him in a state which indicated that he had used it with effect.

"Camp Burgos,
"20th September, 1812.

"LIGHT BATTALION ORDERS.

"Major Cocks cannot pass over the events of yesterday and last night without returning his most hearty thanks to the officers, non-commissioned officers, and privates of Colonel Stirling's brigade. To praise valour which was so conspicuous is as unnecessary as to distinguish merit which was so universally displayed is impossible; but Major Cocks must say, it never was his lot to see, much less his good fortune to command, troops who displayed more zeal, more discipline, or more steady intrepidity."

After the capture of the "Horn-work," the measures taken to reduce the castle of Burgos consisted of a succession of assaults, ending, with one exception, in repulses, owing to the absence of a battering train.

In one of these assaults Major Andrew Lawrie of the 79th, a most gallant and able officer, was killed whilst entering the ditch and in the act of encouraging his storming party of Guards and Germans to the assault by escalade; and Major the Honourable E. C. Cocks met with a like fate whilst in the act of rallying his picquet during a night sortie by the French garrison.

Lord Wellington, by whom this officer was much esteemed for his bravery and early military talent, attended the funeral with his staff; and the deep sorrow which his lordship expressed was participated in by all who had known the deceased officer.

Major Cocks had been recommended for the brevet rank of lieutenant-colonel for his conduct in command of the light battalion on the 19th of September, but his death deprived him of the gratification of seeing his promotion in the Gazette.

Besides Majors Lawrie and Cocks, the Cameron Highlanders, in the various operations during the siege, had 1 sergeant and 27 rank and file killed; Captain William Marshall, Lieutenants Hugh Grant, Kewan Leslie, and Angus McDonald, 5 sergeants, 1 drummer, and 79 rank and file wounded. Lieutenant Hugh Grant died of his wounds.

The enemy, having received strong reinforcements from France, advanced from different points to raise the siege, which was now relinquished; and the British army, having broken up camp at Burgos, commenced a hasty retreat into Portugal, which it entered on the 19th of November and immediately went into winter quarters.

On the 1st of December the regiment was quartered at Vodra, where on the 25th it was joined by a draft from the 2nd battalion of 2 sergeants and 42 rank and file, under Captain William Bruce.

1813.

The regiment occupied quarters at Vodra till the 9th of February, 1813, when it moved to Sameice. On the 20th of February Lieutenant-Colonel Neil Douglas joined from the 2nd battalion, and assumed command of the regiment in succession to Lieutenant-Colonel Fulton retired, and he personally commanded it until the termination of the war.

On the 30th of April the regiment was removed to Medoens, where it was joined by a draft of 2 sergeants and 39 rank and file from the 2nd battalion, under the command of Captain Malcolm Fraser.

About the middle of May the army broke up from winter quarters to resume active offensive operations. At this time the enemy, occupying various strongly-fortified positions on the left bank of the Douro, the 79th with the left wing of the army commanded by Sir Thomas Graham, crossed the river at Torre del Moncorvo, then marched along the northern bank, while the remainder of the army advanced upon Salamanca, upon which the enemy precipitately evacuated his strong posts on both banks of the river. The army continued to advance, and on the 4th of June was concentrated between Valladolid and Palencia.

The works of Burgos, which had been so gallantly defended the preceding year, had been destroyed by the enemy, and the army moved to the left and crossed the Ebro unopposed near its source, when it advanced directly to Vittoria, where, in the general action which followed on the 21st of June, the enemy was completely routed, with the loss of all his guns, ammunition waggons, baggage, and camp equipage of every description. His flight was followed up to Pampeluna, where he left a strong garrison, and then continued his retreat to the frontiers of France.

In the honours of the battle of Vittoria the 79th had no share, as it formed part of Major-General Sir E. Pakenham's division, which was detained at Medina del Pomar to cover the train of ammunition and stores. This division immediately after the battle was directed to march upon Salvatierra, in order to intercept a strong French corps, under Marshal Clauzel, which was endeavouring to form a junction with the main body of the French army in its retreat.

Marshal Clauzel effected his escape and his desired junction with the main body of the French army, and the enemy having now concentrated his forces, and formed what he denominated l'Armée d'Espagne, again advanced in great force to the relief of Pampeluna, then closely blockaded by Lord Wellington.

Major-General Pakenham's division was therefore recalled, and, having re-joined the army on the 28th of July, took up a position across the valley of the Lanz, immediately in rear of the left of the 4th division, with its right resting on the village of Oricain and its left on the heights on the opposite side of the valley. It was scarcely formed in order of battle when it was attacked by a very superior French force, which it repulsed with severe loss. The action spreading soon became general along the heights occupied by other divisions, nearly every regiment charging with the bayonet; and the result of the battle of the Pyrenees, as this action was called, was a repulse of the enemy at all points.

The loss of the regiment was 1 sergeant and 16 rank and file killed; Lieutenant J. Kynoch, 2 sergeants, 1 drummer, and 37 rank and file wounded. Lieutenant-Colonel Neil Douglas had his horse killed under him.

For this battle the regiment received the royal authority to bear the word "Pyrenees" on its colours and appointments. Lieutenant-Colonel Neil Douglas had a gold medal conferred upon him, and Major Andrew Brown was promoted to the brevet rank of Lieutenant-Colonel for gallantry displayed when in command of the brigade picquets at the commencement of the action.

The 79th with its division followed up the enemy by Alta Biscar and Alduides, until the army finally encamped near the Pass of Mayo. Here, on the 12th of September, the regiment was joined in camp by a draft from the 2nd battalion of 2 sergeants and 40 rank and file under the command of Lieutenant Ewen Cameron. Whilst the regiment remained here the strong fortresses of St. Sebastien and Pampeluna fell. On the 9th of November the army was put in motion, and, passing the French frontier on the 10th, the regiment shared in the battle of "Nivelle," when the enemy was completely driven from the strong line of entrenchments thrown up to resist the passage of the allied army. The fine line formed by the Cameron Highlanders, when ascending the hills to meet the enemy, excited the admiration of Sir Roland Hill, who was pleased to remark the steady advance of the regiment under fire. The conduct of the regiment gained a clasp for Lieutenant-Colonel Sir Neil Douglas, who commanded it in action, and it subsequently received the royal authority to have the word "Nivelle" inscribed on its colours and appointments. Its loss was 1 rank and file killed, Ensign John Thomson and 5 rank and file wounded.

On the 16th the regiment encamped at Ustaritz, where it was joined by a draft of 4 sergeants and 46 rank and file from the 2nd battalion, under the command of Captain J. H. Christie.

On the 9th of December it advanced from Ustaritz, and on the 10th it shared in the successful attack upon the enemy's fortified line of entrenchments on both banks of the river Nive, when it had 5 rank and file killed; Lieutenant Alexander Robertson, 2 sergeants, and 24 rank and file wounded. Lieutenant-Colonel Neil Douglas had an additional clasp conferred upon him for this service, and the regiment by royal authority received permission to have the word "Nive" added to the other inscriptions on its colours and appointments.

The enemy being no longer able to cover Bayonne retired to a position on Gave d'Oleron, when the inclemency of the weather suspended all further operations. The regiment then went into quarters at St. Pierre d'Yurbe till the 20th of February, 1814, when it marched to St. Jean de Luz to receive its clothing, of which it stood greatly in need.

1814.

At this time the enemy, being compelled to abandon his position on the Gave d'Oleron, retreated upon Orthes, from which he was driven on the 25th of February with great loss, after an obstinate resistance, retreating, closely followed by the allies, on Toulouse. In the honours of the battle of Orthes the 79th did not participate, as it had not rejoined the division from St. Jean de Luz at the time.

At daybreak on the morning of the 10th of April the 6th division, under the command of Lieutenant-General Sir H. Clinton, crossed the Garonne, and, following the route of the 4th division, after a march of some hours arrived within two leagues of the enemy's encampment, when the troops were halted to cook provisions. Having by this flank movement turned the enemy's position, which was a height between and running parallel to the canal of Languedoc and the river Ers, fortified by entrenchments and redoubts, the army again resumed its march and crossed the Ers at Croix d'Orrade. Shortly afterwards the division halted near the northern extremity of the height, and arrangements were made for an attack. The 6th division, still following Sir Lowry Cole's—the 4th—advanced by the left bank of the Ers, and soon after the attack on the redoubts—de l'Est and de l'Ouest—was made by General Don Manuel Freyre's corps of Spaniards, which was drawn up in close column, headed by a complete rank of officers. These troops advanced to the attack with great steadiness, but on a near approach to the glacis of the works which were occupied by the enemy, they met with so warm a reception that they retired in the greatest disorder.

The 6th division still continued its movement, filing by threes at the double close under the enemy's guns, from which a heavy cannonade of round and grape shot was now opened, occasioning considerable loss. The Highland brigade, under Sir Denis Pack, consisting of the 42nd, 79th, and 91st regiments, to which were added the 12th Portuguese, halted about mid-way to the position, formed line to the right, and proceeded to ascend the hill. The Light companies were now ordered out to cover the brigade, General Pack bravely leading them on in person. The Grenadier company of the 79th was brought up as a reinforcement to the light troops; and after a vigorous resistance the enemy was driven to a considerable distance down the opposite slope of the ridge. The pursuit was then discontinued, and a slackened and desultory fire of advanced posts succeeded.

The brigade had, in the meantime, formed on the Balma road across the height, the light companies were recalled, and final arrangements made for an attack on the two centre redoubts of the enemy's position, designated respectively "La Colombette" and "Le tour des Augustins."

The attack of the former, or most advanced redoubt, was assigned to the 42nd, and the latter to the 79th, the 91st and 12th Portuguese being in reserve. Both these redoubts were carried at the charge in a most gallant style in the face of a terrific fire of round shot, grape, and musketry, by which very severe loss was sustained. About 100 men of the 79th, headed by several officers, now left the captured work to encounter the enemy on the ridge of the plateau; but, suddenly hearing a discharge of musketry in the redoubt captured by the 42nd in their rear, and also seeing it again in the possession of the enemy, they immediately fell back on the redoubt des Augustins. The Colombette had been suddenly attacked and entered by a fresh

E

and numerous column of the enemy, and the 42nd was compelled to give way and retire, closely followed by the enemy, along a deep narrow road leading through the redoubt des Augustins occupied by the 79th. The 79th joined in the retreat, and both regiments for a moment quitted the works.

Lieutenant Ford and seven men of the 79th were cut off in their retreat, and must have been taken prisoners but for the presence of mind of one of the privates who called out "sit down," which hint was immediately acted on, and they were mistaken for wounded—a French officer expressing his regret that he could not assist them.

At this critical juncture, Lieutenant-Colonel Douglas having re-formed the 79th, the regiment again charged the enemy, and succeeded not only in re-taking the Augustins redoubt but also the Colombette. For this service Lieutenant-Colonel Douglas received, on the field, the thanks of Generals Clinton and Pack commanding the division and brigade; and the regiments in reserve having now come up, the brigade was moved to the right, for the purpose of carrying, in conjunction with the Spaniards, the two remaining redoubts on the left of the position. While, however, the necessary preparations were being made for this attack, the enemy was observed to be in the act of abandoning them, thus leaving the British army undisputed masters of the field. The 79th spent the night in the Colombette work.

The conduct of the regiment was so highly distinguished on this occasion as to call forth the particular commendation of the Marquis of Wellington in his despatch, in which it will be observed that only four regiments are specially mentioned, all of them belonging to the sixth division; and when it is considered that the rear face of the Colombette, captured by the 42nd, commanded the city of Toulouse within half cannon-shot, and that the front face of the Tour des Augustins, captured by the 79th, commanded the valley of the Ers, the importance of the services performed by these two regiments will be at once admitted. The following extract from the despatch above alluded to will confirm these observations.

Extract from the Marquis of Wellington's despatch to Earl Bathurst, dated—

"Toulouse, 12th April, 1814.

"Marshal Beresford continued his movement along the ridge, and carried, with General Pack's brigade of the sixth division, the two principal redoubts and fortified houses in the enemy's centre. The enemy made a desperate effort from the canal to regain these redoubts, but they were repulsed with considerable loss; and the sixth division continuing its movement along the ridge of the height and the Spanish troops continuing a corresponding movement upon the front, the enemy was driven from the two redoubts and entrenchments on the left, and the whole range of heights was in our possession. We did not gain this advantage, however, without severe loss, particularly in the brave sixth division. The 30th, 42nd, 79th, and 61st regiments lost considerable numbers, and were highly distinguished throughout the day.

"The loss of the 79th was Captains Patrick Purvis and John Cameron, Lieutenant Duncan Cameron, and 16 rank and file killed; Lieutenant Colonel Neil Douglas had a horse shot under him; Captains Thomas Milne, Peter Innes, James Campbell, and William Marshall; Lieutenants William McBarnet, Donald Cameron, James Fraser, Ewen Cameron (1), Ewen Cameron (2), John Kynoch, Duncan McPherson, Charles McArthur, Allan McDonald; Ensign Allan McLean, and Lieutenant and Adjutant Kenneth Cameron, 12 sergeants, 2 drummers, and 182 rank and file wounded; 1 rank and file missing. Lieutenants William McBarnet, Ewen Cameron (2), and 23 rank and file died of their wounds within a few days of the battle.

> "'We found the heroes on the plain,
>   Their eyes were fixed, their hands were chill;
> Still bore their breasts the life-blood stain,
>   The blood was on their bonnets still,
> They died as hearts like theirs should die,
>   In the hot grasp of victory.'

"The regiment went into action 36 officers, 31 sergeants, 13 drummers, and 414 rank and file, and came out 18 officers, 19 sergeants, 11 drummers, and 215 rank and file."

Mr. Mackenzie, in his "*History of the Camerons*," publishes the following interesting letter from Lieutenant-Colonel Duncan Cameron of the 79th to Major-General Alan Cameron, written a day or two after the battle :—

"Toulouse, France,
"13th April, 1814.

"MY DEAR GENERAL,

"I take the very first opportunity I could command since our coming to this place on the 10th, to write you. We fought a heavy battle that day (Sunday) with Soult, which we fervently trust will finish this interminable contest. I am sorely grieved at the loss of so many dear relatives and comrades in this action—in which I know you will join. Your two nephews John and Ewen, my cousin Duncan, and Captain Purvis were killed, and Lieutenant McBarnet is not likely to outlive his wounds. Adjutant Kenneth Cameron is also severely wounded; indeed I think Colonel Douglas and myself are the only two among the officers that escaped. We buried Captain Purvis, John, Ewen, and Duncan in one grave, in the citadel of Toulouse, and I have ordered a memorial slab to mark their resting place. News is about that Napoleon has abdicated, but not confirmed. I will, however, write again and acquaint you of anything. I hope your own health has improved. My best regards.

"I am, yours ever sincerely,
"DUNCAN CAMERON,
"Brevet Lieut.-Colonel."

"To Major-General Cameron,
Gloucester Place, London."

In a French work, entitled "*Précis Historique de la bataille de Toulouse*," the loss of the Highland regiments of the 6th division is thus noticed; and, although much exaggerated, is worthy of observation, as showing the degree of importance attached by the enemy to the services performed by these troops:—

"Les Ecossais sur tout y firent des pertes énormes. Des debris de trois regiments n'on forma plus qu'un seul. 700 furent enterrés daus un de ces retranchements."

Lieutenant-Colonel Neil Douglas received the decoration of a gold cross for this action, in substitution of all his former decorations; Major Duncan Cameron, the brevet rank of lieutenant-colonel in the army; and the regiment by royal authority was permitted to bear on its colours and appointments the word "Toulouse," in addition to its other inscriptions. As a proof, likewise, of the distinction earned by it during the successive campaigns in the Peninsula, and for its general services throughout the war, it was subsequently authorised to have the word "Peninsula" inscribed on its colours and appointments.

The news of the abdication of Napoleon Buonaparte and the restoration of the Bourbons having been received the day after the battle, hostilities were suspended, and the regiment was quartered in several villages in the South of France. While in cantonments, it received a draft of 2 sergeants and 64 rank and file from the 2nd battalion, under the command of Captain Robert Mackay.

On the 3rd of July it embarked at Pauiliac, a small port on the Gironde, to return to England; and on the 26th of the same month it landed and marched into barracks at Cork.*

On the 25th of December following it was joined by a draft of 4 sergeants and 257 rank and file from the 2nd battalion, under the command of Captain John Sinclair; and on the 27th of January, 1815, it embarked at the Cove of Cork, together with several other regiments, destined to reinforce the army then acting in North America under the command of Lieutenant-General Sir Edward Pakenham.

1815.

On the 8th of February the expedition sailed, but was driven back the same day by contrary winds. On the 1st of March it again sailed, but adverse winds once more compelled it to put back.

On the 3rd of March the expedition to America was counter-ordered, and on the 17th the regiment sailed for the North of Ireland.

It disembarked on the 27th at Warren's point, near Newry, and from thence marched to Belfast.

The escape of Napoleon Buonaparte from Elba, and his triumphal entry into Paris, again necessitated Great Britain taking up arms against

---

* During the Peninsular war the 79th lost 650 officers, non-commissioned officers, and men, in action, from wounds, disease, &c.

France, and in the month of May the Cameron Highlanders were ordered to Flanders. The regiment marched from Belfast to Dublin, embarked on board some small craft, and sailed for the Downs, where transports were in readiness to receive it. From the Downs it sailed to Ostend, where it landed, and was conveyed along the line of canal from Bruges to Ghent. From Ghent the regiment marched to Brussels and there joined the army of the Duke of Wellington.

The 79th was brigaded with the 28th and 32nd regiments, under the command of Major-General Sir James Kempt, forming the first brigade of the 5th, or Sir Thomas Picton's, division.

At 10 o'clock on the night of the 15th of June the troops in Brussels received orders to hold themselves in readiness to march at a moment's notice. About 12 o'clock the bugles were sounding throughout the city for the troops to assemble, rations were issued for three days, and the division began its march about 4 o'clock on the following morning along the road leading to Charleroi. The mustering of the troops on this eventful night has been celebrated in one of the ablest epics our age has produced, Byron's "*Childe Harold*;" and an individual prominence has been given to the 79th in the touching and magnificent stanzas descriptive of the marshalling of the hardy warriors destined to do battle on the morrow :—

> "And wild and high the ' Camerons gathering ' rose
>   The war note of Lochiel, which Albyn's hills
> Have heard, and heard too have her saxon foes ;
>   How in the noon of night that pibroch thrills
> Savage and shrill ! but with the breath which fills
>   Their mountain-pipe, so fill the mountaineers
> With the fierce native daring which instils
>   The stirring memory of a thousand years,
> And Evan's, Donald's fame rings in each clansman's ears."

At 8 o'clock a.m. the division halted in the Forest of Soignés, near the village of Waterloo, three leagues from Brussels, and soon after the Duke of Wellington, accompanied by his staff, was observed passing to the front. The troops began to cook their provisions, but before this was done orders were given for the division to resume its march at once. Cannonading was now heard distinctly in front, and the troops pressed forward under a burning sun and amidst clouds of dust through Gemappes to Quatre Bras, where the column halted on the road and piled arms for a quarter of an hour. From a rising knoll at the head of the column a full view could be obtained of the enemy, who appeared to be advancing obliquely to the left, about half-a-mile off. A brisk cannonade was going on in the direction of the Prussian army on the left. In front a battalion of Belgians was retiring before the enemy and exchanging shots with him. In support of this battalion two companies of the Rifle brigade, attached to the division, were sent out.

The two brigades then moved to the left, lining the Namur road, the banks of which were here ten or fifteen feet high on either side. The Cameron Highlanders formed the extreme left of the British army, and the 92nd Highlanders the right of the division, being posted immediately in front of Quatre Bras. Scarcely had the division got into position when the enemy advanced to the attack. The light companies of the first brigade, with the 8th company and marksmen of the 79th, were ordered out to skirmish and keep down the fire of the enemy's sharp-shooters, which was causing a heavy loss particularly amongst the officers. It was now a quarter to three o'clock. The light companies in front maintained their ground for an hour against the ever-increasing number of the enemy; but as his sharp-shooters had by this time picked off nearly all the artillerymen who were serving the only two British guns which had as yet come into action, and as he was becoming very threatening in front, the Duke of Wellington, who was present with his staff, directed Sir Thomas Picton to detach a regiment to the front, in order to cover the guns, and drive the enemy from his advanced position. Sir James Kempt thereupon rode up to Colonel Douglas and said that the honour of executing his grace's orders would devolve on the Cameron Highlanders.

The regiment accordingly cleared the bank in front, fired a volley as it advanced, and, charging with the bayonet, drove the French advanced troops with great precipitation and in disorder to a hedge about one hundred yards in rear, where they attempted to re-form, but were followed with such alacrity that they again gave way, pursued to another hedge about the same distance, from which they were again driven in great confusion upon their main column, which was formed on the rising ground opposite. The regiment, now joined by number 8 company, halted and formed up behind the last hedge and fired volleys at the enemy until all the ammunition was expended. Whilst in this critical position it was ordered to retire, which it accomplished without confusion, although it had to re-pass the first hedge and cross a deep ditch, and formed line about fifty yards in front of its original position. Here it was ordered to lie down as it was much exposed to the enemy's fire, and it remained lying down for about an hour, when it was again ordered to its original position in the Namur road. Being afterwards repeatedly threatened by cavalry it had to move forward a little and form square.

In the meantime the other regiments of the division were warmly engaged. The Royals, 42nd, 28th, 44th, and 92nd, were repeatedly charged by the enemy's cuirassiers, who were everywhere repulsed; but, amongst the killed were Colonels Sir Robert Macara and Cameron of Fassiefern, the commanding officers of the 42nd and 92nd. Every regiment, from the sudden and peculiar nature of these attacks, was compelled to act quite independently for its own immediate defence.

The enemy's columns at length began to suffer much from the well-directed fire of the British artillery, which was now coming into action; and, as he had failed in every attack, at dusk he desisted from further fighting, and by 9 p.m. all firing had ceased.

The troops of the division proceeded to form their bivouac for the night on an open space in advance of the Namur road and the position they had occupied during the battle.

The loss of the 79th was Captain John Sinclair, Lieutenant and Adjutant John Kynoch, and 28 rank and file killed; Lieutenant-Colonel Neil Douglas, Brevet-Lieutenant-Colonels Andrew Brown and Duncan Cameron; Captains Thomas Milne, Neil Campbell, William Marshall, Malcolm Fraser, William Bruce and Robert Mackay; Lieutenants Thomas Brown, William Maddock, William Leaper, James Fraser, Donald McPhee, and William A. Riach; Ensign James Robertson, Volunteer Alexander Cameron, 10 sergeants, and 248 rank and file wounded. All the field officers, in addition to severe wounds, had their horses killed under them.

Lieut. General Sir Neil Douglas, K.C.B. K.C.H.

At daylight on the 17th the troops were in full expectation of a renewal of the attack, but a few shots only were exchanged by the picquets. At 1 o'clock p.m. a retreat was ordered by the Brussels road, and, in order to mask this movement, the light companies of the division were thrown out some distance in front. The army continued to retire, covered by the artillery and cavalry, till it had passed Genappe, when it began to rain heavily. The division then halted for about half-an-hour, and at dusk filed off the road to the right, at the farm of La Haye Sainte, and took up its position in corn fields under cover of some rising ground. From the summit of this ground a few shots were fired by the divisional artillery at the enemy's columns, as they occupied the heights opposite to the British position. The division bivouacked in the corn fields, the remainder of the army occupying the continuation of the ridge to the right and left of the division. The divisional artillery (in advance of which were strong picquets) remained posted in front for the night. The left of the division extended towards Ohaim, its right resting on the Brussels road.

It rained heavily all night, and rain was still falling when daylight broke on the morning of Waterloo.

About 8 o'clock a.m. on the 18th it began to clear up, and about 10.30 the enemy was observed to be falling in and preparing for the attack. The division awaited the approach of the enemy lying down in close column at deploying interval. The French advanced in columns under cover of a tremendous cannonade, which was answered with great spirit by the British artillery, who were posted in advance of a road which ran along the crest of the rising ground in front of the division, and on either side of which there was a hedge. Kempt's brigade then deployed into line, threw out its light troops, and advanced up to where the artillery were posted. The light companies and Rifles descended into the valley, and maintained a severe contest with very unequal numbers, until a heavy column of the enemy's infantry, driving them in, advanced direct against that portion of the line occupied by the left wing of the 79th and right wing of the 28th. Picton allowed this column to approach quite close, and then, after one volley, he charged at the head of the two regiments and drove back the French down the hill at the point of the bayonet. It was in this charge that the gallant Picton fell, shot through the temple, his last words (to his aide-de-camp) were—"Thornton, rally the Highlanders!" At this moment Sir William Ponsonby's brigade of cavalry (the 1st, 2nd, and 6th Dragoons), the Union brigade, came up, and passing through the intervals in the division, charged the broken and flying column of the enemy, capturing one eagle and many prisoners.

The Greys passed through the 92nd with loud shouts of "Scotland for ever!" the enthusiasm being so great that many of the 92nd men joined in the charge with them.

Bodies of the enemy's cavalry now advanced to the support of his infantry, and the several regiments of Kempt's brigade formed square. During this formation piper Kenneth Mackay of the 79th, a brave Highlander, stepped outside the bayonets and continued to play round the outside of the square the popular air, "*Cogadh na Sith.*" Soon afterwards the brigade was ordered to retire to its former position on the road, when it again lined the hedge nearest the enemy. Here it was exposed for some time to a galling and destructive fire, both from his artillery, directed on the British guns, and from a numerous body of sharp-shooters placed behind a bank running oblique to the right of the brigade near the Brussels road.

The enemy having failed in his former attempt, about 6 p.m. sent forward by the Brussels road large bodies of cuirassiers and other cavalry, followed by large masses of infantry. This formidable effort was principally directed against the British centre. Orders were now received by the brigade, in the event of being attacked by cavalry, to retire on the 2nd line; and the several regiments being now without a round of ammunition, exhausted by excessive fatigue and reduced to skeletons, although not actually attacked by cavalry, did fall back to the second hedge on the opposite side of the road. General Pack's brigade, however, advanced to their support, and a supply of ammunition being obtained, the regiments of Kempt's brigade again advanced and lined the front hedge. The enemy's right was now hotly pressed by the advancing Prussians, and as that just made by his cavalry and infantry on the British centre had also been brilliantly

repulsed, Napoleon launched his magnificent old guard against the British position at La Haye Sainte in hopes of still saving the battle. The overthrow of the old guard was the signal for a general retreat of the whole French army, and at about 8.20 p.m. the British line moved forward amidst loud and universal cheering.

The shattered remnant of the 79th still occupied the position it had held throughout the day; but, notwithstanding the exhausted state of the regiment, no sooner were the orders for a general advance heard than the same unconquered spirit of enthusiasm appeared to animate both officers and men. Lieutenant Alexander Cameron, who had commanded the regiment for the last two or three hours, waving his sword, called on the men to advance; and with loud cheers the debris of the regiment pressed forward, determined to maintain to the end the position it had held throughout the day.

The pursuit was continued by the Prussian cavalry; but the British halted on the ground which the enemy had occupied during the action. The Cameron Highlanders bivouacked for the night at the farm of La Belle Alliance.

The loss of the 79th was Captain John Cameron, Lieutenants Duncan McPherson, Donald Cameron, and Ewen Kennedy, 2 sergeants, and 27 rank and file killed. Captains James Campbell and Neil Campbell; Lieutenants Alexander Cameron, Ewen Cameron, Alexander Forbes, Charles McArthur, and John Powling; Ensigns A. J. Crawford and J Nash; 7 sergeants, 4 drummers, and 121 rank and file wounded,—being a total numerical loss on both days of 479, exceeding by one that of any other regiment in the army, the 3rd battalion of the 1st Foot Guards alone excepted, which was almost annihilated. Captain **Neil Campbell**, Lieutenants Donald Cameron and John Powling, and 48 men, wounded at Quatre Bras or Waterloo, died of their wounds soon afterwards.

	Officers.	Sergeants.	Drummers.	Rank & file.
Numbers engaged	41	40	11	684
Killed at Quatre Bras	2	0	0	28
Wounded at Quartre Bras	17	10	0	248
Killed at Waterloo	4	2	0	27
Wounded at Waterloo	9	7	4	121
Remaining unwounded at the close of the battle	9	21	7	260

> "La Haye, bear witness, sacred is its height,
> And sacred is it truly from that day;
> For never braver blood was spent in fight
> Than Briton here has mingled with the clay.
> Set where thou wilt thy foot, thou scarce can'st tread
> Here on a spot unhallowed by the dead.
> Here was it that the Highlanders withstood
> The tide of hostile power, received its weight
> With resolute strength, and stemmed and turned the flood;
> And fitly here, as in that Grecian strait,
> The funeral stone might say—Go traveller, tell
> Scotland, that in our duty here we fell."
>
> *Southey's "Pilgrimage to Waterloo."*

The high character which the regiment acquired at Fuentes d'Onor, Toulouse, and Quatre Bras was nobly maintained throughout this eventful day; and its conduct was mentioned in highly flattering terms in the Duke of Wellington's despatch to Earl Bathurst, dated " Waterloo, 19th June, 1815;" and it is worthy of observation, that in this despatch, as in that of the battle of Toulouse, the division of the British army to which the Scottish regiments were attached, is the only one especially mentioned. The following is an extract from the despatch above alluded to :—

"The troops of the fifth division, and those of the Brunswick corps, were long and severely engaged, and conducted themselves with the utmost gallantry. I must particularly mention the 28th, 42nd, 79th, and 92nd regiments, and the battalion of Hanoverians."

In the Prussian official despatch by Marshal Prince Blucher, dated 18th June, 1815, the distinguished conduct of the Scotch regiments is thus adverted to :—

"The English army fought with a valour which it is impossible to surpass; and the repeated charges of the old guard were baffled by the intrepidity of the Scotch regiments."

From the great loss it sustained amongst the superior officers, the command of the regiment eventually devolved upon Lieutenant Alexander Cameron, who was promoted to a company in the gazette subsequent to the battle, and afterwards to the brevet rank of major, for his very conspicuous gallantry on that occasion.

The distinction of a companionship of the Order of the Bath was conferred upon the commanding officer, Lieutenant-Colonel Neil Douglas, Brevet Lieutenant-Colonel Andrew Brown, and Brevet Lieutenant-Colonel Duncan Cameron; Captain Thomas Milne, the senior captain, was promoted by brevet to be a major in the army; each surviving officer and soldier engaged either at Quatre Bras or Waterloo received the decoration of the silver "Waterloo" medal, and was allowed to reckon two additional years' service, whilst it is almost superfluous to add that the regiment received the royal authority to bear the word "Waterloo" on its colours and appointments, in commemoration of its services on this glorious day.

The following is a complete list of the officers, non-commissioned officers, and men who served in the ranks of the Cameron Highlanders at the battles of Quatre Bras and Waterloo:—

STAFF.

Lieutenant-Colonel	Neil Douglas ...	Severely wounded.
Major and Brevet Lieutenant-Colonel	Andrew Brown...	Ditto
,, ,, ,,	Duncan Cameron ...	Ditto
Lieutenant and Adjutant	John Kynoch ...	Killed.
Quarter-Master	Angus Cameron ...	
Surgeon	John Ridesdale...	
Assistant-Surgeon	W. G. Burrell ...	
,,	David Perston ...	
Paymaster	John McArthur ...	
Acting-Adjutant-Lieutenant	George Harrison	
Sergeant-Major	Masterton McIntosh	
Quarter-Master-Sergeant	James Hay ...	
Paymaster-Sergeant	William Lane ...	
Armourer-Sergeant	John Morris ...	
Schoolmaster-Sergeant	William Gray	

GRENADIERS.

Captain	Neil Campbell ...	Died of wounds.
Lieutenant	Alexander Cameron	Wounded.
,,	William Leaper	Severely wounded.
,,	Duncan McPherson	Killed.
Colour Sergeant	James McQueen	Killed.

GRENADIERS—(continued).

Sergeant	Thomas Campbell	Slightly wounded.
,,	Gordon Cowie	
,,	Alexander Gunn	
,,	Colin McDonald	Slightly wounded.
Corporal	William Astbury	Killed.
,,	John Mowat	Killed.
,,	Rose Campbell	
,,	George McNie	
,,	John Walton	Severely wounded.
Private	Donald Andrew	
,,	George Beekie	Severely wounded.
,,	William Black	
,,	Ebenezer Brown	Severely wounded.
,,	David Buckley	Severely wounded.
,,	Henry Burns	
,,	Donald Cameron (1st)	Severely wounded.
,,	Donald Cameron (2nd)	Killed.
,,	Duncan Cameron	Killed.
,,	Donald Campbell (1st)	Severely wounded.
,,	Donald Campbell (2nd)	Killed.
,,	Neil Campbell	
,,	Mark Clarke	Severely wounded.
,,	William Cormick	Dangerously wounded.
,,	Daniel Dillon	
,,	Peter Dunbar	Dangerously wounded.
,,	Samuel Fervel	Slightly wounded.
,,	John Fraser	
,,	John Gall	Severely wounded.
,,	Daniel Gibbons	Killed.
,,	Alexander Gow	Severely wounded.
,,	Alexander Gray	
,,	John Hayter	
,,	David Henderson	
,,	Walter Henderson	Killed.
,,	John How	Killed.
,,	Peter Hutton	
,,	William Harvey	Severely wounded.
,,	James Kerr	Severely wounded.
,,	Robert Jeffrey	Killed.
,,	Thomas Kirkwood	Severely wounded.
,,	John Kennedy	Severely wounded.

79TH CAMERON HIGHLANDERS.

GRENADIERS—(continued).

Private	Peter McArthur	Slightly wounded.
,,	Charles Luss	Killed.
,,	Alexander McLennan	Died of wounds.
,,	Hugh McCaskill	Severely wounded.
,,	Alexander McDonald	Killed.
,,	John McDonald	
,,	Donald McIntosh	Dangerously wounded.
,,	Charles McIntosh	Severely wounded.
,,	Peter McInroy	
,,	Robert McInnes	
,,	Donald McGillivray	
,,	Kenneth McKay	
,,	Robert McKay (1st)	Severely wounded.
,,	Robert McKay (2nd)	Severely wounded.
,,	James McGill	Died of wounds.
,,	John McKechnie	
,,	John McLean	
,,	John McMillan	Killed.
,,	John McPherson	Severely wounded.
,,	Peter McLaren	Slightly wounded.
,,	Allan McLachlan	Slightly wounded.
,,	Neil McPherson	Severely wounded.
,,	John McPhee	Slightly wounded.
,,	William Manson	Severely wounded.
,,	Donald Munro	Killed.
,,	Alexander Moss	
,,	John Moorhead	Severely wounded.
,,	John Mowat	Dangerously wounded.
,,	Thomas Murray	Severely wounded.
,,	Andrew Noble	
,,	Thomas Noble	Severely wounded.
,,	Robert Phillips	Killed.
,,	James Raggs	Severely wounded.
,,	John Reid	
,,	Alexander Ritchie	
,,	David Ross	
,,	Alexander Stewart	Slightly wounded.
,,	Donald Sutherland	Severely wounded.
,,	Hugh Sutherland	Killed.
,,	James Sutherland	
,,	Daniel Southwale	Killed.

GRENADIERS—(*continued.*)

Private	William Swanson	Severely wounded.
,,	Archibald Taylor	Severely wounded.
,,	William Williamson	Severely wounded.

No. I.

Captain	William Bruce	Severely wounded.
Lieutenant	A. Forbes	Slightly wounded.
,,	Donald McPhee	Slightly wounded.
Ensign	A. S. Crawford	Slightly wounded.
Sergeant	Hugh Bannerman	
,,	Ewen Mackenzie	
,,	George Sinclair	
,,	William Swanson	
,,	David Taylor	
Corporal	John McLellan (1st)	Severely wounded.
,,	John McLellan (2nd)	Severely wounded.
,,	John O'Neil	Severely wounded.
Private	William Adams	Slightly wounded.
,,	William Allan	Slightly wounded.
,,	James Anderson	
,,	Thomas Armstrong	Slightly wounded.
,,	George Bain	Killed.
,,	Charles Boag	
,,	George Brian	
,,	John Bruce	Dangerously wounded.
,,	Alexander Cameron	Slightly wounded.
,,	John Cameron	
,,	Angus Campbell	
,,	George Coghill	
,,	William Coleman	Severely wounded.
,,	James Coventry	
,,	James Diver	Severely wounded.
,,	Angus Dickson	
,,	James Givan	Severely wounded.
,,	John Grant	Severely wounded.
,,	Archibald Hamilton	
,,	Archibald Henderson	
,,	James Hume	Slightly wounded.
,,	Stephen Hunt	Slightly wounded.
,,	William Johnston	Severely wounded.

79TH CAMERON HIGHLANDERS.

No. I.—(continued).

Rank	Name	Status
Private	James Jack	Killed.
,,	George Jeffray	
,,	David Kinnaird	
,,	Hugh McBinnie	
,,	John McCetrick	Slightly wounded.
,,	William McReady	
,,	Colin McIntosh	Severely wounded.
,,	George McKay (1st)	
,,	George McKay (2nd)	
,,	Neil McKay	Severely wounded.
,,	George Mackenzie	Severely wounded.
,,	James McLellan	Severely wounded.
,,	Angus McLeod	
,,	Hugh McLeod	Severely wounded.
,,	James McLeod	Killed.
,,	Roderick McLeod	
,,	John McLongish	
,,	James Marshall	
,,	William Martin	Slightly wounded.
,,	Samuel Mitchell	Severely wounded.
,,	Henry Munro	Slightly wounded.
,,	Thomas Moon	
,,	Thomas Mully	Killed.
,,	James Nesbit	Severely wounded.
,,	Thomas Owens	
,,	John O'Neil	Severely wounded.
,,	James Rae	
,,	James Robertson	Slightly wounded.
,,	James Scott	
,,	Andrew Sheddon	Severely wounded.
,,	John Wemyss	Severely wounded.
,,	Thomas Whiteside	Slightly wounded.

No. II.

Rank	Name	Status
Lieutenant	John Powling	Died of wounds.
,,	James Cameron	
Ensign	McPhee	
Colour-Sergeant	Peter Grant	
Sergeant	Lachlan MacLachlan	
,,	John McCrumman	
,,	James McGowan	

F

No. II.—(continued).

Rank	Name	Status
Sergeant	Hugh Cameron	Killed.
Corporal	Colin Henderson	Severely wounded.
,,	Hugh Love	Dangerously wounded.
,,	John McLeod	Slightly wounded.
,,	Angus Bruce	Slightly wounded.
Drummer	James McKay	
Private	James Atkins	
,,	Gilbert Ayre	
,,	Thomas Brakenridge	
,,	Angus Bince	Severely wounded.
,,	George Burgess	
,,	Robert Calder	
,,	Alexander Campbell	Slightly wounded.
,,	John Campbell (1st)	Slightly wounded.
,,	John Campbell (2nd)	Severely wounded.
,,	Alexander Clowes	
,,	William Cummings	Severely wounded.
,,	Daniel Ewart	Severely wounded.
,,	James Fairweather	
,,	David Fish	
,,	Alexander Fraser	Severely wounded.
,,	John Hastie	Killed.
,,	David Harden	Severely wounded.
,,	John Hayes	
,,	Charles Heathy	
,,	Jonathan Hazel	
,,	James Killoch	
,,	David Laird	Severely wounded.
,,	William Lithgow	Severely wounded.
,,	William Lane	Killed.
,,	Magnus Larnoch	Killed.
,,	Donald McBain	Severely wounded.
,,	John McCulloch	Severely wounded.
,,	Donald McKay	
,,	Peter McKinnon	Killed.
,,	Donald Mackenzie	
,,	James Mackenzie	Severely wounded.
,,	John McLeod	Severely wounded.
,,	Norman McLeod	Severely wounded.
,,	Angus McMillan	
,,	John McMillan	Killed.

No. II.—(continued).

Private	Alexander Morton	...	Slightly wounded.
,,	David McWhinnie	...	
,,	Henry Neil	...	
,,	Edward Roberts	...	
,,	James Robertson (1st)	...	
,,	James Robertson (2nd)	...	Severely wounded.
,,	Thomas Robertson	...	
,,	Joseph Southall	...	
,,	John Stark	...	Slightly wounded.
,,	Charles Stewart	...	
,,	Donald Sutherland	...	Slightly wounded.
,,	Thomas Train	...	Killed.
,,	Robert Varmen	...	
,,	John Westwood	...	
,,	Alexander Weir	...	
,,	Robert Young	...	
,,	William McKay	...	
,,	Robert Ashton	...	Killed.

No. III.

Captain	Thomas Mylne	...	Severely wounded.
Lieutenant	W. Maddock	...	Severely wounded.
,,	Ewen Cameron	...	Severely wounded.
Ensign	C. J. McLean	...	
Sergeant	John Cummings	...	Slightly wounded.
,,	John Gray	...	Slightly wounded.
,,	Alexander Lamont	...	Severely wounded.
,,	William Gurney	...	Died of wounds.
Corporal	Andrew Horn	...	
,,	James Mowatt	...	Severely wounded.
,,	William Newbigging	...	Slightly wounded.
,,	Peter Ross	...	Slightly wounded.
,,	James Marshall	...	Killed.
Drummer	John Broughall	...	
,,	Peter Campbell	...	
Private	William Allan	...	Slightly wounded.
,,	Alexander Anderson	...	
,,	William Anderton	...	
,,	William Baird	...	
,,	James Barr	...	Dangerously wounded.
,,	John Blunt	...	Slightly wounded.
,,	Thomas Bryson	...	Slightly wounded.

No. III.—(continued).

Private	Matthew Boyd	
,,	David Binst	
,,	Duncan Cameron	
,,	William Campbell	
,,	Michael Connell	
,,	George Drysdale	Slightly wounded.
,,	John Easton	Slightly wounded.
,,	James Fisher	Dangerously wounded.
,,	John Guyler	Dangerously wounded.
,,	McBain Hamilton	Slightly wounded.
,,	Thomas Henderson	
,,	William Horton	
,,	John Johnston	Slightly wounded.
,,	Edward Kelly	Slightly wounded.
,,	Norman Leslie	
,,	John Lumsden	Slightly wounded.
,,	Donald McColl	Dangerously wounded.
,,	Murdoch McCraw	Dangerously wounded.
,,	Charles McDonald	Severely wounded.
,,	Dugald McDonald	Dangerously wounded.
,,	John McDonald	
,,	Malcolm McDonald	Severely wounded.
,,	Norman McDonald	
,,	Murdoch McFarlane	Dangerously wounded.
,,	Hugh McGillivray	Slightly wounded.
,,	John McGregor (1st)	Severely wounded.
,,	John McGregor (2nd)	Severely wounded.
,,	Peter McIntosh	Dangerously wounded.
,,	Donald McKain	Dangerously wounded.
,,	John McKay	Severely wounded.
,,	George McKenzie	Dangerously wounded.
,,	William McKenzie	
,,	John McKinnon	
,,	Alexander McMillan	
,,	John McNaughten	
,,	Archibald Martin	
,,	William May	
,,	John Miller	Dangerously wounded.
,,	James Mills	
,,	William Miller	Dangerously wounded.
,,	Thomas Mitchell	

No. III.—(continued.)

Private	Hugh O'Donnelly	
,,	John Patterson	Severely wounded.
,,	James Penman	
,,	Robert Petrie	Severely wounded.
,,	James Rogers	
,,	James Shaw	Severely wounded.
,,	John Shaw	
,,	Norman Shaw	Dangerously wounded.
,,	John Smith	Dangerously wounded.
,,	John Taylor	Slightly wounded.
,,	Andrew Thompson	
,,	Neil Turner	Taken prisoner.
,,	James Walsh	

No. IV.

Captain	John Sinclair	Died of wounds.
,,	Robert Mackay	Severely wounded.
Lieutenant	Ewen Kennedy	Killed.
Ensign	James Robertson	Severely wounded.
,,	Alexander Cameron	Severely wounded.
Colour-Sergeant	William McKay	
Sergeant	John Malcolm	
,,	John Murray	Severely wounded.
,,	Samuel Owens	
Corporal	John Donald	
,,	Gavin Hamilton	
,,	Alexander McKay	Severely wounded.
,,	George McPherson	
Private	William Abercrombie	
,,	Michael Alexander	
,,	Peter Angus	
,,	Donald Banks	Died of wounds.
,,	James Barton	Severely wounded.
,,	Samuel Bergam	
,,	John Birnie	Severely wounded.
,,	Joseph Bogle	
,,	Donald Cameron	Severely wounded.
,,	James Campbell	
,,	William Campbell (1st)	
,,	William Campbell (2nd)	

No. IV.—*(continued)*.

Private	William Cooper	Severely wounded.
,,	Thomas Crawford	Killed.
,,	John Fitton	
,,	Andrew Flockart	Severely wounded.
,,	Roderick Fraser	
,,	John Graham	Severely wounded.
,,	Adam Gray	
,,	David Glasgow	
,,	Donald Grant	
,,	John Hamilton	
,,	William Harley	Severely wounded.
,,	William Heatley	Severely wounded.
,,	James Heath	Slightly wounded.
,,	George Henderson	
,,	William Henderson	
,,	John Innes	Slightly wounded.
,,	James Jamieson	Slightly wounded.
,,	Peter Johnson	
,,	John Kennedy	
,,	John King	
,,	Michael Loftus	
,,	Samuel McCunne	
,,	John McDonald	
,,	Thomas McDonald	
,,	James McIntosh	Slightly wounded.
,,	William McIntosh	
,,	Donald McKay	
,,	William McKellar	Killed.
,,	James McKenzie	Slightly wounded.
,,	Kenneth McKenzie	Severely wounded.
,,	Angus McLean	Severely wounded.
,,	James McPherson	
,,	Archibald Mills	Severely wounded
,,	James Paton	Slightly wounded.
,,	Alexander Paterson	Slightly wounded.
,,	John Pirrie	
,,	Peter Pringle	Severely wounded.
,,	John Ross (1st)	
,,	John Ross (2nd)	Slightly wounded.
,,	Robert Russell	Severely wounded.
,,	Thomas Shaw	

No. IV.—(continued).

Private	David Sinclair	Slightly wounded.
,,	James Sutherland	Severely wounded.
,,	William Sutherland	Severely wounded.
,,	Archibald Taylor	
,,	George Wardrop	
,,	Matthew Young	

No. V.

Captain	Peter Innes	
Lieutenant	James Fraser	Severely wounded.
,,	W. A. Riach	Severely wounded.
Colour-Sergeant	John Gibb	Severely wounded.
Sergeant	Neil McIntosh	
,,	George Manuel	Severely wounded.
,,	James White	
Corporal	John Barnett	Severely wounded.
,,	Archibald Clelland	
,,	Donald Fraser	Severely wounded.
,,	Hugh Love	Dangerously wounded.
Drummer	Robert Baldwin	Severely wounded.
,,	John Manners	
Private	Alexander Alexander	Severely wounded.
,,	John Adam	
,,	George Adams	
,,	John Bain	
,,	Alexander Bannerman	Slightly wounded.
,,	William Binnie	Severely wounded.
,,	George Black	
,,	John Blair	
,,	James Brown	Severely wounded.
,,	Thomas Brown	
,,	Matthew Brand	
,,	William Calder	Slightly wounded.
,,	Donald Cameron	Severely wounded.
,,	George Cameron	Slightly wounded.
,,	Alexander Campbell	Killed
,,	William Clarke	Slightly wounded.
,,	George Coghill	
,,	James Dyke	
	James Fairlie	

No. V.—(continued).

Rank	Name	Status
Private	Andrew Falconer	
,,	William Farms	
,,	William Finnie	
,,	Angus Ferguson	Severely wounded
,,	Robert Fletcher	
,,	John Forbes	Killed.
,,	John Gibson	Severely wounded.
,,	James Galloway	Severely wounded.
,,	Peter Grant	
,,	Donald Gunn	Severely wounded.
,,	Alexander Henry	
,,	William Kelly	
,,	Alexander Johnson	Severely wounded. (Died)
,,	Alexander Johnstone	
,,	John Laurie	Severely wounded.
,,	Andrew Lee	
,,	William Lyall	
,,	Alexander McDonald	
,,	James McDonald	
,,	Kenneth McDonald	Severely wounded.
,,	Duncan McGibbon	
,,	Timothy McGunigall	
,,	Michael McKale	Severely wounded.
,,	Alexander McKay	
,,	Holt McKenzie	Dangerously wounded.
,,	John McLeod	
,,	John McLaren	Severely wounded.
,,	William Malcolm	
,,	John Manuel	Dangerously wounded.
,,	John Miller	Died of wounds.
,,	Douglas Mills	Slightly wounded.
,,	James Paterson	Slightly wounded.
,,	John Reid	
,,	William Reid	
,,	George Shaw	Severely wounded.
,,	Nathaniel Scott	
,,	William Stewart	Severely wounded.
,,	John Watson	
,,	Adam Wars	
,,	John Wildie	Dangerously wounded.
,,	Robert Winton	Severely wounded.

79TH CAMERON HIGHLANDERS.

No. VI.

Rank	Name	Status
Captain	James Campbell	Severely wounded.
Lieutenant	John Thompson	
,,	Donald Cameron	Died of wounds.
Ensign	Archibald Cameron	
Colour-Sergeant	James Black	
Sergeant	William Lambell	Severely wounded.
,,	Sinclair Henderson	Severely wounded.
,,	William Lever	Severely wounded.
Corporal	John Gardiner	
,,	John Kennedy	
,,	Duncan McGregor	Slightly wounded
,,	Angus Morton	
,,	James Rowan	Severely wounded.
Drummer	Thomas McDonald	
Private	Thomas Archibald	
,,	John Atkins	Severely wounded.
,,	Thomas Bramner	
,,	Alexander Campbell	
,,	David Campbell	Severely wounded.
,,	Peter Carrick	Killed.
,,	Neil Campbell	
,,	Matthew Cowan	Severely wounded.
,,	John Fife	
,,	Frederick Finlay	Slightly wounded.
,,	William Finlayson	
,,	John Forster	
,,	Donald Gollan	Severely wounded.
,,	Thomas Gibbing	
,,	Donald Grant	Severely wounded.
,,	George Gray	
,,	John Gray	Severely wounded.
,,	George Gwilliam	Slightly wounded.
,,	William Gunn	Severely wounded.
,,	John Harley	
,,	John Hogg	Slightly wounded.
,,	John Houston	
,,	William Humphries	
,,	William Kerr	
,,	Duncan McCuig	
,,	Charles McDonald	Severely wounded.

No. VI.—(continued).

Private	Daniel McGinnerty	Severely wounded.
,,	Denis McGinnerty	
,,	Alexander McIntosh	Killed.
,,	Alexander McKay	
,,	Angus McKay (1st)	Severely wounded.
,,	Angus McKay (2nd)	
,,	George McKay	
,,	Donald McKenzie	
,,	Donald McLeod	
,,	John McPherson	
,,	David McQuattie	Killed.
,,	Andrew Morgan	
,,	William Morland	
,,	James Mowat	Severely wounded.
,,	Charles Munro	
,,	Angus Murray	Severely wounded.
,,	James Robertson	Severely wounded.
,,	Robert Shaw	Severely wounded.
,,	Archibald Smith	Severely wounded.
,,	Alexander Smith	
,,	William Smith	Severely wounded.
,,	Noble Sproul	
,,	Lachlan Stewart	Severely wounded.
,,	John Stewart	Severely wounded.
,,	James Stratton	Severely wounded.
,,	James Stone	Severely wounded.
,,	Donald Taylor	Slightly wounded.
,,	Henry Travers	Severely wounded.
,,	Dixon Vallance	Severely wounded.
,,	William Walton	Severely wounded.
,,	David Watt	Severely wounded.
,,	Alexander White	
,,	William Wilson	Severely wounded.
,,	John Reid	Severely wounded.

No. VII.

Captain	John Cameron	Died of wounds.
Lieutenant	Charles McArthur	Slightly wounded.
,,	John Mackenzie	
Colour-Sergeant }	Duncan McDonald	

79TH CAMERON HIGHLANDERS.

No. VII.—(continued).

Rank	Name	Status
Sergeant	Donald Mackenzie	Dangerously wounded.
,,	Charles Rose	Dangerously wounded.
,,	John Sutherland	
Corporal	James Barclay	Severely wounded.
,,	Duncan Grant	
,,	David Kerr	
,,	John McDonald	Dangerously wounded.
Drummer	William Christmas	
,,	James McColl	Severely wounded.
Private	Robert Anderson	
,,	Travers Baillie	
,,	Andrew Barrie	
,,	William Bee	Dangerously wounded.
,,	Joseph Brothers	
,,	William Brummage	
,,	William Carradice	
,,	Thomas Chrystal	
,,	James Culross	Severely wounded.
,,	Charles Craig	
,,	John Dempster	Dangerously wounded.
,,	John Donnelly	Severely wounded.
,,	Colin Fletcher	Severely wounded.
,,	Hugh Fraser	
,,	John Fletcher	
,,	Jesse Fulton	Severely wounded.
,,	Charles Gore	Dangerously wounded.
,,	Adam Gordon	Slightly wounded.
,,	Andrew Greig	Dangerously wounded.
,,	Edward Hieson	
,,	Robert Hill	
,,	John Hutchison	Killed.
,,	James Jamieson	Dangerously wounded.
,,	Robert Keldy	Dangerously wounded.
,,	Andrew Kennedy	
,,	William Kennedy	Killed.
,,	Angus Kerr	
,,	Thomas Kirkbride	Slightly wounded.
,,	John Macbain	Slightly wounded.
,,	Gilbert McArthur	Killed.
,,	Donald McColl	Dangerously wounded.
,,	Duncan McFarlane	

No. VII.—(continued).

Rank	Name	Status
Private	David McGregor	
,,	Robert McGregor	Died of wounds.
,,	David McIntosh	
,,	Peter McIntyre	Slightly wounded.
,,	John McIvor	Slightly wounded.
,,	George McKay	
,,	Hugh McKay	
,,	Ewen McKenzie	
,,	Donald McKercher	Severely wounded.
,,	James McLaren	
,,	Hugh McLennan	Severely wounded.
,,	Donald McLeod	
,,	Donald McPherson	Severely wounded.
,,	Robert Munro	
,,	Peter Munool	
,,	William Mitchell	
,,	Alexander Mulligan	
,,	Charles Paterson	
,,	James Pollock	
,,	Alexander Reid	Slightly wounded.
,,	William Reid	Dangerously wounded.
,,	Allan Scott	
,,	William Sutherland	
,,	William Swanson	
,,	John Watson	Dangerously wounded.
,,	Henry Wheeler	Severely wounded.
,,	Robert White	

No. VIII.

Rank	Name	Status
Captain	Malcolm Fraser	Severely wounded.
Lieutenant	Kewan Leslie	
Ensign	John Nash	Slightly wounded.
Colour-Sergeant	William Baxter	Severely wounded.
Sergeant	Peter McLaughlin	Severely wounded.
,,	Donald Sutherland	Slightly wounded.
,,	John Wright	Slightly wounded.
Corporal	Thomas Birch	Slightly wounded.
,,	James Campbell	Slightly wounded.
,,	Alexander Clarke	
,,	Jeffrey Goddard	**Severely wounded.**

79TH CAMERON HIGHLANDERS.

No. VIII.—(continued).

Rank	Name	Status
Corporal	George McKenzie	Severely wounded.
,,	Alexander Stewart	Severely wounded.
,,	Henry Fogerberry	Slightly wounded.
Private	David Allan	
,,	William Athos	Slightly wounded.
,,	William Calder	Slightly wounded.
,,	Donald Campbell	Severely wounded.
,,	Thomas Clifton	
,,	James Cooper	
,,	Archibald Cumming	Severely wounded.
,,	Henry Dargan	
,,	David Duncan	
,,	Robert Elliot	
,,	Donald **Faulkner**	Killed.
,,	Robert Ferguson	Slightly wounded.
,,	Thomas Finner	Severely wounded.
,,	Roderick **Grant**	Severely wounded.
,,	James Hill	Killed.
,,	Samuel Hinney	Slightly wounded.
,,	James Inglis	
,,	Allan Irons	Slightly wounded.
,,	Thomas Jackson	Severely wounded.
,,	James Kerr	Severely wounded.
,,	John Lamont	Slightly wounded.
,,	William Lightbody	Severely wounded.
,,	Abraham Keshaw	Killed.
,,	John McDonald (1st)	Severely wounded.
,,	John McDonald (2nd)	Killed.
,,	James McDonald	
,,	Robert McGillivray	Slightly wounded.
,,	Robert McIndoe	Slightly wounded.
,,	William **McIntosh**	Severely wounded.
,,	James McKay	Killed.
,,	Robert McKay	Slightly wounded.
,,	William McKay	
,,	John McKenzie (1st)	Slightly wounded.
,,	John McKenzie (2nd)	Killed.
,,	William McKechnie	
,,	Isaac McKenzie	
,,	Lachlan McLachlan	Severely wounded.
,,	Ewen McLachlan	Killed.

No. VIII.—(continued).

Private	John McLeod	...
,,	Neil McMillan	Slightly wounded.
,,	Donald McPhee	Slightly wounded.
,,	John Mulchrist	Slightly wounded.
,,	John Neil	Slightly wounded.
,,	Robert Neil	Slightly wounded.
,,	William Paul	...
,,	David Ross	Slightly wounded.
,,	William Robertson	Killed.
,,	Robert Sinclair	Severely wounded.
,,	Thomas Stewart	Severely wounded.
,,	John Walker	Severely wounded.
,,	John Wands	Severely wounded.
,,	Daniel Weir	Severely wounded.
,,	Donald Williamson	Severely wounded.
,,	William White	Severely wounded.
,,	Colin Cameron	Slightly wounded.

LIGHT COMPANY.

Captain	William Marshall	Severely wounded.
Lieutenant	Thomas Brown	Severely wounded.
,,	Fulton Robertson	
Colour-Sergeant	William Dewar	
Sergeant	Donald McPhee	...
,,	Donald McLeod	Severely wounded.
,,	Finlay Robertson	Severely wounded.
,,	Charles Campbell	
,,	Angus McKay	Severely wounded.
Corporal	James Aitchison	Severely wounded.
,,	John Burns	Severely wounded.
,,	Angus Kennedy	
,,	Matthew Lithgow	Dangerously wounded.
,,	John McKenzie	
,,	George Sutherland	
Drummer	Thomas Bently	
Private	James Atcherson	
,,	David Bannerman	Severely wounded.
,,	James Bramer	Severely wounded.
,,	John Blithe	Killed.
,,	John Brockie	Severely wounded.

LIGHT COMPANY—(continued).

Private	John Bruce	Killed.
,,	Lachlan Campbell	
,,	Archibald Campbell	Severely wounded.
,,	William Chambers	
,,	Robert Clelland	Slightly wounded.
,,	William Clunes	
,,	Henry Cormich	Severely wounded.
,,	Alexander Cruikshank	
,,	George Cowie	Severely wounded.
,,	Benjamin Davidson	Severely wounded.
,,	Matthew Dickie	
,,	James Duffy	Severely wounded.
,,	John Doyle	Severely wounded.
,,	John Dunn	
,,	Thomas Gardner	Severely wounded.
,,	John Gibson	Severely wounded.
,,	Donald Gunn	
,,	John Gunn	Severely wounded.
,,	Matthew Hayes	
,,	George Hill	
,,	Murdoch Jack	Severely wounded.
,,	Henry Jolly	
,,	John Lachlan	Severely wounded.
,,	William Lennox	Severely wounded.
,,	John Lloyd	
,,	Donald McDonald (1st)	Slightly wounded.
,,	Donald McDonald (2nd)	Slightly wounded.
,,	James McDonald	Dangerously wounded.
,,	Andrew McEwen	
,,	Duncan McFarlane	Severely wounded.
,,	Alan McGillivray	
,,	Swain McIntosh	
,,	Murdoch McIntyre	
,,	Donald McKay	
,,	Charles McKay	Severely wounded.
,,	William McKay (1st)	Severely wounded.
,,	William McKay (2nd)	
,,	Donald McKenzie	
,,	Lachlan McKinnon	
,,	Donald McLeod	Severely wounded.
,,	Duncan McLeod	Severely wounded.

LIGHT COMPANY—*(continued)*.

Private	John McLeod (1st)	...
,,	John McLeod (2nd)	Severely wounded.
,,	William McMillan	Severely wounded.
,,	Charles McPherson	Severely wounded.
,,	James McPheaters	Slightly wounded.
,,	Alexander McTavish	...
,,	James McMiller	...
,,	George Moor	..
,,	Peter Mungan	...
,,	Allan Nesmyth	
,,	James Pocock	Severely wounded.
,,	William Poole	
,,	Donald Ross	
,,	John Ross	...
,,	David Scott	
,,	William Sherrat	
,,	William Shaw	Killed.
,,	Matthew Shepherd	Killed.
,,	James Smith	Severely wounded.
,,	Donald Sutherland	Severely wounded.
,,	John Sutherland	Slightly wounded.
,,	William Thorburn	Severely wounded.
,,	Peter Wardrop	Severely wounded.
,,	David White	Slightly wounded.
,,	James Young	Severely wounded.
,,	Connor McColl	...
,,	Andrew Fyne	Killed.
,,	William Rose	Slightly wounded.
,,	John Smallbrook	Severely wounded.
,,	George Sutherland	Slightly wounded.

On the 19th the regiment advanced with the army in pursuit of the enemy, and on the 8th of July it arrived at Clichy, near to which it encamped within a league of Paris, the capitulation of which, together with the surrender of Napoleon to Captain Maitland, R.N., closed a war which, for its duration, its sanguinary character, and the combination of events it involved, is unparalleled in history.

On the 24th of July, 1815, the army was reviewed by the Emperors of Austria and Russia, the King of Prussia, the distinguished allied Commanders, and a great concourse of English and Foreign nobility.

On the 5th of August a draft of four sergeants and 88 rank and file joined from the 2nd battalion, under the command of Captain James Campbell. In compliance with a special request from the Emperor of Russia, who was personally desirous of examining the dress and equipments of the Highland regiments, on the 17th of August Sergeant Thomas Campbell of the Grenadiers, a man of gigantic stature, with Private John Fraser and Piper Kenneth Mackay, all of the 79th, accompanied by a like number of each rank from the 42nd and 92nd Highlanders, proceeded to the Palace Elysée in Paris, then the residence of the Emperor Alexander. The following is Sergeant Campbell's account of what took place at this presentation :—

"In the month of August, 1815, I was ordered to proceed, with Private John Fraser and Piper Kenneth Mackay, to the Palace Elysée in Paris, then the residence of the Emperor of Russia, where we were joined by Sergeant McGregor, Private Munro, and Piper McKenzie, of the 42nd Highlanders, and Sergeant Grant, Private Logan, and Piper Cameron, of the 92nd Highlanders. About half-an-hour after our arrival at the Palace, Lord Cathcart sent a valet to conduct us to the grand hall, where we met his lordship, whom I immediately recognised. He was pleased to order me to take charge of the party while he went to the Emperor to acquaint him of our arrival, and in about ten minutes after the Emperor entered the hall accompanied by his two brothers, as well as Prince Blucher, Count Plutoff, and several other distinguished personages. The Emperor made a very minute inspection of us, and his curiosity led him to call upon me, as being the most robust of the party, to step to the front, when he ordered the rest to sit down. As soon as I stepped to the front I was surrounded by the astonished nobility, and the Emperor commenced his inspection and questions as follows : First, he examined my appointments and drew my sword ; inquired if I could perform any exercise with that weapon, which I told him I could not, and at the same time Lord Cathcart made a remark that it was a deficiency in the British army which he had never taken into consideration before.

"Second, he examined my hose, gaiters, legs, and pinched my skin, thinking I wore something under my kilt, and had the curiosity to lift

G

my kilt up to my navel, so that he might not be deceived. The questions were: If I was present at the actions of the 16th, 17th, and 18th of June? How many officers and men the regiment lost on the 16th, 17th, and 18th of June? Whether I was in Egypt? If I wore the kilt in winter, or if I did not feel cold in that season? If I was married? If my parents were alive?

"The Emperor then requested Lord Cathcart to order me to put John Fraser through the "manual and platoon" exercise, at which performance he was highly pleased. He then requested the pipers to play up, and Lord Cathcart desired them to play the Highland tune, "*Cogadh na Sith*," which he explained to the Emperor, who seemed highly delighted with the music.

"After the Emperor had done with me, the veteran Count Plutoff came up to me, and, taking me by the hand, told me in broken English that I was a good and brave soldier, as all my countrymen were. He then pressed my hand to his breast, and gave me his to press to mine. After all was over, I was ordered to take the party to Lord Cathcart's quarters, where we had refreshment, and received a piece of money each from his lordship, and also his approbation for our appearance.

(*Signed*) "THOMAS CAMPBELL,
"Sergeant, 79th Highlanders."

Finally, the 79th having been one of those regiments selected to remain in France for three years with the army of occupation, it was formed into a brigade with the 4th and 52nd regiments, under the command of Sir Denis Pack, and added to the 2nd division of the army, commanded by Lieutenant-General Sir H. Clinton.

On the 10th of December, 1815, it proceeded to occupy cantonments in the Pas de Calais, where it remained for the three following years in perfect harmony with the inhabitants.

On the 25th of December, 1815, the second battalion was reduced at Dundee barracks.

During the residence of the regiment in France as a part of the British contingent it was successively reviewed with the other corps of the army of occupation by the Emperor of Russia, the King of Prussia, their Royal Highnesses the Dukes of Kent and Cambridge, and the Duke of Wellington.

1818.

At length so profound a tranquillity pervaded France, that the allied Sovereigns agreed to withdraw their respective contingents. On the 29th of October, 1818, the Cameron Highlanders arrived at Calais, where they embarked for England, and the following day landed at Dover, and marched to Chichester, arriving there on the 8th of November.

1819.

The regiment remained at Chichester till the month of March, 1819, when it was removed to Portsmouth. In the month of June in the same year it proceeded to the island of Jersey, where it was quartered until the month of March, 1820.

1820.

In March, 1820, the regiment embarked for Plymouth, and occupied Cumberland and Granby barracks.

Soon after the arrival of the regiment in Plymouth the following letter and enclosure was received by the officer commanding from Colonel de Butts, R.E., commanding the troops in Jersey :—

"Government House, Jersey,
"15th April, 1820.
"SIR,
" In transmitting the enclosed address of the States of Jersey, I have great pleasure in congratulating you and the battalion under your command upon so flattering a testimony to their conduct in this island.
" I have the honour to be, etc.,
(Signed) " AUG DE BUTTS,
" Colonel Commanding."
" The officer commanding
"79th Highlanders, Plymouth."

> "At the States of the Island of Jersey,
> "The 5th day of April, 1820.

"The States being informed that the 79th regiment of foot quartered in this island, under the command of Lieutenant-Colonel Brown, is called to another part of His Majesty's dominions, view its departure with those feelings of regret which the happy experience of its exemplary conduct must necessarily produce.

"The discipline and order which have uninterruptedly distinguished this excellent corps have excited the admiration and deserved the approbation of the States and the inhabitants, who have observed with peculiar satisfaction that not one single violation of the laws, not even the slightest irregularity, has occurred during its abode in this island.

"To the bravery and gallantry so repeatedly displayed in the field by the regiment in the late war, it has now added, in a most eminent degree, the no less useful qualities which characterize good soldiers in the days of peace.

"Under these impressions, the States think it incumbent upon them to return their warmest thanks to Lieutenant-Colonel Brown, the officers, non-commissioned officers, and privates of the 79th regiment, forming part of this garrison, and they take this opportunity of wishing them all manner of success and prosperity wherever their King and country may require their services.

(Signed) "FRANCIS GODFRAY,
"Greffr., L.S."

In the month of May, 1820, the regiment embarked at Plymouth for Ireland, and, having landed at Balnacurry, it marched to Fermoy barracks.

1821.

In the month of June the regiment moved to Limerick, furnishing detachments to Newport and Kildimo.

1822.

The regiment was quartered in Limerick until May, 1822, when it was moved to Templemore, furnishing detachments to Cashel, Nenagh, and Thurles.

When the **Cameron Highlanders were about to leave** Limerick, an address, signed **by the Magistrates and Council,** was presented by a deputation from **that body to Lieutenant-Colonel** Douglas, commanding the regiment, **of which** the following **is a copy :—**

" To Colonel Neil Douglas, 79th regiment **(or Cameron Highlanders).**

"With emotions of regret **we have heard that you are to** march hence to-morrow, and we cannot allow **you to depart from this** city without offering you the **respectful** and **heartfelt tribute of our** regard and admiration.

" During a residence amongst us of nearly two years, you have, with **little intermission,** commanded **this garrison, and your important duties have performed with** the temperate energy and calm dignity of the **accomplished soldier.**

"'The mild manners and military deportment of the officers, as well as the excellent discipline and moral order **of the brave men** whom you so **well command, are happily evinced in the** general esteem which their uniform **good conduct has excited in this** city ; and we beg of you to convey **to them the expression of our highest approbation.** On leaving Limerick, **you will carry with you our best wishes** for your glory and safety, **and we** sincerely desire **for you what your** virtue and valour so justly **entitle** you to enjoy—the blessing of private happiness, and **the well-merited reward of public honour."**

1823.

In the **month of April, 1823, the regiment was removed from** Templemore **to Naas, from whence** it furnished detachments to Drogheda, Dundalk, **Baltinglas, Irim, and** Kilcock.

In October of the same year **it moved** to Dublin, and was quartered in the Royal barracks.

1824.

In October, 1824, the Cameron Highlanders marched from Dublin to Kilkenny, supplying detachments to Carlow and **Cullen.**

1825.

In April, 1825, orders were received for the augmentation of the regiment from eight to ten companies, with a strength of 740 rank and file, preparatory to its proceeding on foreign service to Canada, leaving four companies on home service as a regimental depot. In the month of May the regiment was removed from Kilkenny to Cork with a view to its embarkation.

On the 25th, 26th, and 27th, of August the service companies embarked accordingly under command of Colonel Sir Neil Douglas, in three divisions, on board H.M.S. *Romney* and the *Cato* and *Maria* transports, the depôt companies remaining at Cork under the command of Major William Marshall. The various divisions arrived in safety at Quebec in the month of October, and were quartered in the Jesuit barracks.

In September the depôt companies moved from Cork to Glasgow, where they remained until February, 1826.

1826.

In February, 1826, the depôt companies embarked at the Broomielaw for Ireland and sailed to Belfast, where they were billeted for ten days. They then proceeded to Armagh, occupying barracks there for fourteen days only, when they marched to Newry barracks. Here they remained until May, when they moved to Cavan.

1827.

In May, 1827, the depôt proceeded from Cavan to Belfast barracks, detaching one company to Downpatrick and one to Carrickfergus.

1828.

In February, 1828, the depôt was removed on board two steam vessels from Belfast to Dublin, where it landed and marched into barracks at Birr. On the 9th of March Sir Alan Cameron, K.C.B., the first colonel and founder of the corps, died at Fulham.

The following paragraph appeared in the *Gentleman's Magazine*, from the pen of Colonel Sir William Napier, on the occasion of Sir Alan's death :—

"Died at Fulham, on the 9th ult., at an advanced age, General Sir Alan Cameron, Colonel, 79th regiment. By birth a Highlander; in heart and soul a true one; in form and frame the bold and manly mountaineer. His adventurous career in early life, and subsequent distinguished gallantry in the field, gained him considerable celebrity, together with the unbounded admiration of his countrymen. The son of a private gentleman, but ardent and determined in accomplishing whatever he undertook, he brought to the ranks of the British army more men and in less time than any other who, like himself, was commissioned to raise regiments in 1793-4. During the American war he had the misfortune of being taken prisoner, but from which he escaped after two years confinement by an act of desperate daring. Fate, however, brought him in the course of his life the rare distinction of being successively commandant of the capitals of two countries, Denmark and Portugal, 1807-8. Although of late years he was not able to go among his friends, yet they were always, and to the last, found at his house and around his hospitable table. The number of this man's acts of friendship to his countrymen cannot be estimated, therefore the blank his death has created will be better understood than described."

Mr. Mackenzie says: "In the army he was held universally popular, where, in consequence of his familiar habit of addressing the Irish and Highland soldiers with his gaelic salute of "*Cia Mar tha thu,*"—How are you? he was known as "*Old Cia Mar Tha.*"

On the 24th of March, 1828, Lieutenant Sir Ronald Ferguson, G.C.B., was appointed colonel of the regiment, in succession to Lieutenant-General Sir Alan Cameron, K.C.B.

In the beginning of June, the same year, the service companies proceeded from Quebec to Montreal, from whence they furnished small detachments to occupy St. Johns, Coteau-du-lac, and Isle Aux Noix.

On the 18th of June, 1828, the regiment was presented with new colours, the gift of its gallant colonel, Lieutenant-General Sir R. C. Ferguson, G.C.B. The presentation took place on the Champ-de-

Mars, in presence of a very numerous assemblage of the inhabitants of Montreal and its vicinity, who were eager to witness the ceremony.

At a quarter to one o'clock the parade was formed, and the troops wheeled into line to receive his Excellency the governor, Lieutenant-General the Earl of Dalhousie, the Montreal troop of Volunteer cavalry being on the right, the Montreal Volunteer rifle company in the centre, and the 79th Highlanders on the left. Precisely at one o'clock His Excellency came on the ground accompanied by his staff, and was received with a general salute. The Grenadier company, commanded by Captain Young, marched to the quarters of Colonel Sir Neil Douglas, received the new colours whilst the drums beat the "point of war," and planted them in front of the saluting flag, in charge of two sentries. The regiment then formed three sides of a square. His Excellency, with his staff and Lady Douglas, then came forward, the colours were unfurled, and the ceremony of consecration performed by the Rev. Mr. Stevens. After which, Lady Douglas, placing the colours in the hands of Sir Neil Douglas, addressed him as follows:—

"The honour has this day devolved upon me of presenting to the 79th Highlanders a new set of colours. I need not say how nobly and gloriously the regiment has supported those which are now so decayed, and which—like veteran warriors—have been worn and shattered in their country's cause; the deeds of the regiment are again emblazoned on those which I now present to you. Take them to your hearts! and while the breasts of soldiers glow with honourable zeal for their beloved country, I am confident that the 79th will ever protect these with a devotion worthy of their native land, with steady courage and fidelity to their beloved Sovereign."

Lieutenants Thomas and Lachlan Cameron of the Grenadiers, having advanced, received the colours. Sir Neil Douglas then addressed Lady Douglas, His Excellency, and the 79th, in the following terms:—

"It affords me great pleasure in this ceremony passing through your hands; and I thank you very much for the handsome manner in which you have performed it.

"My Lord, in my own name, and that of the 79th, I beg to return our warmest thanks for the kind support you have this day afforded us, and to assure your lordship that every individual in the regiment feels most grateful for this additional favour to the many which we have already received at your lordship's hands.

"Soldiers! on this great anniversary I am proud to receive these new standards, and to your keeping I with confidence commit them, feeling assured, from the experience of many trying and difficult occasions, how safe the precious deposit will remain in the keeping of men, who, with pride I say it, have ever conducted themselves in the most gallant and intrepid manner. Receive them then 79th, continue to signalise yourselves for order and regularity in quarters, as you have ever done for courage in the field; and be assured, that your reward will be the favour of your Sovereign and the esteem and goodwill of your fellow citizens."

His Excellency the Earl of Dalhousie, addressing Sir Neil Douglas, replied as follows :—

"While the 79th continues to perform its duty as it has hitherto done under my own observation, I shall ever feel gratified in my expression of the approbation of its conduct."

His Lordship then addressed the regiment as follows :—

"79th, the colours which you have now received bear upon them the names of bright and chivalrous deeds. I would desire to impress upon you, on this momentous occasion, the obligation you are under to protect these standards with your lives, to remain by them in circumstances of difficulty and danger, as well as in the bright hour of victory; and as you have every reason to be proud of the reputation you have acquired for valour in the field, let it be your emulation to hand down that reputation untarnished to your successors. This end you will most assuredly attain by obedience to your superiors, gallantry in the field, steadiness in quarters, and devotion to the person of His Majesty the King."

The Grenadier company, with the new colours, now marched round the square, while the band played the National Anthem—the regiment presenting arms as they passed along; the same company also marched to the barracks, and deposited the old colours in Sir Neil Douglas's quarters. At the conclusion of these ceremonies, the regiment marched past in slow and quick time, and then returned to barracks.

1829.

In the month of April, 1829, the depôt of the regiment marched from Birr to Dublin, embarked for Liverpool, and, upon arrival there, proceeded to Burnley, in Lancashire.

In the month of May the regiment moved from Montreal to Kingston, from whence it supplied detachments to Fort Henry, Point Frederick, and Prescott.

In the month of October the regimental depôt moved from Burnley to Liverpool, where it embarked for Scotland, and, landing at Glasgow, marched to Stirling Castle.

1830.

On the 3rd of August, 1830, Sir Neil Douglas left Kingston to return to England for the recovery of his health, which was much impaired by the effects of several severe wounds. On this occasion a tribute, most gratifying to his feelings, was paid to this highly-distinguished soldier by the corporation of Kingston, which presented him with the following address,—whilst many of the veteran soldiers of the regiment were moved to tears at the departure of their warm-hearted and much-loved commander, who had so often led them to victory, and who had been in uninterrupted command of the regiment for the previous eighteen years of his life :—

"To Colonel Sir Neil Douglas, K.C.B., A.D.C. to His Majesty.

"SIR,

"We, the undersigned inhabitants of the town of Kingston, cannot witness your departure from among us without testifying to you in this public manner our unfeigned respect and esteem. We deeply regret that ill-health deprives the town of Kingston of the presence of an officer, distinguished, not more by his merits in the service of his king and country, than for the kindness of his disposition, the urbanity of his manners, and his uniform endeavours to promote cheerfulness and happiness around him. In returning to your native country, we trust you will derive much benefit from a change of air and of climate, and hope that, with health restored and undiminished happiness, we shall again shortly see you at the head of the distinguished corps which you have so long commanded.

"Wishing yourself and Lady Douglas and children the best protection of a kind Providence, and a safe and pleasant voyage,

"We remain, with much regard, &c., &c.,

(Signed)

"THE MEMBERS OF THE CORPORATION OF KINGSTON."

In the month of September, 1830, the depôt of the regiment marched from Stirling to Glasgow, and in the following month it again marched from Glasgow to Edinburgh Castle.

1831.

The regiment was removed from Kingston in the month of May, 1831, and ordered to Toronto, where it was called upon to furnish the following detachments:—No. 3 company, under Captain Riach, to Amherstburgh; No. 4 company, under Captain Forbes, to Fort George; and 2 sergeants and 40 rank and file, under Lieutenant Matheson, to Penitanguishine.

In the same month the depôt companies marched from Edinburgh Castle to Granton, and proceeded by steamer to Aberdeen, where they landed and occupied barracks.

The undermentioned non-commissioned officer and men died whilst the regiment was quartered in Kingston and Toronto in 1830 and 1831:—

Corporal	Donald Keith	Private	John McGarraty
Private	William Sinclair	,,	Samuel McGarraty
,,	John Cockburn	,,	William Brown
,,	William Blissett	,,	Donald McPhee
,,	James Chisholm	,,	Hugh Cameron
,,	John Walker		Alan Cameron

1832.

In the month of May, 1832, the depôt of the regiment marched from Aberdeen, in two divisions, to Perth, where it occupied barracks.

On June 5th Lieutenant-Colonel McDougall joined from England, and assumed command of the regiment.

During the months of July and August cholera appeared in the regiment, and there were several deaths; but, by the 10th of September it had entirely disappeared. The following officers, non-commissioned officers, and men were publicly thanked in regimental orders for their courage and devotion in attending to the sick: Captains Young and Forbes; Doctor Fraser; Sergeants Begg, McGregor, and McGee; Corporal Rennie; Privates George Thompson (who died of the disease), William Gould, James Deans, James Mitchell, John Wilson, and John Neilson.

In November, 1832, the flank companies of the regiment were detached to Montreal, under Lieutenant-Colonel McDougall, in aid of the civil authorities, in consequence of a succession of political riots in that city.

1833.

In May, 1833, the regiment was removed from Toronto to Quebec, where it was quartered in the Jesuit barracks. On this occasion it furnished detachments to Grosse Isle and Sorel.

In the same month the depôt of the regiment was removed from Perth to Dundee barracks; and in the month of December, in the same year, it again moved from Dundee to Perth.

On the 18th of May, Captain Riach's detachment, No. 3 company, was ordered to return to head-quarters from Amherstburgh; and, on the occasion of his leaving that station, he was presented with the following flattering address from the magistrates and residents of the town:—

"To Captain Riach, commanding at Amherstburgh.

"Sir,

"Understanding that the detachment of the 79th regiment under your command is about to be removed from this post, we cannot refrain from expressing our regret at the loss which our little society will sustain by being deprived of you and your amiable lady, who, by your courtesy, have added so much to its happiness, have recommended **yourselves to** the affections of all, and will leave a pleasing and **lasting memorial in every heart.** We hope you will **receive this, inadequate** though it is, **as a testimony of our esteem, and** a token of our sense of your worth.

"To the other officers under your command we must also pay our deserved tribute of praise, on account of their affability of **deportment** and agreeable manners.

"The uniform, peaceable, **and orderly conduct of all under your orders—non-commissioned officers and privates—claims our highest** approbation ; **and may we request that you will** communicate to them **our sense of their merits, and our hope, that, in addition to the glory which your regiment has acquired by its arms in the** tented field, it will ever, by the same propriety of conduct which those stationed here have observed, merit the good wishes of all in time of peace.

"Wishing **yourself,** lady, and family, long life, prosperity, and happiness,

"We have the honour to **be,**

"Sir,

"Your obedient humble servants,

(Signed)

"The Magistrates and Gentlemen of **Amherstburgh.**"

As the detachment was returning **down Lake Erie, to** Quebec, a sad accident occurred ; **the** boiler **of the steamer burst, causing the** death of two of the crew and **serious injuries to several men of the** 79th.

On the 6th of September, 1833, Brevet Lieutenant-Colonel Duncan McDougall succeeded to the command of the regiment, by the retirement of Sir Neil Douglas, K.C.B., A.D.C., on half pay.

1834.

In June, 1834, the depôt of the regiment marched from Perth barracks to Stirling Castle.

On January 23rd the old Château (Castle of St. Louis) at Quebec, was burnt to the ground. The 79th and other troops in the garrison did their utmost to subdue the flames; but the cold was so intense that all the water in the engines was frozen, and it was found impossible to save the building.

1835.

On the 13th of March, 1835, Major Robert Ferguson was promoted to the lieutenant-colonelcy of the regiment, in succession to Lieutenant-Colonel McDougall, retired.

In June, 1835, the regimental depôt embarked on board two steam vessels at Stirling, and proceeded to Aberdeen, where it landed and went into barracks. In July, cholera broke out in Quebec, and there were several fatal cases in the regiment.

1836.

In May, 1836, the depôt was removed from Aberdeen to Edinburgh Castle; and in the month of August of the same year it marched from Edinburgh to Paisley barracks.

The Cameron Highlanders were stationed in Quebec during the remainder of their foreign service. In the month of September, 1836, the regiment embarked for England, under the command of Lieutenant-Colonel Robert Ferguson, and on the 11th of October landed at Leith and marched to Glasgow, where it was joined by the regimental depôt from Paisley. Whilst stationed at Glasgow the regiment furnished a detachment to Dumbarton Castle.

Previous to its embarking for England, the following general order was issued by Lieutenant-General Sir John Colborne, K.C B., commanding the forces in North America:—

"Quebec, 3rd September, 1836.

"The 79th Highlanders being about to embark for home, after a long absence from their native land, the Lieutenant-General commanding thinks it his duty, on their embarkation, to express in general orders his satisfaction at their exemplary conduct during the period they have served in Canada.

"The Lieutenant-General offers them his best wishes for their welfare, and is persuaded that in whatever service they may be employed

Officer Levee Dress

they will always continue to maintain the high reputation which they have ever so justly borne.

(Signed) "JOHN EDEN, Lieutenant-Colonel,
"D.A. General."

1837.

In the month of June, 1837, the regiment marched from Glasgow to Edinburgh Castle, where it furnished a small detachment to Greenlaw barracks. It remained at Edinburgh till the month of June in the following year, when it was ordered to Dublin. The regiment accordingly marched to Glasgow by divisions, where—steamers being in readiness for their conveyance—they embarked immediately, and upon landing at Dublin were quartered in Richmond barracks.

1839.

In consequence of the disturbed state of several of the manufacturing districts in England in the month of May, 1839, the regiment received orders to proceed with all possible despatch to Liverpool, there to await further orders. It accordingly embarked in two divisions on the 30th and 31st, and landed at Liverpool on the following days respectively, when it was billeted throughout the town. On the 3rd of June it was conveyed by rail to Manchester, where it was again billeted—detachments being ordered to Halifax and Newcastle-under-Lyne. After a month's residence in billets, the regiment occupied a temporary barrack prepared for its reception in Tib Street, when it furnished an additional detachment to Rochdale.

1840.

In the month of June, 1840, the head-quarters of the regiment moved to Haydock Lodge—near Warrington—with detachments at Bolton, Liverpool, Wigan, and Stockport.

In the month of August following the regiment received orders to hold itself in readiness to proceed on foreign service to Gibraltar, and consequently a regimental depôt was formed at Stockport on the 10th of September, under Major Andrew Brown. On the 9th of

November the detachments at Wigan and Bolton, consisting of two companies, were withdrawn, and having formed a junction at Warrington, proceeded under the command of Captain T. L. Butler by railway to Deptford, where they embarked, together with the service companies of the first battalion Rifle Brigade, under orders for Corfu, on board the transport *Abercrombie Robertson*, and landed at Gibraltar on the 2nd of January, 1841.

On the 26th of November, 1840, the head-quarters marched from Haydock Lodge, and, with the several detachments forming the service companies, assembled at Warrington on the morning of that date, and proceeded by railway to Weedon barracks, which the regiment occupied until the 31st of December following, when it was removed in two divisions by railway to Deptford, and embarked on board the *Boyne* and *Prince Regent* transports, under the command of Major the Honourable Landerdale Maule. In a few days both vessels proceeded to sea, and arrived at Gibraltar on the 25th and 26th of January, 1841, respectively.

1841.

On the 27th of April, 1841, Major-General the Honourable John Ramsay was appointed Colonel in succession to General Sir Ronald Ferguson, G.C.B., deceased.

In the month of May, 1841, the depôt moved from Stockport to Paisley barracks, where it remained until June, 1842, when it proceeded to Aberdeen.

On the 8th of June, 1841, Major Andrew Brown succeeded to the lieutenant-colonelcy of the regiment, *vice* Lieutenant-Colonel Robert Ferguson, retired.

On the 29th of October, 1841, Colonel John Carter, K.H., from the 1st Royals, obtained the command of the 79th by exchange with Lieutenant-Colonel Andrew Brown.

1842.

On the 14th of June, 1842, Major the Honourable Landerdale Maule was promoted to the lieutenant-colonelcy of the regiment, in succession to Colonel Carter, K.H., retired on half pay.

On the 14th of July, 1842, Lieutenant-General Sir James Macdonnell, K.C.B., was appointed colonel, *vice* Major-General the Honourable J. Ramsay, deceased.

1844.

In February, 1844, the depôt companies were removed from Aberdeen to Stirling Castle, and in April following proceeded to Londonderry in Ireland. In the month of July in the same year they again changed stations, having been removed from Londonderry to barracks at Naas.

1845.

In the Month of September, 1845, the regimental depôt was moved from Naas to Belturbet barracks.

On the 1st of September the undermentioned non-commissioned officers and men were publicly thanked by the Governor of Gibraltar, in orders, for their great gallantry in saving the lives of two soldiers, who had been capsized in a boat in the harbour.

Corporal John Ross		
Private John Aitken		
,, Archibald Livingston		
,, Robert McDiarmid		
,, Thomas Scotland		79th.
,, Hugh Hamilton		
,, William Martin		
,, William Craig		
,, Lewis Gagely		
,, Thomas Robinson		Sappers and Miners.
,, McIvor		
,, McMahon		1st Royals.
,, Gray		

1846.

The depôt companies were ordered from Belturbet to Mullingar in July, 1846, from whence in August following they proceeded to barracks at Castlebar.

1847.

In May the depôt was removed from Castlebar to Boyle barracks, and in November of the same year its station was again changed from Boyle to Mullingar.

1848.

On the 7th of June the regiment embarked on board H.M.S. *Resistance* at Gibraltar for Canada, under the command of Lieutenant-Colonel the Honourable Landerdale Maule; and, after a prosperous voyage, arrived at Quebec on the 27th of July following. On the 28th the regiment disembarked and occupied the Citadel barracks.

Previous to the embarkation of the regiment for Canada a handsome marble tablet was erected by voluntary contribution of the officers and men in the Wesleyan Chapel at Gibraltar (where divine service was held for the Presbyterian soldiers of the garrison), to the memory of those non-commissioned officers and soldiers, who died during their period of service on the Rock. The following is the inscription thus recorded on the tablet:—

TO THE MEMORY

OF THE UNDERMENTIONED

NON-COMMISSIONED OFFICERS AND PRIVATES

OF THE

CAMERON HIGHLANDERS,

A.D. 1841—1847.

Cuimhne

Nan Sonn Nach Maireann.

79th REGIMENT.

913	Sergeant	W. Brodie	4th Company		Obit	23rd February	1841
467	Colour-Sergeant	T. Mercer	Light	,,	,,	24th May	,,
1163	Private	S. Gardner	2nd	,,	,,	24th August	,,
1661	,,	J. Taylor	Gr.	,,	,,	19th November	,,
1869	,,	D. Stewart	2nd	,,	,,	19th December	,,
406	,,	W. Abbot	1st	,,	,,	7th January	1842
1724	,,	D. Cumming	Light	,,	,,	19th March	,,
1865	,,	D. Ross	4th	,,	,,	31st May	,,
1081	,,	J. Robertson	3rd	,,	,,	3rd July	,,
251	,,	R. Fowls	4th	,,	,,	20th August	,,
889	,,	J. Kerr	2nd	,,	,,	21st October	,,

1131	Private	G. Cloriac	Gr. Company	Obit		9th November	1842
1400	,,	W. Dickson	3rd	,,	·	24th February	1843
1578	,,	T. Millar	1st	,,	·	7th April	,,
1031	,,	Wm. Connell	1st	,,	·	20th May	,,
325	Corporal	G. Hall	3rd	,,	·	22nd August	,,
1318	,,	A. Gemmell	1st	,,	·	10th April	1844
904	Private	A. McDonald	Gr.	,,	·	17th February	1845
1791	,,	J. Leadine	3rd	,,	·	27th February	,,
1683	,,	G. McGregor	Gr.	,,	·	22nd February	1846
595	,,	Samuel Young	1st	,,	·	24th August	,,
833	,,	J. McPherson	Light	,,	·	22nd October	,,
818	,,	D. Spence	2nd	,,	·	3rd November	,,
1475	,,	Chas. Dunnet	2nd	,,	·	10th February	1847
1830	,,	G. Litster	Gr.	,,	·	17th March	,,
885	,,	W. Baxter	1st	,,	·	5th April	,,
1152	,,	J. Stirling	1st	,,	·	14th June	,,
1646	,,	H. Muir	1st	,,	·	13th September	,,

In the month of November, 1848, the station of the regimental depôt was changed from Mullingar to Nenagh.

1849.

On the 8th of February, 1849, Major-General James Hay, C.B., was appointed colonel in succession to Lieutenant-General Sir James Macdonnell, K.C.B., appointed to the colonelcy of the 71st Foot.

Sergeant Donald Mackenzie, who was discharged from the 79th Highlanders in 1832, died in France in 1849, where he was residing with the relations of his wife, a Frenchwoman. He left an orphan daughter totally destitute, and Sir Duncan McDougall, with that kind interest he always manifested in everything connected with the 79th, not only whilst the lieutenant-colonel of the corps, but also since he ceased to command it, received the child into his own family, and originated in London a subscription for the purpose of purchasing the right of admission for an orphan, during a period of 21 years, into the Royal Caledonian Asylum. The sum of one hundred guineas was accordingly subscribed for this purpose by officers lately belonging to the 79th and those serving in the regiment.

In the month of July there was one case of cholera in the regiment at Quebec.

1850.

In the month of April, 1850, the depôt of the regiment was removed from Nenagh to Kinsale; in May following it was ordered to Cork, and in June, the same year, it embarked at Cork for England, landed at Liverpool, and proceeded by railway to Preston. The depôt occupied barracks at Preston until the month of November, when it proceeded by railway to Berwick-upon-Tweed.

1851.

In April, 1851, the depôt companies were removed from Berwick-upon-Tweed by railway to Stirling Castle.

In the month of June, 1851, the service companies received orders of readiness to embark for England, and on the 4th of August they embarked accordingly, under the command of Lieutenant-Colonel the Honourable Landerdale Maule, in the freight-ship *Herefordshire*, and, after a highly favourable voyage, arrived in Leith Roads on the 30th of the same month. On the 1st of September the regiment disembarked, the head-quarters proceeding to Stirling Castle and forming a junction with the depôt, whilst three companies were detached to Perth and three to Dundee.

When the regiment was about to embark for England a highly complimentary letter was addressed to Lieutenant-Colonel the Honourable Landerdale Maule by the Magistrates and Council of Quebec, of which the following is a copy:—

"Quebec, 29th July, 1851.

"To Lieutenant-Colonel the Honourable Landerdale Maule,
   "Commanding the 79th Highlanders.

"The Magistrates of this city have learned with regret that the expiration of your period of service here will shortly cause the removal of yourself and your distinguished regiment from amongst them.

"They avail themselves of this occasion to acknowledge their obligation to you for your willing and efficient co-operation with them upon all occasions when your aid was required to assist them in the performance of their duties, nor can they pass over without acknowledgment the cordial manner in which you and your officers have at

79TH CAMERON HIGHLANDERS.

all times contributed to the amusements of the citizens of Quebec.

"It is with great pleasure that the Magistrates bear testimony to the excellent conduct of the men of your regiment during their sojourn in Quebec, where they will be long and favourably remembered.

"With our warmest wishes for your welfare, and that of the officers and men of your corps, we beg to subscribe ourselves, &c.

"SIGNED BY THE WHOLE OF THE

"MAGISTRATES AND COUNCIL."

Previous to the embarkation of the regiment at Quebec for England, a handsome marble tablet was erected by voluntary contributions of the officers and men in the Scotch Presbyterian Church of St. Andrew's in that city, to the memory of those non-commissioned officers and soldiers who died during their period of service in Canada, bearing the following inscription :—

LXXIX.

CAMERON HIGHLANDERS.

TO THE MEMORY OF

THEIR COMRADES,

WHO DEPARTED THIS LIFE WHILST SERVING

IN CANADA,

A.D. 1848—1851.

Cuimhne

Nan sonn nach Maireann.

			Gr. Company			Obit		
1179	Drummer	John Tabram	Gr. Company		-		5th August	1848
1701	Lance-Corporal	J. McLeod	4th	,,	-	,,	23rd September	,,
1369	Private	Peter McLean	2nd	,,	-	,,	30th September	,,
827	,,	Archd. Fletcher	4th	,,	-	,,	6th January	1849
1189	,,	Robert Kerr	3rd	,,	-	,,	8th July	,,
937	,,	James Porter	3rd	,,	-	,,	11th July	,,
2137	,,	Wm. Drummond	3rd	,,	-	,,	13th July	,,
1602	Corporal	James Ewart	3rd	,,	-	,,	13th July	,,
1104	Private	John Keith	2nd	,,	-	,,	14th July	,,
2431	,,	Wm. Jarvie	4th	,,	-	,,	17th July	,,
1240	,,	Alex. McLachlan	1st	,,	-	,,	18th July	,,

2327	Private	Wm. Kitchen	Gr.	Company	Obit	6th August	1849
2395	,,	John McKinnon	1st	,,	,,	7th September	,,
2123	,,	James Fleming	1st	,,	,,	8th December	,,
792	,,	John Garn	4th	,,	,,	22nd February	1850
836	Lance-Sergeant	Wm. Fairley	2nd	,,	,,	19th March	,,
1401	Qr.-Mr. Sergeant	Jas. Wilson	Gr.	,,	,,	30th May	,,
2655	Private	Neil Campbell	4th	,,	,,	25th December	,,
894	Sergeant	Archd. Ewing	Gr.	,,	,,	5th February	1851
1731	Private	G. L. Dickinson	4th	,,	,,	18th March	,,
828	,,	Duncan Matheson	Gr.	,,	,,	28th April	,,
——	,,	Wm. Fleming	Gr.	,,	,,	21st May	,,
976	,,	Angus Gunn	3rd	,,	,,	26th May	,,
2508	,,	Angus Gunn	1st	,,	,,	10th June	,,

1852.

On the 25th of February, 1852, the regiment moved from Stirling to Edinburgh, from whence it supplied a small detachment to Greenlaw barracks, leaving detachments at Stirling, Perth, and Dundee. In the month of May the three latter detachments were withdrawn, and joined at Edinburgh Castle.

On the 24th of December, 1852, Major Edmund James Elliot succeeded to the command of the regiment as lieutenant-colonel, by the retirement of the Honourable Landerdale Maule on half pay.

1853.

In April, 1853, the regiment proceeded by railway from Edinburgh to Bury, in Lancashire, where the head-quarters with two companies were stationed, having detachments at Burnley, Ashton-under-Lyne, Stockport, and the Isle of Man. On the 13th of June following the regiment changed quarters from Bury to Preston, where the several detachments joined, with the exception of one company at the Isle of Man. On the 28th of June the regiment was again removed from Preston to Weedon, and the detachment from the Isle of Man having re-joined on the 14th of July, the 79th proceeded by railway from Weedon to Staines and marched to the encampment at Chobham, where it was brigaded with the 19th and 97th regiments, under the command of Colonel Lockyer, K.H.

The regiment remained for some time under canvas at Chobham, performing various field operations with the other troops—consisting of three brigades, with artillery and cavalry, forming one division under the command of General Lord Seaton, G.C.B. During the period of its service at Chobham camp, the division had, on more than one occasion, the honour of being reviewed by Her Majesty the Queen, their Royal Highnesses Prince Albert and the Duke of Cambridge, the General commanding-in-chief, and many other distinguished persons. On the 20th of August the encampment was broken up, when the 79th marched to Farnborough station and proceeded by railway to Portsmouth, where it occupied the Cambridge and Colewort barracks.

1854.

In consequence of the declaration of war with Russia, on the 1st of March, 1854, the 79th received orders to hold itself in readiness to embark for Turkey to join the army assembling under the command of General Lord Raglan, G.C.B.

Immediate preparations were accordingly made to complete the regiment to the requisite strength by the admission of volunteers from other corps.

On the 24th of March, 1854, Lieutenant-General W. H. Sewell, C.B., was appointed Colonel, *vice* Lieutenant-General James Hay, C.B., deceased.

Before embarking for active service new colours were supplied to the regiment at Portsmouth, and were formally delivered over on parade by Lieutenant-Colonel Elliot on the 21st of April, but the ceremony usually observed on such occasions was in this instance dispensed with by Lieutenant-Colonel Elliot, who unfurled and delivered the colours without comment on the private parade ground of the regiment in the Cambridge barracks.

The 79th having been completed to its numerical strength, and all necessary arrangements made to proceed on active service, it embarked at Portsmouth, under the command of Lieutenant-Colonel E. J. Elliot, in Her Majesty's ship *Simoom*, on the 4th of May, and after a most prosperous voyage arrived at Scutari on the 20th. On the following day the regiment disembarked and encamped on the plain of Scutari, near the Turkish barracks, where it was brigaded with the 93rd Highlanders, under the command of Brigadier-General Sir Colin Campbell.

On the embarkation of the regiment for Turkey two companies were left at Portsmouth as a depôt, which very soon afterwards joined the depôt battalion stationed at Winchester.

On the 1st of June the whole army then at Scutari had the honour of being reviewed by the Sultan Abdul Medjid, with the Grand Vizier and several other Turkish Ministers of State, the English and Foreign Ambassadors to the Porte, Marshal St. Arnaud, the French Commander-in-Chief, and a very numerous staff, when His Majesty the Sultan was pleased to express himself to Lord Raglan in terms of the highest approbation regarding the appearance and equipment of the troops.

On the 7th of June the arrival of the 42nd Royal Highlanders in the *Hydaspes* completed the Highland brigade, which—with the brigade of Guards under General Bentinck—formed the 1st division of the eastern army, which was commanded by H.R.H. the Duke of Cambridge.

On the 13th of June the 1st division embarked at Scutari for Varna, the 79th embarking on the steamer *Cambria*, the 42nd on the *Hydaspes*, and the 93rd on the *Melbourne*.

On the 14th the division arrived in Varna Bay, and on the 15th the Highland brigade disembarked in the boats of H.M.S. *London*, *Bellerophon*, *Arethusa*, and *Sidon*, and encamped on a magnificent plain overlooking Lake Devno, situated a mile south of Varna, on ground just vacated by the light division, which had moved to Aladyn.

The regiment here received a great acquisition in the person of Dr. Richard James Mackenzie, a gentleman of the highest professional acquirements, who—resigning a lucrative practice in Edinburgh—with true professional zeal, embarked for Turkey, provided with an introductory letter from the Earl of Aberdeen to Lord Raglan. Returning from visiting the Turkish hospitals on the banks of the Danube, Dr. Mackenzie was offered by his lordship the temporary rank and pay of an army surgeon, which he accepted, and at his own request he was attached to the 79th, Dr. Scot, the surgeon, being an early college friend.

On the 1st of July the division marched from the camp at Varna and moved to Aladyn, where it again encamped on ground recently vacated by the light division, which had proceeded seven miles further to the village of Devno.

On the 6th of July the division was reviewed by His Excellency Omar Pasha, the Turkish commander-in-chief, who expressed himself highly pleased with the appearance and discipline of the troops.

The division remained encamped at Aladyn till the 28th, when, owing to the prevalence of fever and the appearance of Asiatic cholera, it was removed to a new encampment at a distance of six miles, on an elevated table land near the village of Givrakla, in close proximity to a large forest.

Whilst stationed at Givrakla the regiment had the misfortune to lose its two senior field officers, Lieutenant-Colonel E. J. Elliot, who commanded the regiment, and Brevet Lieutenant-Colonel James Ferguson, both of whom died of fever.

Colonel the Honourable Landerdale Maule, assistant-adjutant-general to the 2nd division, who for many years commanded the regiment, also died about the same time. These three deaths, which occurred within a few days of each other, caused deep feelings of regret in the regiment.

On the 13th of August Major John Douglas was promoted to the lieutenant-colonelcy of the regiment, in succession to Lieutenant-Colonel E. J. Elliot, deceased.

The division remained in this encampment until the 20th of August following, during which time the men were employed in making gabions and fascines and throwing up entrenchments.

On the 16th of August the Guards and 42nd Highlanders moved from Givrakla to Varna, and on the 22nd the 79th and 93rd followed them. On the 23rd the regiment encamped at Galata Bornou, on the western side of the Bay of Varna, four miles from the town.

On the 29th of August the division embarked for the invasion of the Crimea, the 79th, under Lieutenant-Colonel Douglas, on board the sailing transport *Dunbar*, the 42nd in the *Emu*, and the 93rd in H.M.S. *Terrible*.

Other portions of the army continued to embark until the 4th of

September, when the whole fleet of transports and men-of-war rendezvoused at Baltschik Bay, where it formed a junction with the French army under Marshal St. Arnaud and the Turkish contingent under Suleiman Pasha. On the 7th the combined expeditionary army of the allies sailed from Baltschik Bay, each steam-vessel taking two sailing transports in tow, and arrived at Kalamita Bay, on the coast of the Crimea, on the 13th.

On the 14th of September at daybreak, orders were issued to prepare for landing, which was effected during the day without opposition. At 2 p.m. the 1st division had completed its disembarkation, and at 4 o'clock it marched four miles inland from the place of landing, and bivouacked for the night near to Lake Touzla. On the following day a portion of the tents were landed, and the time from this date until the 18th was occupied in disembarking cavalry, artillery, and stores from the fleet, and in making preparations for an advance. On that day the tents were struck and shipped on board the *Orinoco*, as it was found impracticable to convey them with the army for want of transport. Consequently the troops bivouacked on the night of the 18th, and at midnight orders were issued to march at 6 o'clock on the following morning. Accordingly the troops were under arms at the appointed hour, but, from some delay in embarking the sick, the army did not start until 8 a.m., when it proceeded on its march across immense plains in the direction of Sebastopol. The order of march was in double columns of companies from the centre of divisions at half or sub-division distance, the front and left flank being covered by skirmishers of the 2nd battalion Rifle brigade, the 8th and 11th Hussars, 13th Light Dragoons, and the 17th Lancers. This order of march was adopted in order that, by wheeling suddenly to the right or left, a line of four-deep could at once be formed to either flank. The artillery formed by divisions and marched on the right of the infantry. The Turks were nearest to the sea, with their right flank protected by the men-of-war, which steamed along parallel to the army; the French were in the centre, and the British furthest away from the sea on the left.

After several halts to allow the stragglers to re-join, at half-past three o'clock the army arrived at the Bulganak River, a small stream intersecting the road to Sebastopol, traversed by a bridge which was found to be in good repair. As the column approached the bridge a distant cannonade was heard, and the galloping of horse artillery to the front indicated that the enemy was in view.

Upon arriving at the crest of some rising ground about a mile beyond the river, the brigades of the 1st Division formed line, and were ordered to lie down. The horse artillery were in advance of the infantry, and the cavalry were posted in some hollow ground still further to the front. The glistening of sabres and bayonets reflected in the sunshine now brought to view a dark mass of the enemy, which was drawn up upon some high ground about a mile in advance, with a battery of artillery in position on its left.

Fire was now opened between the English artillery and that of the enemy, and was maintained for upwards of half-an-hour, when a strong column of French infantry advanced in order to turn his left flank, upon which he withdrew in perfect order.

The brigades then withdrew over the summit of the ridge nearer to the Bulganak, and, piling arms, prepared to bivouac for the night. Strong picquets were thrown out in front, and, as it was now six o'clock, watering parties were ordered, and the troops prepared to refresh themselves with tea and biscuit, it being found impossible to cook the ration meat, the only fuel procurable being weeds, as not a bush was visible along the whole line of march. Thirteen miles of ground had been traversed, and the army was now within five miles of the strong position which the Russians had taken up upon the river Alma.

At dawn on the 20th the army got under arms, and at 6 a.m. it was announced to the troops that the position occupied by the enemy was to be attacked. The sick being embarked on board the fleet at 8 a.m., the army advanced in two columns, having the 2nd division on the right (communicating with the French left), supported by the 3rd; the light division on the left, supported by the 1st; with the 4th division in reserve. The advance was covered by the 2nd battalion Rifle Brigade in extended order, and the left flank by the cavalry and reserve artillery.

After several halts to enable the staff to reconnoitre the enemy's position, the army came within full view of the enemy, occupying a ridge of heights on the left bank of the Alma, completely commanding the road to Sebastopol and disputing the passage of the river.

The right bank of the Alma was now approached by the village of Burliuk, which is intersected by a road passing to a ford at the river, flanked by vineyards to the right and left, and edged by trees and brushwood. Opposite to the ford, a rugged and winding mountain road ascends to the crest of the hill, with ravines diverging to the right and left; and below the village a good bridge was left standing, connecting the Sebastopol road. On the plateau near the summit of the ridge, and nearly opposite to the bridge, a very powerful redoubt was occupied by the enemy in force, and to the right and left of this there were two others on commanding points, the spaces connecting all three being filled by columns of infantry. At half-past one p.m. the action commenced by the redoubt on the enemy's left opening fire on the French columns, which were destined to attack and turn his left flank; the other two redoubts—the attack upon which was assigned to the British army—opening fire as the troops came within range. The fire was returned with spirit by the field batteries, which were in position close to the stone wall of the vineyard, but with little effect on the heavily armed redoubt; however, from the accuracy of the artillery practice, the round shot and shell directed against the enemy's infantry, dropped right into his columns, causing much disorder and inflicting severe loss. The village of Burliuk was all this time in flames, having been fired by the enemy on the approach of the British; and the skirmishers of the Rifle Brigade, rushing through the burning village, and entering the vineyard beyond, spread themselves along the margin of the river, and engaged the Russian riflemen on the opposite side of the bank.

The several divisions now formed line, and the light and 2nd proceeded to the attack, whilst the 1st division advanced close to the vineyard wall and was ordered to lie down under a heavy cannonade for a quarter-of-an-hour, when it received orders to advance in support of the light division. The 1st division, clearing the stone wall at a bound, entered and traversed the vineyards; and, fording the river, crossed to the opposite bank.

Sir Colin Campbell, with much judgment, availed himself of the overhanging brow of an abrupt rising ground to the right of the mountain pass, by which the Highland brigade was directed to ascend, and forming the troops in quarter distance column, advanced in this formation, thereby gaining ground for a considerable distance under cover, and avoiding one of the most conspicuous points on which the guns of the enemy were trained. On reaching the slope of the hill, the three regiments rapidly formed in echelon lines, and in admirable and imposing array advanced to the attack. On the right the 42nd Royal Highlanders preserved the communication with the brigade of Guards, in the centre were the 93rd Sutherland Highlanders, and the 79th formed the extreme left of the whole allied line. The magnificent mile of line displayed by the Guards and Highlanders, the prominent bearskins, the undulating waves of the clan tartans, the stalwart frames and the steady and confident bearing of those young and eager soldiers can never be forgotten by those who witnessed the scene, whilst it contributed materially to the discouragement of the enemy, whose columns perceptibly wavered as the line approached. To waver is to be defeated, and the enemy's masses of four-and-twenty deep absolutely reeled and staggered to and fro under the murderous fire of the Scottish line, which was delivered with great effect at a distance of 200 yards.

Kinglake, in his *Invasion of the Crimea*, thus describes the advance of the 79th :—

" Above the crest or swell of ground on the left rear of the 93rd, yet another array of the tall, bending plumes began to rise up in a long, ceaseless line, stretching far into the east, and presently, with all the grace and beauty that marks a Highland regiment when it springs up the side of a hill, the 79th came bounding forward. Without a halt, or with only the halt that was needed for dressing the ranks, it sprang at the flank of the right Sousdal column, and caught it in its sin—caught it daring to march across the front of a battalion advancing in line! Wrapped in the fire thus poured upon its flank, the hapless column could not march, could not live. It broke, and began to fall back in great confusion ; and the left Sousdal column being almost at the same time overthrown by the 93rd, and the two columns which had engaged the 'Black Watch' being now in full retreat, the spurs of the hill and the winding dale beyond became thronged with the enemy's disordered masses. A cheer now burst from the Highlanders, and the hill-sides were made to resound with that joyous assuring cry, which is the natural utterance of a northern people as long as it is warlike and free."

In fifteen minutes the centre or great redoubt was stormed and captured by the troops of the light division, and the enemy simultaneously abandoned the one on his right, which was occupied by two companies of the Cameron Highlanders, commanded by Major Clephane, the guns being withdrawn by the enemy. The French troops had now succeeded in turning the enemy's left, and he retired in confusion from all parts of his position. The allied line then advanced, and the horse artillery galloping up the ravine opened fire upon his columns, which were in full retreat down the opposite side of the ridge, which was crowned on all parts by the British infantry. At 5 p.m. all firing ceased, when the army moved forward and occupied a second chain of hills in advance of the first, leaving the ground recently covered by the enemy considerably in rear, and the troops proceeded to form their bivouac.

The loss of the Cameron Highlanders in the battle of the Alma was 2 rank and file killed and 7 rank and file wounded. The distinction of a Companionship of the Bath was conferred upon Lieutenant-Colonel John Douglas, who commanded the regiment; Captain Andrew Hunt was promoted by brevet to be Major in the army, and the 79th subsequently received, with other regiments, the royal authority to have the word "Alma" inscribed on its colours and appointments. The whole of the 21st and 22nd was occupied in the interment of the allied and Russian dead, and in conveying the wounded on board the fleet. At 7 a.m. on the 23rd the combined armies again advanced, and at 3 p.m. arrived at the Katscha river and villages, both of which were found deserted by the inhabitants. As both the bridges had been left entire, the British army crossed by them at the village of Eskel, and bivouacked on a chain of hills beyond the river. The French and Turkish armies passed by the lower bridge, near the embouchure of the river with the sea, and bivouacked on the high ground to the British right.

At 7 a.m. on the 24th the army marched with the French and Turkish troops on the right flank, but were halted in a wide plain until nearly noon, when, the sick being embarked, it again advanced, and arrived at 3 p.m. at the Belbec river and village; and, crossing by the bridge which was left entire, ascended by a precipitous and winding mountain road to a high table land, where it bivouacked a mile beyond the river. In its onward march to Kalamita Bay the army continued to suffer from Asiatic cholera; and it is with deep regret that the writer has to record the loss from this cause of Doctor R. J. Mackenzie, who died on the heights of the Belbec at 8 a.m. on the 25th, sincerely and deeply regretted by all ranks of the 79th, and by a wide circle of private friends, who were much attached to him for his personal qualities and disinterested motives in serving with the army. The victim of his ardent love of his profession, Doctor Mackenzie followed the army on foot, undergoing much fatigue and sharing its every privation. So highly were his services appreciated by the 79th, that after the battle of Alma, on his coming up to the regiment from attendance on the wounded, several of the men called out "Three cheers for Dr. Mackenzie!" which was promptly and warmly responded to. As an instance of the important services rendered to the army generally by Dr. Mackenzie, it may be here stated that, after the battle of Alma, he performed no fewer than twenty-seven capital operations with his own hands, two of them being amputations at the hip joint. The relatives of the unfortunate gentleman will be pleased to learn, that after the notification of peace a neat tombstone, with an appropriate inscription and fenced in by a stone wall, was erected to his memory by the regiment on the heights of the Belbec, near to his resting-place.

The army prepared to move at 7 a m. on the 25th, but counter-orders were issued, and it remained inactive until 11 in the forenoon, when it proceeded on its march, in columns of divisions, through a dense forest of underwood, which harassed the men and greatly impeded the march of the troops. The order of the previous day's march was reversed, the French and Turkish troops being on the

British left—whilst the artillery, cavalry, and commissariat covered the only road which led through the wood. Precisely at noon Sebastopol came in view, distant about three miles directly in front, when the line of march was suddenly changed to almost due south-east, leaving Sebastopol to the right and rear. The army continued to struggle onwards under a fierce sunshine, and at 4 p.m. the 1st division, following the route of the light division, debouched from the wood upon the highway from Simpheropol to Sebastopol, at a spot marked in the map as "Mackenzie's Farm." At an angle in the road were numerous carriages, a few prisoners, and two ammunition waggons, captured by the cavalry advance guard from the rear of a Russian division half-an-hour previously. Proceeding on the march down a very precipitous mountain road, a most magnificent and extensive plain came in view, surrounded by very high mountains, intersected by numerous ravines, and covered with dwarf trees and brushwood. Numerous traces of the late brush with the enemy, in the shape of clothing, bridles, and saddlery, with broken carriages and their contents, were strewed along the road, encumbering the march; and at nightfall the division crossing the Tchernaya by the Traktir bridge, about 8 o'clock arrived at its bivouac on a high hill overlooking the valley it had just left.

At 7 a.m. on the 26th the march was resumed, the various divisions descending to the high road, and advancing in columns of sections of companies till they crossed the Woronzoff road and entered the plain of Balaclava, where they formed in columns of divisions and advanced, preceded by the Rifle Brigade in extended order. About noon the column halted in the plain, while the skirmishers of the Rifle Brigade ascended the steep acclivities on both sides of the harbour, and a troop of Horse Artillery entered Balaclava by the lower road. At 1 p.m. the sharp crack of the Minié rifle, with the fire from the Horse Artillery and booming of guns from the fleet outside the harbour, intimated that the old Genoese fort, held by the enemy, had been attacked. In fifteen minutes it surrendered, when the fleet entered the harbour, and the army at once proceeded to form its bivouac.

A base of operations being thus secured, the army proceeded by divisions and encamped together with the French troops on the south side of Sebastopol, as it had been resolved to proceed with the siege of that important fortress.

On the 1st of October the 1st division marched from Balaclava and encamped on the right of the light division before Sebastopol, to assist in the duties of the siege. The 93rd Highlanders were detached from the brigade, and encamped on a rising ground to the right of the road leading from the valley to the town and harbour of Balaclava, 1,200 men of the Royal Marines were landed from the fleet and encamped on the opposite height, numerous batteries were erected, and a chain of redoubts constructed across the entrance to the plain commanding the Woronzoff road. The defence of these redoubts was entrusted to Turkish artillery and infantry. On the 3rd and 4th, tents were landed and distributed to the army in sufficient proportion to afford cover to the troops, and all necessary preparations for the siege proceeded with vigour.

With a view to facilitating the recruiting of Scotchmen for the Highland regiments serving in the Crimea, the Highland depôts attached to the battalion at Winchester, were, in the month of September, removed to several stations in Scotland. The 79th depôt, under the command of Captain T. B. Butt, proceeded by railway from Winchester to London, and again by rail from London to Aberdeen, where it occupied barracks.

On the 8th of October Sir Colin Campbell was appointed to the important command of the troops and position of Balaclava, and was succeeded in command of the Highland brigade by Colonel D. A. Cameron of the 42nd, as colonel on the staff, and subsequently as major-general with local rank.

Early in this month Lieutenant F. A. Grant died of cholera before Sebastopol.

On the 9th the army again broke ground before Sebastopol, when the 79th and other regiments of the division furnished strong covering and working parties to guard the trenches and batteries.

On the 17th the English and French batteries opened fire upon the Russian defences, and the regiment furnished, along with others, ten volunteers, and the brigade one subaltern officer, to act as sharp-shooters in picking off the enemy's gunners and engaging his riflemen. Lieutenant Edward William Cuming of the 79th was the volunteer officer from the brigade, and he rendered good service in the performance of this very important duty.

At 7 a.m. on the 25th the report of guns from the plain of Balaclava, followed by the galloping of numerous staff officers, and the order for the 1st division to "fall in," apprised the army that an attack was meditated in the direction of Balaclava. The 1st, and afterwards the 4th divisions, with their field batteries under the command of Lieutenant-General Sir George Cathcart, moved rapidly to the scene of the attack, witnessing the events of the battle as they proceeded to the valley by the heights along the rear of the French position.

From a hill on the left bank of the Tchernaya, a heavy battery of the enemy's guns was playing upon the Turkish redoubts at the head of the valley, from which the fire was returned with spirit at a distance of three-quarters of a mile. Heavy columns of Russian infantry, with a numerous artillery, emerging from the defile of Tchorgoum, crossed the low ground and advanced in beautiful order, preceded by a cloud of skirmishers, towards the Woronzoff road, covered by the fire of their artillery, which slackened as they approached the road. Before, however, the sharp-shooters had neared the redoubts, the Turks abandoned them and fled across the plain towards Balaclava, the recreant Moslems in their rapid flight rushing through the 93rd Highlanders, who were formed in line on a rising ground in front of the village of Kadikoi, with the invalid battalion commanded by Lieutenant-Colonel Daveney on their left. Suddenly from six to eight squadrons of Russian cavalry dashed up the slope, crossed the road, and galloping through the plain, sabred many of the fugitive Turks. Onward they swept in the direction of the 93rd, which opened fire in line at a distance of 400 yards, when they wheeled about, and, galloping off, disappeared in the gorge of a chain of hills in the direction of the village of Kamara.

The repulse of this attack upon the 93rd was followed by the splendid charge of the British heavy cavalry brigade, commanded by General Scarlett, upon another formidable body of the Russian cavalry. It was a fearful shock, but the combat was short and decisive, and in seven minutes the enemy broke and retired across the plain in great disorder, leaving numbers of killed and wounded on the ground, 60 prisoners, and 40 horses.

The 1st division now arrived on the battle-field, and soon afterwards the 4th division and a brigade of French infantry. They immediately formed in two lines in order of battle, while the light cavalry brigade, under the Earl of Cardigan, took post rather in advance of the left of the line of infantry. The guns of the 4th division now opened fire on the captured redoubts, which the enemy soon abandoned; and Liprandi, declining the proffered battle, withdrew his infantry in the direction of Kamara. The light cavalry brigade was then ordered to advance and endeavour to prevent the Russians from carrying off the guns taken from the Turks, but, from some fatal mistake, it was led at a gallop along the valley, swept by the Russian guns, to the left of the ridge of hills occupied by the Turkish redoubts, and was directed against a Russian battery at the extreme end of the valley. The brigade rushed on under a murderous fire from all arms, and actually rode through the spaces between the guns, sabring the enemy's artillerymen; but, alas! the triumph was short-lived, and the splendid light brigade now found itself exposed to a front and flank fire of musketry, to a cross fire from several masked batteries, and to an attack in flank by a large force of the enemy's cavalry. In fifteen minutes after reaching the enemy's guns, it was obliged to retire, after suffering a loss of more than half its numbers in men and horses.

The infantry divisions now piled arms in the plain to await events; and, as Liprandi evinced no disposition to renew the combat, the 4th division and the brigade of Guards of the 1st division were withdrawn at nightfall to their encampment before Sebastopol. The 42nd and 79th were moved to a new position on the heights on the north side of the valley of Balaclava, communicating with the Royal Marines, the 93rd occupying their former encampment on the left of the road leading into the town and harbour, whilst three Turkish battalions were posted at intervals to complete the communication at various points. Preparations to throw up a strong line of entrenchments along the heights above Balaclava were immediately commenced, and several batteries of heavy guns were erected by the Royal Marine artillery.

At 6 a.m. on the 5th of November, the enemy having ascended by several ravines leading to the heights opposite Inkerman, under cover of a dense fog, attacked the right of the English line before Sebastopol in overwhelming force, covered by a powerful artillery, which he had placed unperceived in position during the previous night, whilst a sortie was directed against the left flank of the allies to divert the French troops from reinforcing the English right. A feigned attack was simultaneously made upon the rear of the French position by the valley of Balaclava, the troops occupied in its defence being menaced by a complete division of cavalry and infantry, with two batteries of artillery drawn up in column on the left bank of the Tchernaya, and a squadron of Cossack cavalry was thrown out from this division in extended order to nearly within musket shot of the line of entrenchments.

After a bloody and obstinately contested action of six hours' duration, the division of General Bosquet arrived to the support of the British, and the battle of "Inkerman" terminated in a repulse of the enemy with heavy losses and the withdrawal of his forces within the walls of Sebastopol.

1855.

The Highland brigade, in conjunction with the Royal Marines and Turkish infantry, and latterly with 600 Zouaves in support, continued encamped on the heights of Balaclava until the 21st of May, 1855.

Although the Highland brigade was thus at an early period of the campaign unavoidably withdrawn from the siege operations before Sebastopol, it had all important duties to perform besides those inseparable from the unremitting vigilance imperatively called for in the defence of the base of operations of the army. In the month of December, 1854, and January and February, 1855, all the available duty men of the Highland brigade were usually employed at daylight every morning in the severe fatigue of conveying to the army before Sebastopol round shot, shell, and provisions, the load assigned to each man being generally a 32-lb. shot, carried in a sack, or 56 lbs. of biscuit. The preparation of gabions and fascines for the works of the siege, numerous public fatigue duties in the harbour of Balaclava and elsewhere, as well as the labour required for strengthening the entrenchments, likewise devolved upon the brigade.

In the month of January, 1855, the arrival of numerous vessels from England freighted with wooden huts for the army enabled the Cameron Highlanders to proceed with their erection, and on the 10th of January the first hut was finished and occupied by the sick. Others were completed in succession, and on the 28th of February the regiment was fully hutted.

On the 20th of February the brigade, one wing of the 2nd battalion Rifle Brigade, the 71st Highlanders, and the Royal Marines were employed in a reconnaissance of the position and force of the enemy near Tchorgoum. The troops were ordered to fall in at midnight, but the weather, which had been fine for the previous week, suddenly changed, rain falling in torrents as midnight approached. The movement was therefore deferred till 2 a.m. on the 21st, at which hour the rain was succeeded by a drifting snowstorm, accompanied with a piercing north-east wind, which blew right in the faces of the men, and the morning being intensely dark, objects were scarcely visible at the distance of a few yards. Notwithstanding these unfavourable circumstances, and the non-appearance of General Vinoy's French brigade, which was to have co-operated, Sir Colin Campbell moved the troops into the plain and advanced cautiously, preceded by the 71st in extended order, until close upon the Tchernaya, where daybreak found them benumbed with cold and blinded by snowdrift, at the same time that the French troops were perceived coming up in support. The delay enabled the enemy's picquets to give the alarm, and the intended surprise proving a failure, the troops returned to their encampment at 10 a.m. utterly exhausted, and in numerous instances frost-bitten in the ears and tips of the fingers.

In the months of January, February, March, and April, sickness prevailed in the regiment to a great extent, appearing principally in the shape of low fever and dysentery, arising—in the first instance—from privation and exposure, subsequently aggravated by the moist nature of the ground on which the huts were erected, small springs oozing to the surface underneath the flooring, generating fungi and grasses. At length the sick list became so numerous that it was decided to vacate the huts, and encamp the regiment under canvas about 300 yards higher up the slope, at the foot of the Marine heights, on a beautiful plateau, having a south-western aspect, and pervaded in all parts by the sea breezes. As soon as this change was effected a remarkable decrease occurred in the sick list, and fever ceased to develop itself.

On the 22nd of May an expedition, commanded by Lieutenant-General Sir George Brown, G.C.B., consisting of the Highland Brigade, the 71st Highlanders, 800 men of the Royal Marines, with artillery and Land Transport, together with the French division of Lieutenant-General D'Autemarre, and a division of Turkish infantry, embarked at Balaclava and Kamiesch for the purpose of capturing Kertch and Yenikale, and of acting in concert with a fleet of gunboats, intercepting the enemy's communications by the sea of Azof. The 79th embarked under the command of Lieutenant-Colonel John Douglas, in H.M.S. *Furious*, which, with other vessels of the expedition, arrived off Ambalaki bay, six miles from Kertch, at 2 p.m. on the 24th. The troops landed without opposition, and marching for three miles ascended a ridge of hills, and bivouacked for the night.

As the troops were disembarking, a succession of explosions, occurring at intervals, informed the expedition that the enemy had blown up his magazines.

At sunrise on the 25th the troops advanced towards Kertch, where they halted until guards were established and several government buildings set on fire. The Russian troops had previously evacuated and fired their barracks on the approach of the expedition. The column then proceeded on its march to Yenikale at the entrance to the sea of Azof, where—no resistance being offered—the town was taken possession of by the allied forces at 4 p.m., and the troops proceeded to bivouac on high ground in its immediate vicinity.

On the 20th the tents were landed, and strong working parties were immediately employed, under the able superintendence of Colonel Gordon, R.E., in throwing up entrenchments and constructing redoubts at various points for the defence of the position of Yenikale. On the 29th the 79th was detached to occupy the Quarantine barracks, four miles equidistant from Kertch and Yenikale, in order to keep open the communications between these two stations. The barracks thus occupied were situated close to the water's edge, on the east side of the bay of Kertch, having a fine pier for small craft, and vast piles of buildings, consisting of hospitals, store-houses, stabling, &c., in excellent condition. The outer wall was loopholed for musketry and a breastwork erected exterior to the main gate by Lieutenant Anderson, R.E., and a party of sappers.

The regiment continued in undisturbed possession of the Quarantine barracks until the 12th of June, when it received orders to burn the barracks and other buildings and embark for Balaclava. It accordingly proceeded in boats from the Quarantine station to the bay of Kertch, where it embarked on board the *Colombo*, the last company previous to pushing off having fired the various buildings, which soon blazed fiercely, sending forth vast columns of smoke across the bay as long as the *Colombo* remained in sight.

At 4 p.m. the fleet of transports sailed, having the whole of the British expeditionary force on board, excepting the 71st Highlanders, who were left, with some French troops and a large force of Turkish artillery and infantry, to defend the entrenched position of Yenikale and Pavlovskaya. On the 14th the *Colombo* anchored off Balaclava, and the regiment, landing on the 15th, marched to its old encampment for the night; but the position of Balaclava and the line of the Tchernaya being now held by the Sardinian army, the Highland Brigade marched the following day and joined their old companions in arms, the brigade of Guards before Sebastopol again re-uniting the division, the command of which was assumed by Major-General Sir Colin Campbell.

The 79th with its division was hereafter employed in the siege operations before Sebastopol. During the assault of the advanced works, styled respectively the Malakoff and the Redan, by the French and English troops simultaneously on the 18th of June, the division was drawn up in reserve in advance of Picquet House Hill, ready to act as circumstances might require; but upon the failure of both attacks its services were not called for, and it returned to its encampment at 4 p.m. having been sixteen hours under arms.

On the 28th of June Lord Raglan, the commander-in-chief of the British army, expired, universally and deeply regretted, and was succeeded in command by Lieutenant-General Sir James Simpson, the chief of staff.

The formation of an additional division to the army having been determined on in consequence of the accession of several regiments as reinforcements, on the 16th of August the 9th, 13th, 31st, and 56th regiments of the line were incorporated with the brigade of Guards into the 1st division, commanded by Major-General Lord Rokeby; the 1st and 2nd battalions of the Royals, and the 72nd Highlanders, joining the 2nd brigade, who were, together with the old Highland brigade, now designated the Highland division, and continued under command of Lieutenant-General Sir Colin Campbell.

The 79th continued to share in the operations of the siege of Sebastopol. On the 16th of August the enemy attacked the French and Sardinian positions on the Tchernaya in great force, but were repulsed at all points with severe loss. On the 24th of August information was received from spies by General Simpson to the effect that the enemy meditated a renewal of the attack on the French and Sardinian positions. The 1st brigade of the Highland division, and the 72nd Highlanders from the 2nd brigade, were therefore ordered as a reinforcement to proceed to the vicinity of Kamara and await orders. At 1 a.m. on the 25th it accordingly marched from its encampment before Sebastopol, and arrived before dawn at the appointed locality; but, the anticipated attack not being realised, it was withdrawn, when it received orders to proceed on the following morning and occupy the position it had previously left. The brigade therefore marched at dawn on the 26th with tents and baggage, and encamped on a beautiful slope beyond the village of Kamara in close proximity to the Sardinian head-quarters.

The brigade continued encamped at Kamara until arrangements were made for a second assault on the exterior defences of Sebastopol. At 7 a.m. on the 8th of September it marched to take part in the assault, crossed the valley of Balaclava, ascended by the Karanyi road, and reached the Guards' encampment at 10.30 a.m., where the men were relieved of their knapsacks and feather-bonnets, which were piled by companies and delivered in charge to a guard of the 71st Highlanders. The brigade resuming its march at 11.30 a.m. entered the first parallel by the middle or French ravine, and gradually moving onward by the approaches under a tremendous fire, at 4 p.m. reached the fifth or most advanced parallel fronting the great redan, where it was disposed of in the following order: the 79th under the command of Lieutenant-Colonel R. C. H. Taylor on the right, with the 72nd on its left, both in line in the fifth parallel. The 42nd and 93rd in the same order in the fourth parallel, the 42nd supporting the 79th and the 93rd the 72nd. The works of the redan had by this time been stormed by details from the light and 2nd divisions, the officers and men of which, after exhibiting a devotion and courage not to be surpassed, were compelled to retire with severe loss, whilst the simultaneous attack, executed by the French troops against the works of the Malakoff, was crowned with success.

The brigade continued to occupy the advanced trenches under a heavy fire throughout the remainder of the day, and at 9 p.m. it was intimated to officers commanding regiments that it was to assault the redan at dawn on the following morning. At 10 p.m. the enemy's fire slackened, and only a dropping fire of musketry succeeded until midnight, when it ceased altogether. From 11 p.m. until 1 a.m. on the 9th, a succession of explosions occurred within the city, and by 2 a.m. Sebastopol was one vast sheet of flame and smoke, rendering objects distinctly visible in the town and harbour. At about 5 a.m. it was accurately ascertained that the enemy had abandoned all his works and was in full retreat across the harbour by a bridge of boats. At 6 a.m. two companies of the 79th, under Captain Hodgson, took possession of the redan and its works, and at 8 a.m. the Highland brigade was relieved by several regiments of the 4th division, when it returned to its encampment, which it reached at 3 p.m., having been thirty-three hours under arms.

The loss of the Cameron Highlanders on the day of the assault and in the various operations during the siege, was 17 rank and file killed; Lieutenant D. H. McBarnet, Assistant-Surgeon Edward Louis Lundy, 3 sergeants, 1 drummer, and 39 rank and file wounded. For its services during the siege the distinction of a Companionship of the Bath was conferred upon the junior Lieutenant-Colonel, R. C. H. Taylor; Majors R. D. Clephane and McCall were promoted by brevet to be lieutenant-colonels in the army; Captains W. C. Hodgson and H. W. Campbell were promoted to the brevet rank of major; and it received, in conjunction with other regiments engaged, the royal authority to have the word "Sebastopol" inscribed on its colours and appointments.

The division remained under canvas until the 17th of November, when the 79th, with the other regiments of the 1st brigade, struck tents and occupied wooden huts erected on new ground contiguous to the old encampment at Kamara.

1856.

The regiment continued to occupy its hutted encampment at Kamara, organising its camp equipment and preparing for the anticipated campaign when the season for active operations again commenced; but on the 2nd of April the signature of the treaty of peace with Russia was announced to the army by a salute of 100 guns, and a friendly interchange of civilities was established between the allied and Russian armies.

On the 17th of April, 1856, the Highland division marched from its encampment to the heights before Sebastopol, where the English and French armies were reviewed by His Excellency General Luders, the Russian commander-in-chief, and a very numerous staff. After the review it marched back to its encampment, which it reached at 9 p.m.

On the 8th of May it became known that Sir Colin Campbell was about to return to England, and at 9 a.m. on the 9th the old Highland brigade, consisting of the 42nd, 79th, and 93rd regiments, was formed up in three sides of a square of close columns, on ground contiguous to the encampment at Kamara, when General Sir Colin Campbell, G.C.B., and Major-General D. A. Cameron, C.B., with their respective staffs rode up, and Sir Colin, taking off his hat, delivered the following farewell address to the troops:

"Soldiers of the 42nd, 79th, and 93rd! old Highland brigade; with whom I passed the early and perilous part of this war, I have now to take leave of you; in a few hours I shall be on board ship, never to see you again as a body—a long farewell! I am now old, and shall not be called to serve any more, and nothing will remain to me but the memory of my campaigns and of the enduring, hardy, generous soldiers with whom I have been associated, whose name and glory will long be kept alive in the hearts of our countrymen. When you go home, as you gradually fulfil your term of service, each to his family and his cottage, and you tell the story of your immortal advance in that victorious echelon up the heights of Alma, and of the old brigadier who led you and loved you so well; your children and your children's children will repeat the tale to other generations, when only a few lines of history will remain to record the discipline and enthusiasm which have borne you so stoutly to the end of this war. Our native land will never forget the name of the Highland brigade, and in some future war the nation will call for another one to equal this which it can never surpass.

"Though I shall be gone, the thought of you will go with me wherever I shall be and cheer my old age with a glorious recollection of dangers confronted and hardships endured—a pipe will never sound near me without carrying me back to those bright days when I was at your head, and wore the bonnet you gained for me, and the honourable decorations on my breast, many of which I owe to your conduct. Brave soldiers; kind comrades! Farewell!"

At the conclusion a spontaneous cheer burst from officers and men, which was continued until Sir Colin, much affected, withdrew, accompanied by Major-General Cameron and their respective staffs, when the troops returned to their several encampments.

On the evening of the 9th of May Sir Colin was entertained at a farewell dinner given in his honour by the officers of the Highland division.

On the 6th of June the division paraded and marched to the headquarters of the general commanding at the camp before Sebastopol in order to attend the ceremony of an investiture of the Order of the Bath, held by General Lord Gough as the representative of Her Majesty the Queen. After the conclusion of the ceremony the troops were reviewed by Marshal Pelissier, the French commander-in-chief, and Lord Gough, when the division returned to its encampment.

In terms of the treaty of peace, the evacuation of the Crimea was now rapidly proceeded with. On the 15th of June the Cameron Highlanders embarked at Balaclava on board the steam-transport *Victoria*, which sailed immediately. After touching at Malta and Gibraltar, the vessel arrived in safety at Spithead on the 3rd of July. On the 5th, at 4 a.m., the regiment disembarked in the dockyard at Portsmouth, under the command of Lieutenant-Colonel John Douglas, C.B., and proceeded immediately by rail to the camp at Aldershot.

For their services in the Crimea every officer, non-commissioned officer, and man of the regiment engaged received the Crimean and Turkish War Medals; and, in addition to the distinctions already mentioned the following decorations were conferred on members of the regiment :—

THE LEGION OF HONOUR.

Lieutenant-Colonel McCall
Brevet-Major Hodgson
Captain H. W. Campbell
Lieutenant and Adjutant J. Young
Sergeant W. Davie

THE MEDJIDIE.

Lieutenant-Colonel John Douglas, C.B.	4th class
Lieutenant-Colonel R. C. H. Taylor, C.B.	5th class
Captain A. C. McBarnet	,,
Captain E. W. Cuming	,,
Captain H. H. Stevenson	,,
Lieutenant J. M. Leith	,,
Lieutenant W. McGill	,,
Surgeon T. Goldie-Scot	,,

SARDINIAN MEDAL.

Lieutenant-Colonel J. Douglas, C.B.
Lieutenant-Colonel R. C. H. Taylor, C.B.
Major R. D. Clephane
Captain H. H. Stevenson
Quarter-Master R. Jameson

FRENCH WAR MEDAL.

(Elected by their Comrades.)

Colour-Sergeant James Spencer
Colour-Sergeant Alexander Goodbrand
Sergeant William Gunn
Sergeant William Davie
Private James Wilkie
Private Robert Bruce
Private James Sloane

MEDAL FOR DISTINGUISHED CONDUCT IN THE FIELD, WITH ANNUITY OR GRATUITY.

Sergeant-Major Thomas Bunyan	£20 annuity
Qr.-Master-Sergeant Duncan McIntyre	£15 gratuity
Lance-Sergeant James Smith	£10 ,,
Lance-Sergeant William Thom	£10 ,,
Lance-Sergeant Daniel Baker	£10 ,,
Sergeant James Johnston	£10 ,,
Private Alexander Sandison	£5 ,,
Private George Kirk	£5 ,,
Private Robert Andrew	£5 ,,
Private Donald Angus	£5 ,,
Private John Morton	£5 ,,
Private Charles Webb	£5 ,,
Private Thomas Gow	£5 ,,
Private James Douglas	£5 ,,
Private Robert Buchanan	£5 ,,
Private James Dow	£5 ,,

A monument was erected in the Dean Cemetery, Edinburgh, by the regiment to the memory of their comrades who fell in the campaign. The monument is of granite, and has the following inscription upon it:—

IN MEMORY OF

COLONEL THE HONOURABLE LANDERDALE MAULE,

LIEUT.-COLONEL E. J. ELLIOT, LIEUT.-COLONEL JAMES FERGUSON,

CAPTAIN ADAM MAITLAND,

LIEUTENANT F. A. GRANT, LIEUTENANT F. J. HARRISON,

DR. R. J. MACKENZIE;

ALSO 369 NON-COMMISSIONED OFFICERS AND MEN

OF THE

79TH HIGHLANDERS,

Who died in Bulgaria and the Crimea, or fell in action during

the Campaign of 1854-55

On the 8th of July the whole of the troops then encamped at Aldershot had the honour of being reviewed by Her Majesty the Queen, their Royal Highnesses Prince Albert and the Duke of Cambridge, besides numerous other persons of distinction. At the termination of the review Her Majesty addressed a selected number of officers, non-commissioned officers and men from each of the regiments present which had served in the Crimea, in highly complimentary terms, thanking them for the devotion and gallantry they had displayed in her service and their country's cause. At the conclusion of the Royal speech Her Majesty was loudly cheered by the officers and men she addressed.

On the 10th of July the regiment was removed by railway from the camp at Aldershot to Dover Castle, in order to join the division assembling at Shorncliffe and Dover under the command of Major-General Sir H. W. Barnard, K.C.B. It was again brigaded with the 42nd and 93rd Highlanders, under the command of its former brigadier, Major-General D. A. Cameron, C.B.

On the 30th of September the 79th was removed to barracks at Canterbury, within the divisional command, in consequence of the breaking up of the encampment on Dover heights rendering a new distribution of the troops necessary.

On the 5th of December the regimental depôt was removed from Aberdeen to Stirling Castle, where it joined the depôt battalion formed there under the command of Lieutenant-Colonel E. A. G. Muller.

1857.

On the 28th of February the 79th was called upon to furnish 70 volunteers to the 93rd Sutherland Highlanders.

On the 31st of March the regiment marched from Canterbury to the camp at Shorncliffe, where it joined the brigade of Lieutenant-General Lord West, consisting of the 44th, 72nd, and 98th regiments, but its services in camp were of brief duration for on the 23rd of June orders of readiness for its removal to Dublin were received.

On the 25th the regiment accordingly proceeded by railway from Shorncliffe to London, where it was temporarily quartered by wings in Portman Street and St. John's Wood barracks, preparatory to its being present at a review to be held in Hyde Park by Her Majesty the Queen for the inauguration of the new order of the Victoria Cross, and for the purpose of presenting the same to several officers and men of the Crimean army.

At 9 o'clock on the morning of the 26th, in presence of an immense assemblage from the metropolis and surrounding neighbourhood, the troops were formed in Hyde Park in review order. They consisted of the Household Brigades of Cavalry and Infantry, 6th Dragoons, 11th Hussars, one troop of Horse Artillery and two Field Batteries, one battalion of Royal Marines, 79th Highlanders, 2nd battalion Rifle Brigade, one company Royal Sappers and Miners, and one troop of Military Train,—the whole representing a division of 10,000 men, commanded by General Sir Colin Campbell, G.C.B. Precisely at 10 o'clock a royal salute from the Field Batteries announced the approach of Her Majesty, who arrived on horseback, accompanied by their Royal Highnesses Prince Albert and the Duke of Cambridge, and followed by a brilliant staff. As Her Majesty advanced towards the line she was received by a royal salute, and she then proceeded to distribute the much-coveted decoration of the new order, in which she was assisted by the Adjutant-General, who called out the rank, name, and corps of each recipient in succession.

On the termination of the ceremony of presentation the troops marched past in slow and quick time, formed line, advanced, halted, and performed the royal salute by presenting arms, which closed the proceedings on this eventful and interesting occasion.

On the morning of the 27th the regiment marched from Portman Street and St. John's Wood barracks to the Euston Square station, from whence it proceeded by railway to Liverpool, and embarked for Dublin on the same day. On the 28th it landed at Kingstown, and was quartered in the Royal barracks, Dublin.

The alarming intelligence of the revolt of several Sepoy regiments, and of the existence of disaffection amongst others, now reached Her Majesty's government, and reinforcements of European troops being urgently called for, the officer commanding the 79th received pressing orders on the 1st of July to make immediate preparations for the embarkation of the regiment for India. By the accession of volunteers from several line regiments, the 79th was completed to 1,000 rank and file, and on the 25th the regiment was inspected by General Lord Seaton, commanding the forces in Ireland.

On the 31st of July, being within a month of the receipt of the order, the head-quarters, band, grenadiers, 1st and 2nd companies, and light company embarked at Kingstown, under the command of Lieutenant-Colonel John Douglas, C.B., on board the *Walmer Castle*, and sailed the following day; the left wing, consisting of the 3rd, 4th, 5th, 6th, and 7th companies, under Major Butt, embarked on the 1st of August in the *Louisiana* and *Tyburnia* transports, and both vessels proceeded to sea on the following day. The men were in the highest spirits, and their good conduct, and the rapid and exemplary manner in which the embarkation was conducted, elicited the following garrison order from the General Officer commanding the Dublin division.

"Town Major's Office, Dublin,
"31st July, 1857.

"The Major-General commanding the division considers it only due to the 79th Highlanders to express his satisfaction at the very soldier-like manner in which the head-quarters of the regiment marched from the barracks and effected their embarkation at Kingstown this morning; and he trusts this notice of his approbation may serve as an inducement to the troops generally, under similar circumstances, to effect their removals in a like creditable manner.

(Signed) "G. MYLIUS,
"Town Major."

The following officers embarked with the regiment :—

Colonel John Douglas, C.B.; Majors T. B. Butt and Hodgson; Captains Maitland, McBarnet, Miller, Stevenson, Percival, Turner, Currie, Leith, Scovell, and McDonald; Lieutenants Mackesy, Durant, Allen, McNair, Crawford, de Carteret, Cleather, F. Campbell, McMurdo, Gawne, Everett, Neil Campbell, Alleyne, Walker, and Wimberley; Ensigns McGuire, Stewart, Dougal, J. Campbell, Duff, Holford, McCausland, and Kerr; Paymaster Cant; Adjutant Young; Quarter-Master McGill; Surgeon J. Goldie Scot; Assistant-Surgeons Drysdale, Roberts, and Kilgour.

The detachments on board the *Louisiana* and *Tyburnia*, under Majors Butt and Hodgson respectively, arrived after a prosperous voyage at Point de Galle, Ceylon, within a day of each other, and were transhipped there to H.M.S. *Simoom*.

The *Simoom* arrived at Calcutta on the 17th of November, and the six companies of the 79th disembarked the following day, being quartered in the Town Hall, which was the largest building in the city.

Lieutenant-Colonel R. H. C. Taylor, C.B., who had come to India by the overland route, now assumed command of the six companies.

Seven young officers of the H.E.I.C. service were on the 1st of December attached for duty to the 79th, and continued to serve with the regiment until the termination of the campaign.

During their stay in the Town Hall at Calcutta the six companies, under the command of Lieutenant-Colonel Taylor, C.B., were reviewed by the Governor-General of India, the steadiness of the men eliciting his warmest approbation. They were on this occasion brigaded with the 42nd Highlanders and the Calcutta Volunteers.

After a voyage of 90 days the *Walmer Castle*, with the headquarters of the regiment, dropped anchor in Madras Roads on the 1st of November, 1857; here the first intimation of the frightful atrocities committed by the revolted Sepoys at Meerut, Delhi, Cawnpore, and other stations in the Bengal Presidency, was received by the regiment, creating a thrill of horror and indignation, and giving rise to a desire for vengeance among all ranks. Notwithstanding that the services of the regiment under these circumstances were most urgently required in Bengal, the *Walmer Castle* was detained at Madras until the 3rd, when—orders being received to proceed to Calcutta—it put to sea, and arrived and dropped anchor there on the 27th of November, 1857.

The head-quarters and right wing disembarked on the 28th, and occupied barracks in Fort William, where they were joined by the left wing from the Town Hall.

After remaining at Fort William for four days the Cameron Highlanders received orders to proceed by rail without delay to Raneegunge, for which place they started on the 2nd of December, under the command of Colonel John Douglas, C.B.; at Raneegunge they occupied temporary straw huts whilst waiting for transport to convey them to the front. On the 16th of the same month the regiment proceeded by detachments to Allahabad by bullock train, and all were assembled there again by the 25th.

1858.

On the 4th of January, 1858, Brigadier-General Campbell, commanding at Allahabad, received information that a large body of the mutineers had assembled at Munseala, in the Secundra district, twelve miles from Allahabad.

Immediate orders were therefore issued for the 79th, some Rifles, and a battery of Artillery to parade at midnight, carrying one day's cooked rations, and to march as rapidly as possible to dislodge the enemy.

The force arrived at Secundragunge at daybreak, where the enemy was found in position with three guns on the opposite side of a ravine. The attack was commenced by the Grenadier and No. 1 companies, which were thrown out in skirmishing order. The defence was very feeble, and the enemy after a few rounds from their guns abandoned them and took to flight, being pursued by the regiment from village

General Sir Richard Taylor, K.C.B.

UNIV. OF
CALIFORNIA

to village. Numbers of the mutineers were cut down by a troop of Horse Artillery acting as cavalry.

At the village of Papahmow a halt was made, as it was ascertained that the rebels had dispersed in all directions and that further pursuit was useless.

During the engagement large numbers of the enemy were taken prisoners, and his loss in killed and wounded amounted to 600.

In this affair the 79th had no casualties.

The regiment returned to Allahabad the same day, having accomplished a remarkable march of forty-eight miles in twenty-three hours. Much praise has been given to British soldiers, and justly so, for their power of marching long distances, but it is open to question if the same amount of ground was ever before covered by a regiment in such a short space of time.

The Governor-General in Council was pleased to express in general orders his approbation of the conduct of Colonel Douglas, Colonel Taylor, and the officers, non-commissioned officers, and men of the 79th on this occasion.

On the 21st of January, 1858, the regiment proceeded by rail to Mahazeepore, 50 miles from Allahabad, where the railway ended, from whence it marched by wings to Futtehpore; the right wing making the journey in two marches, and the left wing in one. After a halt of two days the 79th, with the 7th Hussars and "E" troop R.H.A., marched towards Cawnpore, arriving there on the 27th of January.

On the 4th of February the 79th crossed the Ganges at Cawnpore, and marched to Bunnee, on the 5th it moved on to Oonaoo, and on the 6th to Busseeretgunge. From that date until the 11th the regiment was employed continuously in escorting convoys to the front, and on the completion of this duty it moved to Bunnee, and joined the division under the command of Brigadier-General Sir Hope Grant. As Colonel Douglas, C.B., was now appointed to the command of a brigade, the command of the 79th devolved upon Colonel Taylor, C.B.

On the 2nd of March the 79th moved to Camp Bunterah, near Lucknow, where it joined the force assembling under Sir Colin Campbell for the siege of that city.

The defences of the city of Lucknow consisted of three successive lines, all facing east; the first running along the canal, supported by a strong battery at the Hazret Gunge; the second from the Imambara on the right, round the mess house, to the Moti Mahul on the right bank of the Goomtee; the third protected the Kaiserbagh. Still further to the west the Residency formed an inner line of defence for the mutineers. The southern and western sides of the city were covered by impenetrable masses of building, which rendered them practically unassailable, but the enemy had apparently neglected the defences on the northern side, which was skirted by the river Goomtee.

Sir Colin Campbell therefore resolved to direct a front attack upon the eastern defences with a portion of his force, whilst the remainder, crossing the Goomtee, effected a turning movement on the northern side of the city.

On the 2nd of March a portion of Sir Colin's force, including the 42nd, 79th, and 93rd Highlanders, marched to the Dilkoosha, just outside Lucknow, and commenced to erect batteries to shell the enemy's first line of defence on the canal. On the 3rd the remainder of the force closed up to the Dilkoosha, and Sir Colin took up a position with his right resting on the Goomtee at the village of Bibiapore, and his left on a point about two miles beyond the Dilkoosha. On the 4th he directed that two pontoon bridges should be thrown across the Goomtee at Bibiapore to effect his flanking movement on the opposite bank. These bridges were completed on the 5th, and the same night the 3rd division (Lieutenant-General Walpole's) and some cavalry, the whole under General Sir James Outram, G.C.B., crossed to the left bank of the river.

The 3rd division comprised the 5th brigade, consisting of the 23rd Fusiliers, 79th Highlanders, and 1st Bengal Fusiliers, under the command of Brigadier-General Douglas, C.B., of the 79th, and the 6th Brigade, consisting of the 2nd and 3rd battalions of the Rifle brigade, and the 2nd Punjaub Infantry, under the command of Brigadier-General Horsford.

Sir James Outram's orders were to push up the left bank of the Goomtee and to turn and render untenable the enemy's strong positions on the right bank, thus preparing the way for Sir Colin's direct attack from the Dilkoosha.

On the 6th Sir James Outram's force advanced, and the 2nd Dragoon Guards engaged some of the enemy's cavalry. The 79th, under Lieutenant-Colonel Taylor, C.B., advanced in line in support of the Bays, and were for some time under fire of the enemy's guns, having Ensign Thain of the regiment wounded.

The force bivouacked for the night at Chinhat, throwing out strong picquets. These were attacked at daylight on the 7th by the enemy, who brought out several guns. The regiment turned out immediately in support of the picquets, and advanced in line for about a mile, but as the enemy retired again into Lucknow it returned to camp.

On the 8th of March Outram erected several batteries to fire across the river and shell the enemy on the right bank.

On the 9th, Lieutenant-General Walpole drove the enemy from his position on the left bank, and occupied a building called the Yellow House, which was carried at the point of the bayonet by two companies of the 79th and Bengal Fusiliers; then, pressing on in pursuit of the rebels, he seized the Badshahbagh, which enabled him to place heavy guns in position to enfilade the enemy's works. The remaining eight companies of the 79th advanced through the Badshahbagh and occupied the chief buildings in the vicinity; the Grenadiers and No. 1 company being located in a large house which commanded the road leading to the Iron Bridge by which the city of Lucknow is entered.

Outram, having now occupied the left bank of the Goomtee as far as the Badshahbagh, signalled the success of his operations to Sir Colin Campbell at the Dilkoosha.

On the morning of the 10th the rebels made a most determined attack on a picquet from the most advanced companies of the 79th, but were repulsed with considerable loss, being unable to get nearer than 50 yards. They then withdrew to a respectful distance, and kept up a galling fire upon the picquet. Brigadier-General Douglas therefore gave orders that they should be cleared out at the point of the bayonet, which was done in a most gallant manner by the Grenadiers and No. 1 company under Captain Stevenson and Lieutenant M'Nair. In this brilliant encounter the party of the 79th had Sergeant W. Davie and Private J. Rankine killed; Privates J. Miller and J. Ritchie dangerously wounded, and two men slightly wounded.

Whilst Outram was thus engaged, Sir Colin remained quiet at the Dilkoosha; but on the 9th his force advanced and took the Martiniere, and this success was followed up later in the day by the capture of the Secundrabagh, Shah Nujeef, and Begum Kothie.

At daybreak on the 11th the 79th advanced and cleared the enemy from the remaining portions of the suburbs on the left bank of the Goomtee, seizing the buildings in the vicinity of the Iron and Stone Bridges. On the same day Sir James Outram opened a heavy fire with the artillery across the river on to the Kaiserbagh.

On the evening of the 12th it was resolved to seize the Iron Bridge and throw a breastwork across it, from which the fire of the enemy could be kept under. Volunteers to construct this breastwork were called for, and Captain Stevenson, Lieutenant Wimberley, Sergeant Mackenzie, and 10 men were selected. At midnight the party proceeded carrying with them gabions and sand bags, and placed them about half way across the bridge at a point indicated by Lieutenant Wynne, R.E., who was in charge of the party. Sand bags were passed rapidly on to the bridge, and the breastwork was completed in a very short time. A party of the Bengal Fusiliers then rushed up and occupied the work, opening fire upon the enemy under cover of which the volunteers withdrew. This little affair was admirably carried out and called forth the praise of General Outram in his despatch.

On the 12th, 13th, and 14th, Outram's force kept up a continuous fire against the Kaiserbagh, and on the 14th it was carried by storm by the 10th regiment and Brasyer's Sikhs. During these days the 79th was posted at the Yellow House.

On the 16th of March Sir James Outram, with the 23rd Fusiliers, 79th, and Bengal Fusiliers, re-crossed the Goomtee by a bridge of casks near the Secundrabagh, and joined the Commander-in-Chief in the city at the Kaiserbagh, leaving General Walpole with the remainder of his division to prosecute the attack from the left bank. On the same day Sir James, acting under Sir Colin Campbell's orders, left the Kaiserbagh and stormed the Residency, which was evacuated in great haste by the mutineers.

On the 17th of March Outram continued his advance, occupying the Hussein Mosque and Deolat Khana without opposition, whilst the

79th captured the Great Imambara. Nine carts, full of powder, were left behind by the enemy in a courtyard adjoining the latter place, and orders were given for its destruction. By some accident, which can never now be explained, the powder exploded, killing and wounding 2 officers and 30 men of the brigade; amongst the killed was Sergeant James Blythe of the 79th.

On this occasion Private Kerr of the regiment, who was acting as hospital orderly, was honourably mentioned in regimental orders by Colonel Taylor for rendering assistance to the wounded under a heavy fire.

On the 19th the 79th, 23rd, and 2nd Punjaub Infantry, with three companies of the 20th regiment moved against the Musaghbagh, which was evacuated as they approached, whilst the light company of the 79th, under Lieutenant Everett, stormed and captured the house of Nawab Ali Khan. The regiment had Lance-Corporal James Malcolm and Privates T. Munro and J. Harrison killed during the day's operations. Four of the enemy's guns and the colours of the 7th Oude Irregular Infantry (which are still in the possession of the regiment) fell into the hands of the 79th.

All resistance in the city was over by the 22nd of March, on which day Sir Colin Campbell published the following congratulatory order to the troops :—

"The Commander-in-Chief congratulates the army on the reduction and fall of Lucknow. From the 2nd to the 21st of March, when the last body of the rebels was expelled from the town, the exertions of all ranks have been without intermission, and every regiment employed has won much distinction. The attack on both sides of the river Goomtee has been conducted by the General and Commanding Officers of the brigades and regiments with vigour and perseverance, the consequence being the great result which has been achieved with comparatively moderate loss. His Excellency returns his warmest thanks to the troops. Every man who has been employed either in the old garrison of Lucknow, in the relieving force, or at the siege which has now been terminated may rest assured that he has deserved well of his country."

During the siege of Lucknow the Cameron Highlanders had 2 sergeants and 5 rank and file killed; Brevet-Major Miller, Ensign Thain, 1 sergeant, and 20 rank and file wounded. For its conduct on this occasion the regiment received the royal authority to have the word "Lucknow" inscribed on its colours and appointments.

Brigadier-General Douglas, C.B., Colonel Taylor, C.B., Captains Maitland and Stevenson, and Lieutenants Walker and Everett were mentioned in general orders for conspicuous conduct during the siege.

The 79th occupied the Imambara until the 2nd of April, when, leaving behind the sick and wounded, it marched to the Dilkoosha, where it was once again brigaded with the 42nd and 93rd Highlanders, under the command of Brigadier-General the Honourable Adrian Hope.

On the 7th of April the Cameron Highlanders with the 9th Lancers, 2nd Punjaub Cavalry, the 42nd and 93rd Highlanders, the 4th Punjaub Rifles, and some Artillery, forming a division under the command of Lieutenant-General Walpole, left Lucknow with orders to advance up the left bank of the Ganges, penetrate into Rohilcund, and disperse the scattered bodies of mutineers there. The march was uneventful until the 15th of April, when the force reached Roodemow, close to the fort of Rooyah, which was occupied by the enemy under Nurput Singh.

On the morning of the 16th an attack was made upon the fort, but no reconnaissance had been made, and the attack was delivered against its strongest and most inaccessible face.

The 42nd, 93rd, and 4th Punjaub Rifles were in advance, the 79th being held in reserve. Throughout the day gallant efforts were made to gain an entrance to the fort, but to no purpose, and at sunset the force, after losing its Brigadier-General, Adrian Hope, and many officers and men, was withdrawn, and bivouacked about a mile from the fort.

The Cameron Highlanders had two men wounded, one of whom died of his wounds.

During the night the enemy evacuated the fort, which was destroyed by the troops on the 17th.

On the 18th the division marched to Bilgwan, on the 19th to

Sandhee, on the 20th to Mungoor, on the 21st to Kakladapore, and on the 22nd it arrived at Sirsa, 40 miles from Rooyah, near the village of Allygunge which was occupied by the rebels. Their position was at once attacked, and they were driven from it with a loss of four guns, the 9th Lancers pursuing them for six miles.

In this engagement the 79th had no casualties.

On the 27th of April Sir Colin arrived at Allygunge and assumed command of the force, which advanced at once upon Bareilly. Shahjehanpore was reached on the 30th of April, and on the 3rd of May the force bivouacked at Fareedpore, one march from Bareilly. Early on the morning of the 5th of May, Sir Colin, with the Highland brigade, General Stisted's brigade, and a heavy battery of Artillery, advanced from Fareedpore, covered by the 2nd Punjaub Cavalry.

The enemy was found strongly posted in front of Bareilly with a stream in his rear; the Highland brigade accordingly advanced in line, supported by two native regiments, the artillery and cavalry being on the flanks, and the enemy was quickly driven from his position across the stream. This the 79th crossed by a bridge, and the regiment advanced for about three-quarters of a mile towards the town. A halt was then made for the artillery to come up, as the suburbs of Bareilly were full of the enemy. During this halt Sir Colin, observing that some of the enemy were trying to turn his left flank, directed one company of the 79th, under Captain McBarnet, to occupy a wood to the left front and to hold it at all costs. This company was almost immediately attacked in the wood, but repulsed and drove back the enemy. A very vigorous charge was also made on the 42nd Highlanders, who bayoneted the whole of their assailants.

The left wing of the 79th, the 42nd, and 4th Sikh infantry now advanced towards the cantonments, where they took up a position for the remainder of the day; the right wing, with the 93rd Highlanders, was directed to seize the suburbs in front, the enemy evacuating them and retiring out of range. The force remained under arms for the remainder of the day, and, as evening approached, picquets were thrown out and the troops bivouacked for the night.

In this action the 79th had Privates John Balmain and Alexander Thomson killed, and two men wounded.

His Excellency Sir Colin Campbell, referring to the conduct of the troops during the progress from Lucknow to Bareilly, thus expresses himself in his despatch to the Governor-General of India :—

"I have the greatest reason to be satisfied with all the troops under my own immediate command. Their alacrity to meet the enemy on all occasions is of course what your Lordship would expect from them, but I must not lose this opportunity of bearing testimony to the constancy displayed by all ranks of the force in the performance of their duties during the great and incessant heat of this season of the year. It is difficult to speak too highly of that cheerful endurance of intense fatigue to which we are indebted for the victories gained at comparatively trifling loss on the day of battle."

Colonel Taylor, C.B., was very favourably mentioned in general orders for his conduct in the action of Bareilly.

News now reached Sir Colin that the garrison which had been left behind at Shahjehanpore was being assailed by a large body of Sepoys. He accordingly despatched the 60th Rifles, 79th Highlanders, and 22nd Punjaub Native Infantry, under the command of Brigadier-General Jones, to its relief. This force left Bareilly on the 8th of May and proceeded by forced marches to Shahjehanpore, where it arrived on the 11th at daybreak, when it was found that the fort and town were both in the enemy's possession, and that the British garrison was holding out in the Gaol. Swarms of the enemy's cavalry at once came out of the town, and, crossing by a bridge of boats, attempted to work round the right flank of the relieving force, but a few well-directed shells fired by the artillery stopped the movement and sent them back again. After a halt of about two hours, to obtain shelter from the scorching mid-day sun, the troops again advanced, and entering Shahjehanpore, which was hastily deserted by the enemy, opened communications with the garrison. The 79th continued its march through Shahjehanpore, and at 9 p.m. halted on the side of the town facing Mahomdie. Picquets were thrown out in front for the night, and the regiment breakfasted, for no one had had any food during the day. The regiment had no casualties in this engagement, but twenty-three men were struck down by sunstroke, many of whom died.

Tents were pitched on the 12th, and the force remained inactive until the 15th, when spies brought in word that the enemy meditated an attack. The troops at once got under arms, but nothing occurred till noon, when two bodies of the enemy's cavalry, debouching from a wood, charged the 79th and two guns which were in a position close to the regiment. The 79th at once formed square and received the enemy with volleys, which drove him back with considerable loss. The enemy displayed great courage, charging right up to the muzzles of the two guns, and the artillerymen were fortunate in reaching the 79th square before the cavalry were upon them.

The force remained in position all day and bivouacked for the night, returning to camp the next morning, when it was ascertained that the enemy had retreated to Mahomdie.

On the 24th of May the 79th marched to Remi, a large fort situated half-way to Mahomdie, which was in the hands of the rebels. It was evacuated as the regiment approached. On the following day the regiment advanced to Mahomdie, and drove the enemy from the position which he had taken up, losing two rank and file wounded. During this day's march the regiment suffered terribly from the heat, and 110 men were struck down by the sun, several of whom died by the road. Ten deaths occurred on the 25th of May, eight on the 26th, and four on the 27th; many others were afterwards invalided. The indefatigable exertions of Surgeon-Major Goldie Scot in attending to the sick on this trying occasion were beyond all praise. By his kindness and attention, and that of the medical officers under him, many lives were saved.

As Colonel Taylor, C.B., had been appointed to the command of a brigade, the command of the regiment at Mahomdie devolved upon Major Butt.

As the relief of Shahjehanpore and the capture of Mahomdie had now been effected, it was resolved to suspend all active operations until the close of the hot season. The 79th therefore returned to Shahjehanpore, arriving there on the 29th of May. On the 30th Lieutenant Robertson and 22 men joined head-quarters from the depôt at Stirling.

On the 3rd of June the regiment marched to Futtehghur, where it went into summer quarters, occupying the fort and barracks.

On the 25th of June one company, under command of Major Maitland, moved from Futtehghur to Maguls-K₁-Serai.

On the 16th July four companies marched to Cawnpore, being followed by the remainder of the regiment on the 28th of the same month.

On the occasion of the departure of the regiment from Futtehghur, Brigadier-General McCausland, commanding the troops at that station, issued the following garrison order :—

"Brigadier-General McCausland cannot permit Her Majesty's 79th Highlanders to leave the station without recording the high opinion he has formed of the regiment for its steady and soldier-like behaviour in quarters, and he requests Colonel Taylor, C.B., commanding, to accept and convey to the officers and men under his command his thanks for their uniform good conduct. They leave the station without having a single complaint made against them from the day they entered it."

On the 23rd of August the left wing, under Major Butt, marched to Allahabad.

Whilst at Cawnpore the regiment was inspected by Brigadier-General the Honourable Percy Herbert, C.B., who expressed his approval of the discipline, interior economy, and soldier-like appearance of the corps.

On the 18th of October the head-quarters, with the remainder of the regiment, moved by rail from Cawnpore to Allahabad, where preparations were now made for a renewal of the campaign.

On the 21st of October the 79th marched to Soraon, and joined the field force assembling in Oude under Brigadier-General Weatherall, C.B.

On the 1st of November the force advanced against Rampore Kussia, which was held by a body of the enemy strongly entrenched, arriving there on the 3rd of the month. Four companies of the 79th were at once directed to storm the enemy's position, the remainder of the regiment following in support. So rapidly did the storming party move to the attack that the enemy was completely surprised, and very small loss was incurred by the regiment, viz :—2 rank and file killed, and 1 sergeant and 6 rank and file wounded.

For its conduct in the attack on this place the 79th was specially complimented in general orders by the Commander-in-Chief.

On the 6th of November the force marched to Ameetha, which was occupied without opposition. Here Sir Hope Grant assumed command, and, as Colonel Taylor, C.B., was again appointed to the command of a brigade, Major Butt took over command of the 79th.

The next move of the regiment was to Fyzabad, where it crossed the Gogra, capturing the enemy's works erected on the banks. The bed of this river contained many quicksands, from which Major Miller and several of the men were extricated with the greatest difficulty, and which presented a serious obstacle to the passage of the artillery.

From the banks of the Gogra the force advanced to Muchligan, where it had another skirmish with the mutineers, driving them into a dense jungle where pursuit was an impossibility. The 79th halted on the outskirts of the jungle, where they destroyed great quantities of the enemy's ammunition and equipment, which he had left behind in his flight. On this occasion Private Robert Winning of the regiment greatly distinguished himself. Coming alone in the jungle upon six of the enemy, he shot one of them down and bayoneted two, the remainder taking to flight.

Continuing its march the 79th passed through Sultanpore, and encamped on the banks of the Raptee river. The passage of this river was effected on the 25th December, and the pursuit of the flying mutineers was resumed.

1859.

On the 3rd of January the regiment was present in the engagement with the rebels at **Bundwa Kote**, when 27 guns were captured.

The troops were now on the frontier of Nepaul where the remainder of the rebels found refuge.

This terminated the Indian Mutiny campaign, and, as tranquillity was restored in the country, the field force was broken up, and the regiments were ordered to return to different stations.

Colonel Taylor, C.B., accordingly gave up his brigade and resumed command of the 79th.

On the 22nd of January the regiment arrived at Lucknow, where it was met at the station by Sir Colin Campbell.

The following day he inspected the regiment, congratulating it on its gallantry during the recent campaign, and praising its dash and bravery at the storming of Rampore Kussia, intimating futhermore that the regiment would now be sent to Mean Meer in the Punjaub. At the close of his address His Excellency was greeted with hearty cheers from both officers and men, after which he bade good-bye to the regiment with evident emotion.

During the Indian Mutiny campaign the Cameron Highlanders lost 158 non-commissioned officers and men from disease or in action.

For its conduct during the suppression of the mutiny the regiment received the thanks of Her Majesty the Queen and both Houses of Parliament. Colonel Douglas, C.B., was appointed a Knight Commander of the Order of the Bath; Major Butt was promoted by brevet to the rank of lieutenant-colonel; Captains Maitland, McBarnet, and Miller received brevet majorities, and every officer, non-commissioned officer, and man was granted the Indian Mutiny medal.

On the 8th of April, 1859, the regiment arrived at Mean Meer, and on the 15th of the same month Lieutenant-Colonel Taylor, C.B., proceeded on leave to Europe, being succeeded in command by Lieutenant-Colonel Butt.

1860.

On the 16th of March, 1860, Lieutenant-Colonel Sir John Douglas, K.C.B., retired upon half pay, and on the 10th of May Lieutenant-Colonel Taylor, C.B., also retired from the regiment. This promoted Lieutenant-Colonel Butt and Major Hodgson to be regimental lieutenant-colonels, and Brevet-Majors Maitland and McBarnet succeeded to the vacant majorities.

On the 1st of November, 1860, a detachment of 100 rank and file, under Captain Harrison, proceeded to Fort Kangra, where it remained until the 21st of January, 1862.

On the 5th of November, 1860, the right wing, 287 of all ranks, under the command of **Major McBarnet**, proceeded to Umritzur.

On the 6th of December the 79th lost its first officer by death since its arrival in India, viz., Captain Newport, who died of cholera at Dum Dum. He had never joined the regiment, having exchanged from the 39th only a short time before his death.

1861.

On the 19th of January, 1861, the 79th left Mean Meer for Ferozepore, where it arrived on the 21st of the same month, being joined on arrival by the wing from Umritzur.

On the 19th of May Lieutenant-Colonel Hodgson, who had succeeded Lieutenant-Colonel Butt in command of the regiment, proceeded to Europe on leave of absence, making over the command temporarily to Major Maitland.

1862.

On the 13th of February the regiment marched from Ferozepore to Nowshera, arriving there on the 18th of March. From here the regiment furnished a detachment of three companies to Fort Attock on the Indus.

On the 13th of March General W. H. Sewell, C.B., colonel of the regiment, died in England, and the 79th passed into the hands of General the Honourable Hugh Arbuthnott, C.B.

The 79th remained at Nowshera until the 23rd of November, 1862, when it was joined by the three companies from Fort Attock and moved to Peshawur, where it arrived on the 24th of the same month.

Lieutenant-Colonel Hodgson, having re-joined from leave of absence, again assumed command of the regiment on the 20th of December.

1863.

Whilst at Peshawur the 79th had the misfortune to lose two of its officers—Lieutenants Dougal and Jones. They had volunteered their services and were permitted to proceed with the expedition against the Sitana fanatics, under the command of Brigadier-General

Sir N. Chamberlain, K.C.B.; the former was killed when on picquet on the 6th of November, 1863, the latter in action on the 18th of the same month. They were both doing duty with the 71st Highlanders.

During the month of December, 1863, four companies of the 79th, under Major Miller, were moved from Peshawur to the Shubkudder Pass, at the entrance to the Khyber, to join a force under Colonel Macdonell assembling to resist a threatened inroad of the Mohmunds. These companies were not engaged with the enemy, but in 1884 the officers, non-commissioned officers, and men received the Indian Medal for the North-West Frontier Campaigns. They returned to Peshawur early in January, 1864.

A small detachment of the regiment, under Lieutenant Neil Campbell, was engaged with the Mohmunds in the affairs of Michnie and Shubkudder. Private Burnett of the 79th was slightly wounded.

1864.

On the 7th of January the Cameron Highlanders marched from Peshawur to Rawul Pindee, arriving there on the 17th of the same month. On the 4th of March the regiment was inspected by His Excellency General Sir Hugh Rose, G.C.B., commander-in-chief in India, who expressed himself much pleased with the high state of efficiency in which he found it.

In April the 79th was called upon to furnish volunteers for a working party on the Murree and Abbottabad road, and on the 28th a party of 300 of all ranks, under the command of Captain Conway Gordon, proceeded to Camp Durrgaw Gully, where it remained until the 18th of July, on which date it was moved into huts at Khyra Gully. It re-joined the regiment on the 2nd of November.

In the month of October the 79th lost by exchange its senior lieutenant-colonel, Colonel Butt, who had been employed as Chief Inspector of Musketry in Bengal; he exchanged with Colonel Best of the 86th regiment. By this exchange Lieutenant-Colonel Hodgson became the senior lieutenant-colonel.

For some time after its arrival at Rawul Pindee the regiment continued to suffer from Peshawur fever, and a considerable number of men were invalided.

1865.

On the 5th of April a draft, consisting of 1 captain, 3 subalterns, and 20 rank and file, joined head-quarters from the depôt companies.

On the 8th of May the head-quarters and 650 of all ranks proceeded as a working party to the Murree hills, where the head-quarters went under canvas at Camp Gora Gully, whilst a detachment of 300 men, under Major Maitland, were stationed at Camp Grogur Gully.

On the 2nd of June the camp was visited by a fearful thunderstorm, and a large tree, which had been struck by lightning, fell upon the Sergeants' Mess, killing Sergeant Angus upon the spot.

The health of the men greatly improved during its stay in the Murree hills, and all traces of Peshawur fever disappeared.

On the 2nd of June the regiment went into huts for the rainy season at Khyra Gully, and remained there until the 24th of October, when it returned to Rawul Pindee.

On the 10th of July Lieutenant-Colonel Hodgson received his promotion by brevet to be full colonel in the army.

1866.

In February the service companies were augmented by a draft from the depôt companies, consisting of 2 colour-sergeants, 3 corporals, and 44 privates.

In the same month a detachment of 104 rank and file, under Captain Everett, was sent to Fort Attock, being relieved about a month afterwards by a similar detachment under Captain Leith.

On the 21st of March Colonel R. M. Best took over temporary command of the regiment from Lieutenant-Colonel Hodgson, who proceeded home on fifteen months' leave of absence.

A detachment of 170 of all ranks was again sent as a working party to the Murree Hills on the 28th of April, under the command of Captain McNair; this detachment returned to Rawul Pindee in October.

On the 28th of October the regiment was moved from Rawul Pindee; the head-quarters and left wing, under Colonel Best, marching to Roorkee, and the right wing, under Major Maitland, to Delhi.

1867.

In January the regiment was augmented by a draft from the depôt companies, consisting of 1 captain (Captain Allen), 2 lieutenants, and 52 rank and file.

The regiment suffered greatly from fever during the spring of 1867, six deaths occurring at Roorkee and three at Delhi, and it was considered desirable to encamp the wing at Roorkee five miles away from the town.

On the 24th of December Lieutenant-Colonel Hodgson returned from leave of absence and resumed command of the regiment.

About the end of the year the wings changed places, the head-quarters remaining at Roorkee.

1868.

On the 27th of April a draft of 2 lieutenants, 3 sergeants, and 78 rank and file joined head-quarters.

In the winter months of 1868 the wings again exchanged stations, the left wing returning to head-quarters and the right wing moving to Delhi.

1869.

On the 31st of January, 1869, the service companies were augmented by a draft from the depôt companies, consisting of 1 lieutenant, 1 ensign, 1 sergeant, and 130 rank and file.

The regiment left Roorkee for Umballa on the 19th of March, 1869, having received orders to join a force collecting at that station to take part in the ceremonial on the occasion of the meeting between Earl Mayo, governor-general of India, and Shere Ali Khan, Ameer of Cabul. The head-quarters and left wing, under the command of Colonel Hodgson, arrived at Umballa from Roorkee on the 21st of March, and were joined on the following day by the right wing from Delhi, under the command of Major G. M. Miller. The 79th was encamped near the Viceroy's tent, having been appointed part of His Excellency's personal escort, and on the 24th of March it furnished the Guard of Honour in front of the Durbar tent on the occasion of the meeting of the Viceroy and the Ameer of Cabul, the remainder of the regiment being employed in lining the streets. It was similarly employed a few days later when the Viceroy paid his return visit to the Ameer.

The head-quarters and left wing left Umballa on the 5th of April, 1869, for Roorkee, and on the 7th the right wing returned to Delhi.

In May the 79th was detailed to form part of the force ordered to assemble at Agra in December, 1869, for the Grand Durbar in honour of His Royal Highness the Duke of Edinburgh, but on account of the prevailing famine the orders were cancelled.

On the 7th of December the head-quarters and left wing, under the command of Colonel W. C. Hodgson, left Roorkee *en route* to Kamptee. They were joined on the 15th of December by the right wing from Delhi at Camp Jubbulpore. Here the regiment remained until the 24th of December, when it commenced to move by companies towards Kamptee, at which station the head-quarters arrived on the 1st of January, 1870.

1870.

During the month of January, 1870, the 93rd Sutherland Highlanders passed through Kamptee *en route* for home, and the following letter was received by the President of the Officers' Mess of the 79th Highlanders :—

"At a meeting held at Camp Nagpore by the officers 93rd Sutherland Highlanders, on the 30th of January, 1870, it was proposed, and carried unanimously, that a letter be written the officers 79th Cameron Highlanders, proposing that, in consideration of the friendship and cordiality which has so long existed between them, the officers of the two corps be perpetual honorary members of their respective messes, and the same should be formally recorded in the regimental records.

"In accordance with the above resolution, the officers of the 93rd Sutherland Highlanders have much pleasure in informing the officers, 79th Cameron Highlanders, that they are henceforth perpetual honorary members of the 93rd mess, and that a formal entry to that effect has been made in the records of the 93rd Highlanders.

(Signed) "R. S. WILLIAMS, Major,

"President Mess Committee

"93rd Sutherland Highlanders."

"Camp Deolali,
"6th February, 1870."

The following reply was sent :—

"At a mess meeting held at Kamptee, India, on the 12th of February, 1870, a letter was read from the officers of the 93rd Sutherland Highlanders, dated Camp Deolali, 6th of February, 1870, and the proposition contained in it, to the effect that, 'in consideration of the friendship and cordiality which has so long existed between the two corps, the officers should be perpetual honorary members of their respective messes,' was accepted as a high compliment to the 79th Highlanders and carried unanimously. The officers of the 79th Cameron Highlanders have therefore the pleasure of informing the officers of the 93rd Sutherland Highlanders that they are henceforth perpetual honorary members of the 79th mess, and that the above resolution has been duly entered in the records of the regiment.

(Signed) "A. B. MURRAY, Lieutenant,

"P.M.C., 79th Highlanders."

"Kamptee, India,
"10th March, 1870."

The following officers were present at this important mess meeting:—

Colonels W. C. Hodgson and Best; Lieutenant-Colonel K. R. Maitland; Major G. M. Miller; Captains J. M. Leith, D. McDonald, J. E Allen, E. Everett, A. N. Clay, N. Campbell, H. Currie, and C H. Miers; Lieutenants R. M. Borthwick, A. B. Murray, W. D. S. Campbell, J. Busfield, G. Quin, C. R. K. Fergusson, A. L. H. Holmes, J. Angus, J. D. K. McCallum, and O. B. Gordon; Ensigns R. H. C. Dalzell, J. M. Brown, N. G. Chalmers, H. McLeod, G. L. C. Money, C. C. Mackenzie, and J. F. Shaw-Kennedy; Paymaster, Major D. Cant;

Quarter-Master W. Simpson; Surgeon A. S. Lithgow; Assistant-Surgeons A. Doig and J. F. Beattie.

The regiment remained at Kamptee for nearly two years furnishing a detachment to Fort Nagpore, and sending many parties of convalescents to the Sanitariums of Wellington and Chindwarrah.

1871.

In 1871 the regiment was called upon to send a detachment to Puchmurree.

On the 2nd of August the junior lieutenant-colonel of the regiment, Colonel R.M. Best, was appointed to the command of the Nagpore Field Force, with the rank of brigadier-general.

In the same month the 79th received orders to be in readiness to proceed to England, and about 177 non-commissioned officers and men availed themselves of the permission given to volunteer into regiments remaining in India.

A sad event occurred whilst the regiment remained at Kamptee. On August 28th Captain Donald McDonald fell down suddenly on parade, when at great gun drill at the Artillery Barracks, and died instantaneously. He was by birth and habits a Highlander, and was most warmly attached to the regiment, in which he had served for seventeen years. Great sorrow was felt by all ranks at his untimely and unexpected death, and a monument was erected by his brother officers over his grave at Kamptee.

On the 22nd of September, 1871, the left half battalion, under the command of Brevet-Lieutenant-Colonel Maitland, marched from Kamptee to Nagpore, and from thence proceeded by rail to Deolali. The head-quarters and right half battalion, under the command of Colonel W. C. Hodgson, followed the next day. The regiment remained a few days only at Deolali, where the men were supplied with sea kits, and on the 30th of September the 79th, preceded by a baggage guard of 200 men, moved by rail to Bombay and embarked for England on board Her Majesty's Indian troopship *Jumna*. The undermentioned officers embarked with the regiment :—

Colonel W. C. Hodgson; Lieutenant-Colonels K. R. Maitland and G. Miller; Captains J. M. Leith, J E. Allen, A. N. Clay,

W. H. McCausland, and H. Currie; Lieutenants R. Mc. G. Borthwick, W. D. S. Campbell, C. R. K. Fergusson, S. C. Bucknall, and J. Angus; Ensigns R. H. C. Dalzell, J. M. Brown, N. G. Chalmers, H. T McLeod, G. L. C. Money, C. C. Mackenzie, J. F. Shaw-Kennedy, and P. J. Graeme; Paymaster, Major D. Cant; Lieutenant and Adjutant A. Hume; Quarter-Master W. Simpson; Surgeon S. A. Lithgow; Assistant Surgeons A. Doig and J. F. Beattie; Chaplain Rev. C. Morrison.

The *Jumna* sailed for England at 12 noon on the 1st of October, and, after a prosperous voyage by the Suez Canal, arrived at Spithead on the 6th of November. On the following day the regiment was transhipped to H.M. Ships *Pigmy*, *Camel*, and *Grinder*, and conveyed to West Cowes, where it disembarked and marched to the Albany barracks at Parkhurst.

During the fourteen years that the regiment had been stationed in India it was inspected by many distinguished general officers, including Sir Colin Campbell, Sir William Mansfield (afterwards Lord Sandhurst), Sir Hugh Rose, Sir Hope Grant, Sir Percy Herbert, Sir Sydney Cotton, and Sir John Garvock, all of whom expressed themselves highly pleased with the appearance, conduct, and discipline of the Cameron Highlanders.

1872.

In February, 1872, Her Majesty the Queen, who was at Osborne, was pleased to express her desire to see the 79th Highlanders in marching order. The regiment accordingly paraded at 10 a.m. on the 16th, and proceeded towards Osborne. When the 79th was within a short distance of the approach to the house, Her Majesty, with several members of the Royal Family, appeared at an angle of the road, and watched the regiment march past with great interest. The regiment, after making a detour towards East Cowes, was returning to Parkhurst by way of Newport, when Her Majesty re-appeared, paying particular attention to the dress and appearance of the men as they marched past her for the second time.

This was the last occasion on which Colonel Hodgson was destined to command the regiment on parade. He died, after a very short illness, on the 1st of March, to the great grief of all ranks of the 79th

Highlanders. He had served in the regiment for 32 years and commanded it for 12 of them, endearing himself to everyone by his invariable kindness.

Colonel Maitland, in announcing Colonel Hodgson's death in regimental orders, thus speaks of him :—

"The officers have to lament the loss of one who was always to them a kind and considerate commanding officer ; and the non-commissioned officers and men have been deprived of a true friend, who was ever zealous in guarding their interests and promoting their welfare. Lieutenant-Colonel Maitland feels that this day will be regarded by all ranks of the 79th Highlanders in after years as a day on which the regiment sustained a loss as sad as it was unexpected."

The funeral took place on the 5th of March and was very numerously attended. Every officer, non-commissioned officer, and man, off duty, of the 79th Highlanders and 103rd Fusiliers was present, and, in addition, the officers of the Isle of Wight Militia and Volunteers, the officials of Parkhurst prison, and many pensioners followed to the grave.

By Colonel Hodgson's death Colonel Maitland succeeded to the command of the regiment, but he retired on half pay on the 19th of October following, and Lieutenant-Colonel Miller was selected to succeed him.

On the 17th of September the Cameron Highlanders had the honour of being reviewed by the ex-Emperor of the French, Napoleon III., and the Prince Imperial, who lunched with the officers. His Majesty made a very minute inspection of the men, and afterward witnessed the regiment perform some manœuvres under Lieutenant-Colonel Miller. At the termination of the inspection he expressed his admiration of the splendid appearance and physique of the men, and of the magnificent manner in which the drill had been performed.

On the 27th of September a detachment, consisting of 1 captain, 1 subaltern, 3 sergeants, and 61 rank and file, was sent to Cliff End Fort, near Freshwater. This detachment re-joined head-quarters on the 1st of November.

1873.

On January 14th a detachment of 1 captain, 1 subaltern, 3 sergeants, and 67 rank and file was furnished to Marchwood Magazines, near Southampton.

During Her Majesty's stay at Osborne the 79th always furnished a Guard of Honour at East Cowes. On the 17th of April, 1873, Her Majesty the Queen bestowed upon the regiment one of the highest honours in her power, when on that day she was graciously pleased to attend at Parkhurst barracks and present it with new colours.

On this occasion the town of Newport was tastefully decorated, and many triumphal arches were erected in the streets. The presentation took place in the drill field, and was witnessed by a large number of spectators.

At 11 a.m. the regiment was formed up on parade under the command of Colonel Miller, the other officers present on parade being :—Majors Cuming and Percival ; Captains Leith, Allen, Everett, Clay, McCausland, Miers, Oldham, Borthwick, and Murray ; Lieutenants Busfield, Methuen, Bucknall, Forbes-Gordon, Annesley, Brown, Chalmers, Money, Mackenzie, Smith, and Graeme ; Sub-Lieutenants Smythe and Hunt ; Paymaster, Major Cant ; Lieutenant and Adjutant Hume ; Surgeon-Major Lithgow and Surgeon Doig.

The ground was kept by the 102nd Fusiliers, which regiment also furnished a Guard of Honour for Her Majesty. General Viscount Templetown, K.C.B., commanding the district, and Sir John Douglas, K.C.B., commanding in Scotland, (with his A.D.C., Lieutenant O. B. Gordon of the 79th,) were present. The Mayor and Corporation of Newport attended officially in their robes of office.

At 11.45 a.m. Her Majesty arrived, attended by their Royal Highnesses Prince Leopold and Princess Beatrice, the Countess of Errol, and other ladies. The Royal party having driven along the line the usual order of presentation was proceeded with.

The old colours were in front of the left of the line under double sentries, the new colours were in rear of the centre of the line in charge of the two senior colour-sergeants—Taylor and Mackin. The old colours were then trooped and carried off parade by Lieutenants Annesley and Money to the strains of "Auld Lang Syne." When

Colours presented to the Regiment by Her Majesty the Queen at Parkhurst 1873.

this ceremony was over the regiment was formed into three sides of a square, with the drums piled in the centre, the new colours being uncased and placed against the drums by the majors. The prayer of consecration was then offered by the Rev. Charles Morrison, formerly chaplain of the 79th in India, who came from Aberdeen expressly for this duty. When this was concluded, Major Cuming handed the Queen's colour, and Major Percival the regimental colour, to Her Majesty, who presented the former to Lieutenant Campbell and the latter to Lieutenant Methuen, saying at the same time :—

"It gives me great pleasure to present these new colours to you. In thus entrusting you with this honourable charge, I have the fullest confidence that you will, with the true loyalty and well-known devotion of Highlanders, preserve the honour and reputation of your regiment, which have been so brilliantly earned and so nobly maintained by the 79th Cameron Highlanders."

Colonel Miller then replied :—

"I beg permission, in the name of all ranks of the 79th Cameron Highlanders, to express our loyal and most grateful acknowledgment of the very high honour it has pleased your Majesty this day to confer upon the regiment.

"The incident will ever remain fresh in the memories of all on parade, of those who are unable to have the honour of being present on this occasion, and of others who have formerly served with the 79th ; and I beg to assure your Majesty that, wherever the course of events may require these colours to be borne, the remembrance that they were received from the hands of our most gracious Queen will render them doubly precious, and that in future years, as at present, the circumstance of this presentation will be regarded as one of the proudest episodes in the records of the Cameron Highlanders."

After Colonel Miller's address the regiment re-formed line, and the colours were received with a general salute, after which they were marched to their place in line in slow time, the band playing "God save the Queen." The ranks having been closed, the regiment broke into column and marched past Her Majesty in quick and double time. Line was again formed, and Lieutenant-General Viscount Templetown called for three cheers for Her Majesty, which was responded to by the regiment in true Highland style. An advance in review order and a royal salute concluded the parade, after which Her Majesty drove away.

After the parade was dismissed the old colours, carried by Lieutenants Annesley and Money and escorted by all the sergeants, were carried round the barracks, and afterwards deposited at the officers' mess.

At the unanimous request of the officers the old colours were offered by Colonel Miller to Her Majesty, and as she was pleased to accept them they were conveyed to Osborne on the 22nd of April. The regiment paraded in review order at 12 noon on that day and was formed in line for the colours to pass along it, each man presenting arms as they passed him, whilst the band played "Auld Lang Syne." The old colours then proceeded by train from Newport to Cowes, being received at Osborne by a Guard of Honour, under Captain Allen and Lieutenants Bucknall and Smith; carried by Lieutenants Annesley and Money, and escorted by Quarter-Master-Sergeant Knight, Colour-Sergeant Clark, two sergeants, and four privates, they were then marched, with the pipers in front, to the door.

The officers then advanced, and—kneeling—placed the colours at Her Majesty's feet, when Colonel Miller read the following statement :—

"I beg to inform your Most Gracious Majesty that these colours were presented to the 79th Highlanders at Portsmouth in the month of April, 1854, by Mrs. Elliot (the wife of the officer at that time colonel of the regiment), a few days before the regiment embarked for the Crimea. They were carried at the Alma, Balaclava, Kertch, and during the operations which led to the capture of Sebastopol, also throughout the campaign of the Indian Mutiny, from November, 1857, when the regiment landed at Calcutta, including the siege and capture of Lucknow, the attack on Fort Rooyah, actions of Secundragunge, Allygunge, Bareilly, and Shahjehanpore, the capture of the fort of Rampore Kussia and Mahomdie, the passage of the Gogra at Fyzabad, and the operations in Oudh across the Gogra and Raptee Rivers.

Major General Miller, C.B.

UNIV. OF
CALIFORNIA

After the submission of the rebels they were borne by the regiment at Mean Meer, Ferozepore, Nowshera, Peshawur, Rawul Pindee, Roorkee, and Kamptee, and were brought home by the corps on its return in November, 1871."

He then added : " It having graciously pleased your Majesty to accept these colours from the Cameron Highlanders, I beg permission to express the gratification which all ranks of the 79th feel in consequence, and to convey most respectfully our highest appreciation of this kind act of condescension on the part of your Majesty."

The Queen replied : " I accept these colours with much pleasure, and shall ever value them in remembrance of the gallant services of the 79th Cameron Highlanders. I will take them to Scotland and place them in my dear Highland home at Balmoral."

The guard then presented arms and the colour party withdrew. Her Majesty afterwards addressed a few words to each of the colour-sergeants.

On the 24th of April Colonel Miller received orders for the troops of the Parkhurst garrison to march towards Osborne on the following day for Her Majesty's inspection. They accordingly paraded at 10 a.m. in review order, and on arriving at Osborne, the brigade was drawn up in line on the road, with the 79th on the right and the 102nd on the left. Her Majesty was received with a royal salute and the troops twice marched past her carriage in fours.

It may here be stated, that, on the day of the presentation of colours to the regiment, Colonel Ponsonby, by command of the Queen, wrote to His Royal Highness the commander-in-chief as follows :—

"Osborne, 17th, April 1873.

" SIR,

" I am directed by the Queen to let your Royal Highness know that Her Majesty this morning presented new colours to the 79th Highlanders at Parkhurst. The usual ceremony took place, and at the conclusion the regiment gave three cheers for the Queen. Her Majesty was extremely pleased with the appearance of the men, and the manner in which they moved, and hopes that your Royal Highness may think it right to communicate the Queen's opinion to Lieutenant-Colonel Miller, the commanding officer. Lord Templetown and Sir John Douglas were present; and the prayer was made by the Rev. Mr. Morrison, formerly Presbyterian chaplain to the corps.

(Signed) " HENRY F. PONSONBY."

" The Field Marshal,
    " Commanding-in-Chief."

Shortly after the presentation of colours the Queen again showed her regard for the regiment by presenting to it four copies of her book. "*Leaves from our Journal in the Highlands:*" one for Colonel Miller, one for the officers, one for the non-commissioned officers, and one for the men.

On the 2nd of June the regiment furnished a detachment to Fort Victoria, consisting of one company, and on the following day the Marchwood detachment re-joined head-quarters.

On the 11th of July, 1873, the following letter was received from the Horse Guards :—

" Horse Guards, 10th July, 1873.

" SIR,

"By direction of the Field-Marshal Commanding-in-Chief, I have the honour to acquaint you that Her Majesty has been pleased to command that the 79th regiment be in future styled '79th Queen's Own Cameron Highlanders,' that the facings be accordingly changed from green to blue, and that the regiment be also permitted to bear in the centre of the second colour, as a regimental badge, the 'Thistle ensigned with the Imperial Crown,' being the badge of Scotland as sanctioned by Queen Anne in 1707, after the confirmation of the act of Union of the Kingdoms.

(*Signed*)   "J. W. ARMSTRONG,
        " Deputy-Adjutant-General."

" Lieutenant-Colonel Miller,
    " Commanding 79th regiment."

On the 12th of July Colonel Miller sent the following acknowledgment to Major-General Ponsonby :—

"Parkhurst Barracks,
"Isle of Wight, 12th July, 1873.

"Sir,

"A letter having been received by me this morning, dated Horse Guards, War Office, 10th July, 1873, intimating by command of His Royal Highness, the Commander-in-Chief, that Her Majesty had been pleased to command that the regiment under my command be styled 'The 79th Queen's Own Cameron Highlanders,' I have the honour to request that you will convey to the Queen, in the name of all ranks of the 79th, our most respectful and grateful acknowledgments for so distinguished a mark of royal condescension, and I beg that you will assure Her Majesty of the gratification felt throughout the regiment in consequence of the above announcement.

"I have the honour, etc,
(Signed) "G. M. Miller,
"Lieutenant-Colonel,
"Commanding 79th Queen's Own Cameron Highlanders."
"To Major-General Ponsonby,
"Equerry in waiting,
"Osborne."

On the 13th of August Lieutenant-Colonel Miller received a notification that Her Majesty had expressed a wish that the regiment should be drawn up as a Guard of Honour at East Cowes on her departure from the Isle of Wight the following day. It accordingly marched to East Cowes the following afternoon and presented arms as Her Majesty left for Balmoral.

On the 18th of September the 79th left Parkhurst for Aldershot, where it arrived the same day, occupying "A" and "B" lines, South Camp. It was attached to the 1st, Major-General Parke's brigade.

On the 25th of November this regiment was called upon to give 2 officers and 130 rank and file as volunteers to the 42nd Black Watch, under orders to form part of an expedition proceeding on active service to the Gold Coast under Major-General Sir Garnet Wolseley.

More than half the regiment volunteered, eager for active service, and the required number were selected.

On the 4th of December the volunteers, under Lieutenants Annesley and McCallum, joined the 42nd at Portsmouth, embarking the same day on the SS. *Sarmatian.*

They arrived at Cape Coast Castle on the 16th of December and disembarked on the 3rd and 4th of January.

1874.

The 79th Volunteers were divided amongst the companies of the 42nd, and with them were present on the 31st of January at the battle of Amoaful, at the attack and burning of the town of Becquah, on Sunday, the 1st of February, at the battle of Ordahsu, and at the capture of Coomassie. The capture of Coomassie and the flight of the King of Ashantee brought hostilities to a close, and the 42nd re-embarked on board the *Sarmatian* and arrived at Portsmouth on the 22nd of March.

On the 30th of March the whole of the troops engaged in the Ashantee War were reviewed by Her Majesty the Queen at Windsor; the men of the 79th, under Lieutenants Annesley and McCallum, forming a company by themselves, marched past with the 42nd, and afterward re-joined the 79th at Aldershot. The officers and men engaged in this campaign received the war medal and clasp for Coomassie.

The 79th contingent had 6 rank and file killed, and Lieutenant Annesley and 31 rank and file wounded.

Medals for distinguished conduct in the field were awarded to Privates William Bell (who lost his right arm), George Cameron, and Henry Jones of the Cameron Highlanders.

On the 7th of March, 1874, the regiment proceeded to Windsor, and lined the streets on the occasion of the arrival of their Royal Highnesses the Duke and Duchess of Edinburgh, returning to Aldershot the same evening.

On the 19th of the same month, the 79th took part in a review before the Czar of Russia, being brigaded with the 42nd, 78th, and 93rd Highlanders, under the command of Major-General Parke, C.B.

In the months of June and July the regiment participated in the summer manœuvres at Aldershot, being attached at different periods to the 1st and 3rd brigades, under Major-General Herbert and Colonel Anderson respectively.

1875.

During the summer manœuvres for 1875, the 79th again formed part of the 1st brigade 1st division 2nd Army Corps, under the command of Major-General Sir John Douglas, K.C.B.

On the 28th of July the regiment left Aldershot for Portsmouth, where it embarked on board H.M.S. *Himalaya*, and sailed for Scotland. It arrived at Leith on the evening of the 30th, and, disembarking on the 2nd of August, occupied quarters in Edinburgh Castle. On arrival at the Castle, Sir John Douglas, K.C.B., commanding the North British district, who was accompanied by Colonel Butt, late of the 79th, briefly addressed the regiment, complimenting the men on the high character they bore, and urging them, on their return to their native land, after an absence of 20 years, not to forget that the regiment was always noted for its general good bearing in quarters, and to remember that it was the duty of each individual one of them to do his utmost to maintain the credit of the Cameron Highlanders.

The streets were densely crowded as the regiment marched from Granton to the Castle.

A detachment of 1 captain, 1 subaltern, 3 sergeants, and 41 rank and file were ordered almost immediately on arrival to Greenlaw.

On the 16th, 17th, and 18th of August the regiment furnished Guards of Honour to Her Majesty the Queen at Holyrood, and on the 17th it lined the streets when she unveiled the statue of the Prince Consort.

On the 25th of September, "H" company, consisting of 1 captain, 1 lieutenant, and 35 non-commissioned officers and men, proceeded on detachment to Dundee, and the same evening "A" company, under the command of Brevet-Major J. M. Leith, with 2 subalterns and 55 of all ranks, left for Ballater to form a Guard of Honour to Her Majesty.

"B" company, consisting of 1 captain, 1 subaltern, and 44 non-commissioned officers and men, was sent on detachment to Stirling on the 2nd of October.

1876.

On the 12th of October the head-quarters and five companies left Edinburgh and embarked at Granton pier on board H.M.S. *Assistance*. The *Assistance* arrived off Fort George the following morning, and the regiment landed and occupied quarters in the fort. On the 24th of November Major Leith's company re-joined from Ballater.

1877.

On the 16th of May, 1877, "A" company, under Brevet-Major Leith, again went to Ballater as a Guard of Honour.

On the 5th of June the detachment from Dundee re-joined head-quarters, and on the 25th "A" company returned from Ballater.

The annual inspection of the battalion was held by Major-General Ramsay Stuart, C.B., commanding the North British district, on the 6th and 7th of July, on which occasion he informed the regiment on parade that he considered it "in splendid order."

On the 25th of July a large draft of 13 corporals, 2 drummers, and 271 privates was sent by the 79th to join the 42nd at Malta, the 42nd being linked to the regiment under the brigade depôt system.

On the 22nd of August "C" company, consisting of 1 captain, 2 subalterns, 3 sergeants, 1 piper, 1 drummer, and 49 privates, went to Ballater as a Guard of Honour to Her Majesty.

The regiment embarked on board H.M.S. *Orontes* on the 18th of October, under the command of Major and Brevet-Lieutenant-Colonel Cuming, and arrived at Greenock on the 21st of the same month. The following day it moved to Glasgow, where the head-quarters and "A" and "B" companies occupied the Gallowgate barracks, the remainder of the regiment going to Maryhill, being joined the same day by "C" company from Ballater.

On the 31st of October Colonel Miller was placed upon half pay, after commanding the regiment for five years. He was succeeded in command by Lieutenant-Colonel E. W. Cuming.

1878.

On the 15th of March the head-quarters moved from the Gallowgate barracks to Maryhill.

On the 20th of the same month "F" company, under Captain Busfield, proceeded to Ballater as a Guard of Honour to Her Majesty.

On the 1st of April the establishment of the regiment was raised to 1 colonel, 1 lieutenant-colonel, 1 major, 8 captains, 8 lieutenants, 8 second-lieutenants, 1 adjutant, 1 quarter-master, 48 sergeants, 40 corporals, 23 drummers and pipers, and 960 privates, exclusive of the depôt companies. On the 28th, 167 of the Royal Ayr and Wigton Militia Reserve were posted to the regiment during the mobilization of the reserves. These reservists remained out with the regiment until the 31st of July.

On the 1st of August the establishment of the regiment was reduced again.

On the 24th of August a Guard of Honour, under Captain A. N. Forbes-Gordon, consisting of 2 lieutenants (Lieutenants Chalmers and Money) and 54 non-commissioned officers and men, proceeded to Ballater.

1879.

On the 14th of January Lieutenant-General Sir John Douglas, G.C.B., was appointed to the full colonelcy of the regiment in succession to General Sir Alfred Horsford, G.C.B., transferred to the 14th regiment.

On the 15th of May the regiment was placed under orders for immediate embarkation to relieve its linked battalion, the 42nd Highlanders, at Gibraltar, and it embarked on board H.M.S. *Himalaya* at Greenock on the 3rd of June, under the command of Lieutenant-Colonel E. W. Cuming. Strength : 3 field officers, 17 captains and subalterns, 35 sergeants, 18 drummers, and 485 rank and file.

During the period that the regiment was stationed at Glasgow 270 recruits were raised at head-quarters and 208 at the brigade depôt (42nd and 79th) at Perth.

The 79th landed at Gibraltar on the 11th of June and occupied the Buena Vista barracks.

On the 6th of November the regiment was inspected by His Excellency the Governor, Lord Napier of Magdala, who expressed his entire satisfaction at the appearance of the corps.

1880.

On the 10th of March, 1880, the regiment moved from Buena Vista to the Town Range barracks, relieving the 93rd Highlanders. Two companies were detached for duty to the North front.

On the 23rd of September a draft of 2 sergeants, 2 corporals, and 153 privates joined the regiment from the 42nd Royal Highlanders. Many of these men had served before in the 79th.

On the 24th and 25th of November the Cameron Highlanders were inspected by Major-General Anderson, commanding the infantry brigade, who expressed great satisfaction at the state in which he found the regiment.

On the 27th of December, on the departure of the 97th regiment for Natal, the head-quarters and four companies occupied the South barracks, leaving three companies at Wellington front and 1 company at the musketry camp at the North front.

1881.

On the 3rd of January the three companies at Wellington front re-joined the head-quarters at the south barracks.

During the month the establishment of the regiment was raised from 600 to 700 privates.

It was early in this year that the scheme of army reorganization was framed. This scheme proposed the abolition of the existing system of linked battalions and regimental numbers, and the substitution of territorial regiments of the line; each territorial regiment to consist of two line battalions, with the Militia and Volunteers of the district.

As the 79th was at this time linked to the 42nd Black Watch, it was proposed to make it the 2nd Territorial battalion of that regiment, and the following telegram was received on January the 28th by the officer commanding from the Adjutant-General :—

"If 79th is linked to 42nd will your regiment adopt tartan of 42nd regiment? Linked regiments must wear the same tartan. Wire reply."

Although the Cameron Highlanders would have been proud to be associated with the old Black Watch, by whose side they have so often stood on many a hard-fought field, yet such a proposal meant the practical extinction of the former, and all ranks were unanimous in declining to entertain it. Lieutenant-Colonel Leith (who was in command of the regiment during the absence of Lieutenant-Colonel Cuming on sick leave) accordingly sent the following telegram in reply :—

"No.—The Cameron Highlanders will not adopt 42nd tartan."

At the same time he wrote and despatched this letter by post :—

To the Adjutant-General, Horse Guards, Pall Mall, London.

"Gibraltar, 30th January, 1881.
"Sir,

"I have the honour to forward a copy of a telegram despatched by me this morning in reply to your telegram received yesterday evening, which, in transmission through Spain, had become somewhat illegible.

"It was with the greatest sorrow that the officers of the 79th Cameron Highlanders heard of the proposal to deprive the regiment of the Cameron tartan, worn by them for so many years and regarded with pride and affection by all ranks. No one serving in the 79th would willingly adopt the tartan of the 42nd regiment, which would virtually mean the extinction of the 79th Cameron Highlanders as a regiment.

"May I most respectfully request that you will have the goodness to move His Royal Highness the commander-in-chief to preserve, if possible, for the regiment that tartan which has been the distinctive dress since they were raised in 1793 by Sir Alan Cameron, and, as the inscriptions on the colours testify, has been worn with honour in many hard-fought battles.

"I have the honour to be, Sir,
"Your obedient servant,
(*Signed*) "J. M. Leith,
"Lieutenant-Colonel,
"Commanding 79th Queen's Own Cameron Highlanders."

Nothing further was heard of the matter until Mr. Childers, the Secretary of State for War, in his comprehensive speech in the House of Commons on the new scheme, announced that the 79th would be the only single battalion regiment in the army, and a short time afterwards the following letter was received:—

"Horse Guards, War Office, S.W.
"5th April, 1881.

"SIR,

"With reference to your letter of the 30th of January last, I have the honour, by desire of the Field Marshal Commanding-in-Chief, to acquaint you that, as the regiment under your command is to have a separate existence under the new linking, it is presumed that the regiment will now retain its tartan.

"I have the honour to be, Sir,
"Your obedient servant,
"R. BLUNDELL, A.A.G."

"To the Officer Commanding
"79th Regiment, Gibraltar."

On the 1st of April the establishment of the regiment was increased from 700 to 800 privates.

On the 1st of July, 1881, the day on which the Army Reorganization Scheme came into effect, the time honoured old number—79th—was discontinued, and the regiment was designated by its title alone—"The Queen's Own Cameron Highlanders." It became the Territorial regiment of the county of Inverness, in which it was first raised, being joined as such with the "Highland Light Infantry Militia," which now became the 2nd battalion of the Queen's Own Cameron Highlanders.

The depôt was located at Inverness, but, as the barracks there were not yet completed, it was sent temporarily to Fort George.

The following officers were at this time serving in the 2nd battalion:—

Colonel Simon Lord Lovat	Captain G. A. Duff
Major W. M. Bankes	,, J. T. Shaw
,, T. A. Macdonald	,, G. R. McKessack
,, W. Donaldson	,, H. L. B. Langford-Brooke

Captain A. D. Mackintosh of Mackintosh	Lieutenant E. Grant
,, C. J. Merry	,, R. W. E. Grant
,, H. W. Kemble	,, C. Marjoribanks
,, W. H. Garforth	,, A. G. Ferguson
,, W. G. S. Menzies	,, N. C. Greenhill-Gardyne
Lieutenant G. T. B. Mostyn	,, R. A. Paterson
,, C. L. McKenzie	,, W. D. Wolrige-Gordon
,, E. G. F. Tytler	Quarter-Master P. Forbes
Lieutenant J. M. Hanbury	Surgeon D. McFadyen
,, C. Aytoun	Adjutant H. J. Knight, Captain, Seaforth Highlanders
,, A. A. S. Anderson	
,, W. T. Fraser-Tytler	

On the 1st of July Lieutenant-Colonel E. W. Cuming was placed upon the retired list; he was succeeded in command by Lieutenant-Colonel J. M. Leith.

On the 17th of November the regiment was inspected by Major-General Adams, who expressed himself thoroughly satisfied with its efficiency.

1882.

On the 1st of May, 1882, the rank of Warrant Officer was introduced in the line regiments.

On the 15th of March a draft of 1 sergeant and 119 rank and file, under the command of Major O. B. Gordon, joined the regiment from the depôt.

Before leaving Gibraltar a handsome mural tablet, with the following inscription, was erected by the regiment in the Presbyterian Church, in memory of their comrades who died during the stay of the regiment on the Rock :—

THE 79TH
QUEEN'S OWN CAMERON HIGHLANDERS.

TO THE MEMORY
OF THE UNDERMENTIONED
OFFICERS, NON-COMMISSIONED OFFICERS, AND PRIVATES,
WHO DIED WHILST THE REGIMENT WAS
STATIONED AT GIBRALTAR,
1879—82.

Cuimhne
Nan Sonn Nach Maireann.

Lieutenant		Colin C. Mackenzie			Died at	Gibraltar,	15th Sept., 1880
2nd Lieutenant		Hon. Charles Cathcart			,,	London,	21st May, 1880
1172	Sergeant	Thomas Sim	"G" Company		,,	Gibraltar,	29th Jan., 1880
1592	Corporal	David Ross	"F"	,,	,,	,,	30th July, 1882
1485	Drummer	William Wallace	"C"	,,	,,	,,	20th Sept., 1881
1988	Private	William Wigham	"H"	,,	,,	,,	15th Sept., 1879
1595	,,	Robert Graham	"F"	,,	,,	,,	20th June, 1880
899	,,	John Gorman	"B"	,,	,,	,,	22nd June, 1881
2357	,,	Thomas Scott	"E"	,,	,,	,,	23rd July, 1881
165	,,	James Foster	"D"	,,	,,	,,	10th May, 1882

In June, 1882, events in Egypt proclaimed a state of war imminent; and the refusal of Arabi Pasha to discontinue working at the fortifications around Alexandria resulted in the bombardment of the forts by the fleet on the 11th of July. The first intimation that the Cameron Highlanders were likely to be sent out was received on the 8th of July, when the Quarter-Master-General telegraphed to Lord Napier, the General Commanding at Gibraltar, enquiring whether they could be furnished with regimental transport if they should be required to embark.

An affirmative reply was sent, and the 79th at once prepared for a campaign. On the 14th the regiment was ordered to embark, and from this time until the day of embarkation everybody was busily engaged in making preparations, every telegram was scanned and eagerly discussed, and an intense feeling of excitement and enthusiasm ran throughout the regiment. Bitter regrets were expressed when an order arrived for no man under 20 years of age to embark, and application after application was sent in for this to be modified, but it was only done in the case of drummers, who were all permitted to go.

The Queen's colour only was taken. Lieutenant Halkett was detailed to remain in charge of women, children, men pronounced unfit for service, and those under 20 years of age. Lieutenant Hacket-Thompson was appointed Transport Officer, and commenced his duties.

On the 7th of August the regiment marched from the South barracks to the New Mole for embarkation on board H.M.S. *Orontes*. It was drawn up on the parade at the New Mole for inspection by Lord

Napier of Magdala. A wing of the 95th regiment, which had received sudden orders to embark for Egypt at the same time, paraded on its right.

After the inspection, Lord Napier addressed the regiment in the following terms :—

"Colonel Leith, and the Queen's Own Cameron Highlanders. You are about to leave Gibraltar for active service, after having been quartered here for more than three years. Perhaps we take a special interest in you from having seen your young striplings grow up into fine men during the time you have been here. You have a very noble list of campaigns on your colours, commencing with Holland, then Egypt, the country to which you are again going; and there are few parts of the world where your colours have not been borne, and on every occasion they have gained honour, and I am sure it will be the same now, if you have the opportunity.

"Your conduct during the long time you have been here has been most satisfactory, your steadiness and regularity in barracks and elsewhere have been remarkable; this is the foundation of a good regiment, and these qualities combined in the fine men I see in your ranks make me confident that the Cameron Highlanders can go anywhere and do anything. I shall have the pleasure and honour of reporting to Her Majesty that the Cameron Highlanders embarked in the best order, and not a single man absent. I now bid you farewell, wishing you every success, being sure that you will upon all occasions do your duty, and that if the opportunity should occur you will cover yourselves with glory."

The regiment then embarked, and at 12 noon amidst a burst of cheering, and the strains of "Auld Lang Syne," the *Orontes* started.

The following officers embarked with the regiment :—

Lieutenant-Colonels J. M. Leith and St. Leger; Majors McCausland, Gordon, and Chalmers; Captains Hunt and Reid; Lieutenants Hacket-Thompson, Blackburn, Hon. Ivan Campbell, Scott, Mackenzie, Malcolm, Grant, D. F. Davidson, Macleod, C. Davidson, Scott-Elliot, Cavaye and J. S. Ewart; Captain and Adjutant K. S. Baynes; Quarter-

Master Howard; Paymaster, Major McNair; Surgeon-Major Will; Warrant Officer, Sergeant-Major J. Campbell.

The regiment was to form one of the Highland brigade, under Major-General Sir Archibald Alison, Bart, K.C.B., in the 2nd division, under Lieutenant-General Sir Edward Hamley, C.B., K.C.M.G.

After an uneventful voyage the *Orontes* arrived off Alexandria about 7 a.m. on the 14th, and it was reported that the regiment would not disembark until the arrival of Sir Garnet Wolseley.

On the 19th of August the regiment disembarked, and proceeded to Ramleh, outside Alexandria, where it went under canvas. The 75th was already encamped, but the other two regiments of the Highland brigade, the 42nd and 74th, were yet to come.

On the 20th and 22nd of August the regiment took part in reconnaissances against the enemy's position at Kafr Dowar. On each occasion it was exposed to a heavy fire of big guns, but there were no casualties.

On the 22nd the Black Watch and 74th Highland Light Infantry arrived, and encamped beyond the 79th lines. Their arrival completed the Highland brigade and the 2nd division.

On the 29th it was announced that the Highland brigade would proceed to Ismailia, and form part of the force which Sir Garnet Wolseley was assembling there.

Orders were given to strike camp on the 30th, and at 2.30 p.m. all arrangements having been completed, the regiment marched to the station, and was conveyed to Alexandria, and proceeded to embark on board the hired transport *Lusitania*, on which were also Lieutenant-General Sir Edward Hamley and his staff.

On the 1st of September anchor was dropped in Lake Timsah, but disembarkation was postponed, and until it took place the regiment was employed on fatigue duties landing stores.

On the 4th, H.M.S. *Malabar* came in, and a draft of reservists in charge of Captain Chapman, Lieutenant Urquhart, and Lieutenant S. Macdougall (93rd Highlanders), joined the regiment. Its strength was 3 sergeants, 9 corporals, 3 drummers, and 150 privates. Amongst them there **were a** few old 79th men, but the majority were from the 93rd, 91st, and other regiments.

On the **8th, orders were** given for the brigade to disembark on the following day; all baggage was to go by train with the tents; two days' rations were to be carried in the carts. Valises were to go by train, and each man was to carry his blanket rolled in place of his great coat, his mess tin, and 70 rounds of ammunition.

At about **1.30** p.m. the regiment disembarked in three tugs, **and after a** slight delay on shore the Highland brigade **started on its march across** the **desert.**

After marching **for about** half-an-hour a slight halt **was made, and** the march again **resumed, and,** with frequent **halts, El Magfar,** distant nine miles, **was reached** about 9 p.m. Numbers **of men fell out** during the **last few miles, but all were present when the march** began **next day.**

Here the brigade bivouacked, the regiment furnishing a picquet, consisting of half of "E" Company, under Lieutenant D. Davidson.

At **4 o'clock next** morning the march was continued two miles to Tel-el-Mahuta, where the brigade halted **for** the day. The heat was terrific, and, as there was no shelter from it, it was quite **overpowering.** At 5 p.m. the brigade moved on to Mahsameh, which **was** reached about 10 p.m.

Starting at 4 o'clock the next morning, Kassassin was **reached about** 8 a.m., **and after the tents had been brought from the station and** pitched, the regiment rested, **to prepare for the decisive** battle **which was now daily expected.**

At 10 a.m. on the 12th the following brigade **order was issued :—**

"**Commanding officers are to be** very particular about the fitness of **water-carts, which** will **be filled** and follow in rear of the battalions, **and to make sure, by the** personal inspection of company officers at 5 p.m. **to-day, that** every man has his water-bottle filled, if possible, with cold tea.

"Commanding officers, through officers commanding companies, must impress upon **their men** the absolute necessity of carrying **and** husbanding rations, which will be issued to them to-day, as, until the period for which these rations are issued expires, nothing more can be obtained from the Commissariat.

"As many spare water-bottles as possible will be sent to the brigade from head-quarters, so that a certain number of each company will carry two water-bottles. To-night the men will carry 100 rounds of ammunition in their pouches, but no blankets. Officers commanding must arrange regimentally as to the best mode of carrying this extra ammunition.

"In each corps the mode must be uniform.

"In the event of a night march taking place the utmost attention must be paid to perfect silence in the ranks: the slightest sound when near the enemy might cause the miscarriage of the best planned enterprise.

"Reserve ammunition of each battalion will follow it into action, and the most careful arrangements must be made by officers commanding for the bringing up of ammunition from the mules to the companies engaged.

"The stretchers assigned to each regiment must follow it in charge of the medical officer, who is responsible for the best arrangements that circumstances will permit for the care of the wounded.

"The Major-General will see commanding officers at head-quarters at 3 p.m."

At about 4 p.m. Lieutenant-Colonel J. M. Leith returned to camp and gave out the following orders:—

"Camp to be struck at 5.45 p.m.; tents, blankets, great-coats, valises, and band instruments to be piled alongside the railway and left in charge of a guard.

"The regiment to fall in at 6.30 p.m. Each man to carry 100 rounds of ammunition.

"The position of Tel-el-Kebir is to be attacked with the bayonet; no one is to load; not a shot is to be fired until over the entrenchments."

Arabi's strongly entrenched position was to be stormed, and the old 79th was to go into battle for the first time since the Indian Mutiny.

The camp was struck at 6.30 p.m., and the Highland brigade formed up in line of quarter columns near the railway—the 42nd on the right, 74th on the left, the 75th next to the 42nd, then the 79th.

The strength of the regiment on parade was—

2 Lieutenant-Colonels	1 Surgeon-Major
3 Majors	1 Chaplain
3 Captains	48 Sergeants
14 Subalterns	47 Corporals
1 Adjutant	23 Drummers and Pipers
1 Quarter-Master	660 Privates

The following officers were with the regiment :—

Lieutenant-Colonels J. M. Leith and St. Leger; Majors McCausland, Gordon (on staff of Sir E. Hamley), and Chalmers; Captains Hunt, Reid, and Chapman; Lieutenants Hacket-Thompson, Blackburn, Hon. Ivan Campbell, Mackenzie, Malcolm, Grant, D. F. Davidson, Macleod, C. Davidson, Scott-Elliot, Cavaye, Ewart, and Macdougall; Captain and Adjutant Baynes; Quarter-Master Howard; Surgeon-Major Will; the Rev. David Arthur; and Sergeant-Major J. Campbell.

The advance was begun by the 74th, and the remainder followed in echelon to Nine Gun Hill. Here the brigade deployed into two lines, each regiment having four companies in the front line, and four in support.

The march upon Tel-el-Kebir was continued at 1 a.m. The right of "A" company (Captain Hunt) was the flank of direction of the brigade. Lieutenant R. Macleod was the right guide; he was directed by Lieutenant Rawson, R.N., who steered by the stars.

The weird night march, long to be retained in the annals of the regiment and the country, can never be forgotten by those who took part in it; the monotonous tramp, the sombre lines, the dimly discerned sea of desert faintly lighted by the stars, were at once ghostly and impressive. The pace was necessarily slow; one halt was made, and shortly afterwards the directing star having become concealed another one was chosen, and the direction slightly changed to the right. The 42nd, 74th, and 75th, did not at once conform, and the consequence was that a halt had to be made as these regiments found themselves almost facing each other.

This line was quickly and silently re-formed, and the advance continued.

Just as dawn was breaking two shots were fired from the left front, and Private James Pollock of the regiment fell dead. It was now evident that the regiment was close upon the enemy. Bayonets were at once fixed.

In a few seconds these two shots were followed by others; the bugles of the Egyptians rang out, shells screamed above, and a line of fire poured from the enemy's trenches. The 79th moved steadily on in an unbroken line, not a shot was fired in reply; but on the "advance" for the brigade being sounded by Sir Archibald Alison's bugler, drummer John Alcorn of the 79th, Lieutenant-Colonel Leith galloped to the front, waving his sword and crying, "Come on, 79th!" and breaking into double time, to the shrill music of the pipes, and cheering as they ran, the regiment charged the enemy's lines. Private Donald Cameron was the first to gain the top of the trench; but fell dead at once, shot through the head. The trench was now full, and, mounting on each other's shoulders and scrambling up, the front line gained the fiery top. Lieutenant Malcolm jumped down amongst some gunners, one of whom wounded him on the head, but he cut his assailant down with his claymore.

Flash after flash continued along the line until the bayonets of the 79th had done their work, and the inside of the trench was full of dead and dying.

The Egyptians retired straight to the rear, kneeling to fire as they ran.

The front line followed the enemy in a confused mass, Pipe-Major Grant playing the *March of the Cameron Men* lustily.

The second line had now mounted the works, and became mixed with the first. An attempt was made by the Colonel and Adjutant to form up the regiment, but a double cross fire from shelter trenches on each side had to be silenced, as it was creating havoc in the ranks.

Daylight was breaking, and the regiment moving to the left cleared the trench, and drove back the enemy in confusion through a small camp in rear of it.

Colour-Sergeants Newell, Young and McLaren, with Corporal Syme, advanced to a redoubt on the left, and, killing three gunners in it, drove across the canal some Egyptian cavalry who were meditating a charge. Following them up they took a Krupp gun, and turning it round fired it upon the retreating foe.

The remainder of the regiment, under Lieutenant-Colonel Leith, with the 42nd, 74th, and 75th, pushed on, and, driving all before them, arrived at the crest of the hill, overlooking Arabi's camp and the railway station. Here a terrible scene of confusion appeared; the Egyptians were leaving the camp by hundreds, some running across the desert, some on the railway, and some in their excitement jumping into the canal.

The Highland brigade, with some of the 46th and 60th Rifles, who had now come up, cleared the camp of all remaining Egyptians, and Arabi's army melted in the distance never to form up again.

Major-General Sir Archibald Alison was greeted with a hearty cheer as he passed, and Lieutenant-Colonel Leith, anxious to find shade for his men, marched the regiment into some of the tents, where it rested.

Sergeant-Major Joseph Campbell at once set out with volunteers to give such assistance as they could to the wounded, and they found their services most acceptable to Surgeon-Major Will, who, in spite of dysentery, from which he had been suffering since the regiment left Ramleh, was lending his entire energies to the care of the wounded, and trying to alleviate their sufferings.

In the storming of Tel-el-Kebir the Cameron Highlanders had Lieutenant A. G. Blackburn, (dangerously) Lieutenant H. H. L. Malcolm, and Lieutenant S. Macdougall (very severely) wounded; 13 rank and file killed; 4 sergeants and 40 rank and file wounded.

The following is a complete list of casualties :—

2049	Private	William Bodle	"H" Company	Killed.
2304	,,	Robert Brown	"E"	,,
1455	,,	Donald Cameron	"E"	,,
127	,,	George Crawford	"B"	,,

117	Private	Alexander Denniston	"A" Company			Killed.
2051	,,	John Hyslop	"A"	,,	...	,,
80	,,	Patrick Kenny	"C"	,,	...	,,
2300	,,	Thomas King	"C"	,,	...	,,
1483	,,	Alexander Paterson	"F"	,,	...	
2156	,,	James Pollock	"F"	,,	...	,,
2087	,,	George Rugg	"A"	,,	...	,,
2354	,,	William Simon	"A"	,,	...	,,
299	,,	William Smith	"E"	,,	...	,,
	Lieutenant	Adam G. Blackburn	...	...	...	Wounded.
	,,	H. H. L. Malcolm	...	...	...	,,
	,,	S. Macdougall	..	...	...	,,
1912	Colour-Sergeant	Francis Chapman	"G" Company			,,
2125	Sergeant	Donald Gunn	"B"	,,	..	,,
999	,,	Kennedy Hewitt	"G"	,,	...	,,
1378	,,	Alexander Mackenzie	"C"	,,	...	,,
2099	Corporal	William Cattanach	"C"	,,	...	Died of wounds.
1873	,,	John McKay	"B"	,,	...	Wounded.
1418	Lance-Corporal	James Cuming...	"E"	,,	...	,,
2062	,,	Francis Tillie	"E"	,,	...	,,
2299	Private	David Alexander	"C"	,,	...	,,
1536	,,	David Bell	"B"	,,	...	,,
1261	,,	Thomas Bottomley	"E"	,,	...	,,
1055	,,	Thomas Brown	"D"	,,	...	,,
83	,,	Martin Burns	"E"	,,	...	,,
2247	,,	William Chapman	"B"	,,		,,
455	,,	James Chassels	"B"	,,	...	,,
84	,,	William Cockcroft	"E"	,,	...	,,
2175	,,	James Dick	"H"	,,	...	,,
124	,,	Charles Drummond	"B"	,,	...	,,
2192	,,	John Duff	"C"	,,	..	,,
1406	,,	James Hart	"E"	,,	...	,,
2338	,,	Henry Herd	"H"	,,	...	,,
292	,,	Peter Kynoch	"G"	,,	...	,,
1424	,,	Archibald McAlister	"G"	,,	...	,,
1500	,,	John McAlister	"D"	,,	...	,,
446	,,	John McKale	"F"	,,	...	,,
908	,,	William Mackenzie	"C"	,,	...	Died of wounds.
1472	,,	Thomas McRae	"G"	,,	...	Wounded.
376	,,	Thomas Meers	"D"	,,	...	,,
146	,,	Alexander Murray	"B"	,,	...	Died of wounds

1565	Private	David Murray	...	"H" Company	...	Died of wounds.
2197	,,	David Nelson	...	"E"	,,	Wounded.
901	,,	John Page ...	...	"F"	,,	,,
68	,,	George Quemby	.	"A"	,,	,,
146	,,	Robert Robertson	...	"F"	,,	,,
550	,,	James Rodgers	..	"A"	,,	,,
426	,,	John Sheppard	...	"A"	,,	,,
2266	,,	John Smith	...	"C"	,,	,,
1026	,,	Robert Spers	...	"D"	,,	,,
215	,,	Archibald Telford		"E"	,,	,,
2343	,,	James Walker	..	"C"	,,	,,
312	,,	Michael White	...	"E"	,,	,,
1439	,,	William Wilson	...	"H"	,,	,,
1662	,,	William Witherspoon		"H"	,	,,
108	,,	Luke Young	...	"E"	,,	,,

The following officers, non-commissioned officers, and men were reported to Major-General Sir Archibald Alison for having specially distinguished themselves during the action :—

Captain and Adjutant K. S. Baynes	Colour-Sergeant McNeil
Lieutenant H. H. L. Malcolm	Sergeant-Piper Grant
Lieutenant S. Macdougall	Sergeant-Drummer Sanderson
Surgeon-Major Will	Sergeant Souter
Sergeant-Major J. Campbell	Sergeant Donald Gunn
Colour-Sergeant Newell	Corporal Syme
Colour-Sergeant Young	Private D. Taylor
Colour-Sergeant McLaren	Private T. Chalmers
Colour-Sergeant Gunn	Private Sheehan

For its conduct during the day the regiment received the royal authority to have the word "Tel-el-Kebir" inscribed on its colours and appointments.

Lieutenant-Colonel Leith, Major McCausland, Captain Hunt, Sergeant-Major Campbell, and the non-commissioned officers and men above-named, were mentioned in Sir Garnet Wolseley's despatches, dated the 2nd of November.

Lieutenant-Colonel Leith was appointed a Companion of the Bath, and received the 3rd Class of the Medjidie.

Major McCausland was promoted Brevet-Lieutenant-Colonel, and received the 4th Class of the Osmanieh.

Captain Hunt was promoted Brevet-Major, and received the 4th Class of the Medjidie.

Lieutenant Blackburn received the 5th Class of the Medjidie.

For their gallant services, Sergeant-Major Campbell, Colour-Sergeant Young, and Sergeant Donald Gunn received medals for "distinguished conduct in the field."

Sergeant Souter was promoted to be lieutenant in the Black Watch.

At 4.30 p.m. the same day the regiment, with the 74th and 75th, marched about five miles towards Zagazig and bivouacked for the night. The following day it moved on to Zagazig, 13 miles distant.

On entering Zagazig, about 6 p.m., the 72nd Highlanders were seen encamped on the other side of the canal, and raised many a cheer as the regiment passed. They formed part of the Indian contingent, and had pushed on in front of the Highland brigade.

The Cameron Highlanders were quartered in a cotton manufactory close to the 75th.

Late that evening orders were received for the regiment to start for Benha by train at 6 a.m. on the following day; it accordingly paraded at 5 a.m., but did not leave till about 9 a.m. "F" company, under the command of Lieutenant Hon. Ivan Campbell, was left as a guard for the baggage, which, with the officers' chargers, was to follow by road.

Arriving at Benha at about 9.30 a.m., a large building in the enclosure of the palace was occupied as a barrack, but, as there was nothing but stones to sleep on, some sugar-canes were cut to make a rough sort of bedding.

At 7 p.m. that day, the 15th, orders were received for the 79th to go to the station and line the railway, to capture a train of men and guns which was expected from Kafr Dowar, but there was no opposition offered, and it was therefore dismissed without marching off.

At 3 p.m. on the 16th Major-General Alison sent up to say that at 4 p.m. the 79th was to go by train to Cairo, and marching to the station, after a short delay caused by the entraining of the 74th, it started, and reached Cairo station about 7.30 p.m.

There the staff officer in charge, Major Fraser, R.E., directed the colonel to march to the Citadel, which was entered about 9 p.m., but no one knew where the regiment was to be quartered, so they slept in some unoccupied rooms, on the stones. No one had been in since the Egyptians marched out, and the smell and dirt was beyond description, but they had to remain there until the 21st, when the regiment marched to Ghesireh and encamped on the right of the 74th.

On the 23rd, the 42nd arrived from Belbeis, and the brigade was completed on the 28th by the arrival of the 75th from Tantah.

On the 13th the brigade was inspected by Sir Garnet Wolseley who expressed himself well pleased with the appearance and drill of the 79th.

On the 15th a draft of reservists, consisting of 4 sergeants, 10 corporals, 2 drummers, and 132 privates, under the command of Major Miers and Lieutenants Abercrombie and Toogood of the 21st Royal Scots Fusiliers, joined from Cyprus.

On the 21st Major-General Sir Archibald Alison handed over the command to Major-General Graham, V.C., and at a parade the same day made the following address:—

"Officers and men of the Highland brigade

"The exigencies of the service require that I should this day lay down that command, which three short months ago I took up with so much pride. I cannot quit the brigade without returning to the officers commanding battalions my most sincere thanks for the warm and uniform support which I have ever received from them, and which has made my command to me a period of constant pleasure.

"I have to thank the officers for the admirable way in which they have always discharged their duties.

"I have to thank the non-commissioned officers and men for their excellent conduct in quarters, and their brilliant gallantry in the field.

"It was the dream of my youth to command a Highland brigade! It has been granted to me in my old age to lead one in battle.

"This brigade has been singularly fortunate in having had assigned to it so important a part in what must ever be considered one of the most brilliant victories which have been won by our arms in modern times.

"There is one thing which I wish to impress upon you, and that is—it was not the fiery valour of your rush over the entrenchments of Tel-el-Kebir, but the disciplined restraint of the long night march over the desert preceding it, which I admired the most—that was one of the most severe tests of discipline which could be exacted from men, and by you it was nobly borne. When in the early dawn we looked down from the summit of the ridge upon the camp of Arabi lying defenceless at our feet, and upon his army dissolving before us, the first thought that came into my mind was, that had my old chief, Sir Colin Campbell, risen from his grave he would have been proud of you. He would have thought that you had well maintained the reputation of the Highland regiments, and the honour of the Scottish name; he would have deemed you the worthy successors of that now historic brigade which he led up the green slopes of Alma! I cannot do better than wish that you may afford to that distinguished officer, Major-General Graham, to whom I have this day handed over the brigade, the same satisfaction that you have given to me. And now, to every commanding officer, to every officer, to every non-commissioned officer, and to every man of the Highland brigade, I wish 'God speed.'"

On the 29th the regiment moved back to the Citadel, of which Lieutenant Colonel J. M. Leith became commandant. It was destined to form part of the Army of Occupation in Egypt.

1883.

On the 21st of February, 1883, the regiment paraded at 11.30 a.m. for the presentation of the war medals by Lady Alison, who was accompanied by Major-General Graham, V.C.

Whilst the regiment was waiting drawn up in line at open order,

Lord Napier of Magdala, who was travelling in Egypt, came up, and was received with a field marshal's salute. It did the regiment good to see him, and they would have liked to have raised a cheer for the fine old soldier who had so much endeared himself to them at Gibraltar, and whose name will never be forgotten by the 79th Cameron Highlanders.

Previous to the distribution, General Graham addressed the regiment, complimenting them on their past career, and regretting the absence of Sir Archibald Alison, who, he said, having been with them in action, would have spoken more accurately of the exemplary services which they had rendered during the recent campaign, and especially as to their gallant storming of Tel-el-Kebir.

He concluded by saying—"You men who have survived that gallant charge, and who are about to receive your medals, must not forget those intrepid comrades whose lives were sacrificed, and especially would I mention Private Donald Cameron, who was first into the trenches, and died shot through the head."

Colonel Leith replied, thanking General Graham for the kind manner in which he had referred to the regiment, and expressing a hope that it would in the future maintain the high reputation which it had hitherto enjoyed.

The medals were then distributed, Lady Alison pinning them on the breasts of those who had specially distinguished themselves.

On the 2nd of June His Highness the Khedive presented his bronze stars to the regiment on Abdin Square.

In the month of June the establishment of the regiment was reduced to 2 lieutenant-colonels, 3 majors, 5 captains, 12 subalterns, 2 staff-officers, 2 warrant-officers, 40 sergeants, 21 drummers, 40 corporals, and 480 privates, and all recruiting for the regiment at home was stopped.

In July the cholera, which had been raging for some time past in Egypt, seized the troops, those who were sick in hospital being the first to be attacked, and in most cases the first to succumb.

Four men of the Cameron Highlanders died on the 24th of July, and on the following day the regiment went into camp on Mokkattam heights, about a mile from the Citadel, leaving " G " company, under Captain Napier, in charge of the barracks.

The effect of the change from the foul atmosphere of the Citadel to the fresh ground was an almost complete cessation of the epidemic, and whilst the regiment was under canvas only two other cases occurred.

The undermentioned men of the regiment died during this outbreak:

Sergeant-Piper J. McGregor Grant
Private John Smith
 ,, James Cameron
 ,, Thomas Dodds
 ,, Michael Carrigan

Private William Morrison
 ,, Hugh McKay
 ,, Robert McRae
 ,, John McLaggan
 ,, John Grant

On the 1st of September the regiment returned to its old quarters in the Citadel.

1884.

In January, 1884, recruiting was again opened for the regiment, but recruits came in slowly, and, on the departure of the first expedition to Suakim, under Major-General Sir Gerald Graham, V.C., K.C.B., the regiment was so weak in numbers, having fallen below home establishment, that it could not take part in it.

Captain and Adjutant Baynes, as assistant-military-secretary; Lieutenant Scott, A.D.C. to Sir Gerald Graham; Lieutenant C. Davidson, as a volunteer with the Gordon Highlanders; and about fifteen non-commissioned officers and men of the regiment accompanied the expedition, being present at the engagements of El Teb and Tamaii. Captain Baynes and Lieutenant Scott were mentioned in Sir Gerald Graham's despatches, and Captain Baynes, in recognition of his services, was promoted to the rank of brevet-major.

During the absence of Sir Gerald Graham at Suakim the command of the Cairo brigade devolved upon Colonel Leith, C.B.

From the 1st of April the establishment of the regiment was raised to 2 lieutenant-colonels, 3 majors, 5 captains, 16 subalterns, 2 staff-officers, 2 warrant-officers, 48 sergeants, 21 drummers and pipers, 40 corporals, and 760 privates.

On the 30th of April "A," "B," "C," "D," "E," and "H" companies, under Lieutenant-Colonel St. Leger, proceeded on detachment to Ramleh, and on the 17th of May "C," "D," and "E" companies returned to Cairo.

On the 9th of June "A," "B," and "H" companies, under the command of Major Chalmers, embarked at Ramleh on board H.M.S. *Alexandra*, and were conveyed to Port Said, where they were quartered in the Dutch House.

On the 5th of August the regiment moved from the Citadel to Abdin barracks, and on the 19th "C" company, under Captain Napier, proceeded to Assioot in Upper Egypt.

On the 15th of September a draft, consisting of 1 sergeant, 1 corporal, and 54 rank and file, under Captain Smith, joined headquarters from the depôt at Fort George.

On the 9th of this month Lord Wolseley arrived in Egypt to assume command of an expeditionary force to proceed up the Nile to the relief of General Gordon, who, early in the year, accompanied by Colonel Stewart only, had undertaken to attempt the withdrawal of the Egyptian garrisons in the Soudan and to restore order in Khartoum, and whose position had now become very critical in consequence of the rapid spread of the Mahdist rebellion.

On the 19th of September General Lord Wolseley inspected the regiment on Abdin Square, and expressed himself much pleased with the appearance of the men.

On the 15th of November the Cameron Highlanders were placed under orders to proceed up the Nile to join the expedition, and, after being joined by the detachment from Port Said, under Major Chalmers, it left Boulac Dacroor station for Assioot on the 18th of that month.

The following officers left Cairo with the regiment :

Colonel J. M. Leith, C.B., Lieutenant-Colonel St. Leger, Majors Everett, Chalmers, and Money ; Brevet-Major Hunt ; Captain Smith ; Captain Halkett ; Lieutenants Urquhart, D. Davidson, Forbes, Scott-Elliot, Cavaye, Riach, Cameron, and McKerrell ; Major and Adjutant K. S. Baynes ; Quarter-Master Howard ; Paymaster, Major J. Brown ;

Surgeon Davies, and the Rev. D. Arthur; Warrant-Officer, Sergeant-Major J. Emslie.

Captain Napier and Lieutenants Malcolm, C. Davidson, Ewart and Findlay, had already proceeded up the Nile on various duties.

The Regimental Reserve depôt, under the command of Lieutenant R. W. Macleod, remained temporarily at Kasr-el-Nil barracks, Cairo.

At Assioot the regiment was joined by "C" company, under Captain Napier, and it at once left by river for Assouan, the head-quarters, "A," "B," "C," and "D" companies embarking on barges Nos. 151 and 182, towed by the steamer *Beherah*, and "E," "F," "G," and "H" companies on barges Nos. 69 and 64, towed by the steamer *Zaignet el Bahare*.

The following are the places at which the regiment stopped for the night during its voyage to Assouan:—

November 20th	...	...	The Village of Abu Tig
" 21st	...	...	The Village of Tushba
" 22nd	...	...	Sohag
" 23rd	...	...	The Village of Masateh, near Girgeh
" 24th	...	...	Esbeh
" 25th	...	...	Keneh
" 26th	...	...	Luxor
" 27th	...	...	Esneh
" 28th	...	...	The Village of Gisr Voardil
" 29th	...	...	The Village of Aklit

On the 30th of November the regiment reached Assouan (the first Cataract). Here Colonel Leith received orders that it was to proceed to Korosko to hold the desert road from that place to Abou-Hamad.

On the 1st of December the regiment disembarked, and proceeded by train to Philae at the top of the first Cataract, where it again embarked for Korosko.

The head-quarters, "F" and "G" companies embarked on the steamer *Benha*, towing barge No. 80; "A" and "C" companies, under Major Hunt, in sailing barge No. 112; "B" and "D" companies, under Captain Halkett, on sailing barge No. 14; "E" company (Major Money) on Dahabeah No. 103; and "H" company (Major Chalmers) on Dahabeah No. 84.

The sailing boats left that evening, and the steamer followed on the 2nd.

The regiment arrived at Korosko on the 4th of December and bivouacked for the night. On the 5th the tents were landed and a camp pitched.

Korosko is a small place, consisting of a few mud huts of the Ababdeh Arabs, and is important as being the northern extremity of the desert route to Abou Hamad and the point from which General Gordon had entered the Soudan.

Colonel J. M. Leith, C.B., was now appointed commandant of the station in succession to Major Rundle of the Egyptian army, who was engaged in raising Arab levies from the Ababdeh tribes, with a view to opening the desert road in conjunction with the Cameron Highlanders.

1885.

On the 23rd of January, 1885, a draft of 31 rank and file reached Korosko from the Reserve depôt at Cairo.

On the 28th of January the sad news of the fall of Khartoum and the death of the heroic General Gordon was communicated to Colonel Leith by Lord Wolseley. The splendid efforts of the desert and river columns had been in vain, and they were ordered to fall back upon Korti.

All anticipations of the Cameron Highlanders crossing to Abou Hamad and taking a more active part in the campaign were now closed, and the desert levies under Major Rundle were disbanded.

On the 8th of February the following telegram was received by Colonel Leith from Major-General Sir Evelyn Wood, V.C., commanding the lines of communication :—

"Your battalion will spend the summer at Korosko; commence at once to hut half a battalion with a view to health and comfort, and report progress when half is completed."

From this it became evident that Lord Wolseley's army would summer in the Soudan and advance upon Khartoum in the autumn.

On receipt of this order the regiment at once commenced to construct huts of mud and palm branches.

On the 29th of February Major and Adjutant K. S. Baynes proceeded to Suakim on the staff of Sir Gerald Graham, V.C., K.C.B., who had been appointed to command the force designed to co-operate with the Nile Expedition.

On the 8th of March a draft of 2 officers (Lieutenants Douglas-Hamilton and Hon. Andrew Murray) and 30 rank and file joined the regiment from the Nile reserve depôt.

On the 31st of March, to the great regret of all ranks, Colonel J. M. Leith, C.B., left the regiment to take up the appointment of assistant-adjutant-general of the Suakim field force. He was succeeded in command by Lieutenant-Colonel H. H. St. Leger.

On the 7th of April Lord Wolseley arrived at Korosko and inspected the hutting in progress.

"B," "C," and "D" companies occupied huts on the 20th of April, and by the middle of May the whole of the regiment was hutted.

On the 11th of May Major G. L. C. Money was appointed assistant-military-secretary to Lieutenant-General Sir Frederick Stephenson, commanding the troops in Lower Egypt.

On the 12th small pox appeared in the regiment, but prompt measures were taken for its suppression and the disease did not spread.

On the 1st of July a draft, consisting of 1 sergeant and 61 reservists, under Captain Hacket-Thompson, arrived at Korosko from Fort George; these men had chiefly come from the 1st, 21st, 72nd, 78th, and 92nd regiments, and there were a few old 79th men.

It had now been definitely decided to withdraw the Nile expedition, and accordingly a frontier field force, consisting of the 20th Hussars, West Kent, Stafford, and Yorkshire regiments, and the Cameron Highlanders, was formed, under the command of Major-General F. W. Grenfell, C.B., A.D.C., to hold the Soudan frontier. This force was disposed as follows :—The West Kent regiment at Halfa; the Cameron Highlanders at Korosko, and the remainder at Assouan.

For its services in the Nile expedition the regiment received the royal authority to have the words "Nile, 1884-85" inscribed on its colours and appointments; Major Everett was promoted to be lieutenant-colonel in the army, and every officer, non-commissioned officer, and man received the medal and "Nile" clasp (or clasp only if already in possession of the medal).

On the 17th of July the regiment was inspected by Colonel Leach, V.C., R.E., commanding the garrison at Korosko, who complimented all ranks on having maintained such a smart and soldier-like appearance under such disadvantageous circumstances.

On the 6th of September the regiment was much grieved to hear of the death of Captain Halkett, which occurred in England. He had been invalided from the Nile suffering from fever.

On the 29th of September a draft consisting of 3 subalterns (Lieutenants W. D. Ewart, Gordon, and MacFarlan), 1 sergeant, and 17 rank and file, under the command of Major R. C. Annesley, joined the regiment from the Nile reserve depôt.

On the 5th of October a telegram was received from Major-General Grenfell, C.B., A.D.C., directing that the Cameron Highlanders should be held in readiness to proceed to Wady Halfa as soon as relieved, in consequence of intelligence received that the Soudan Arabs were advancing upon Akasheh and Wady Halfa.

On the 10th of the same month the regiment was inspected on parade by Lieutenant-General Sir Frederick Stephenson, K.C.B., who was inspecting the frontier stations. He complimented the regiment on its fine appearance and excellent conduct.

On the 13th the 1st battalion of the Yorkshire regiment arrived at Korosko to relieve the regiment; and as soon as the former had disembarked, the Cameron Highlanders embarked on three steamers towing barges. Four companies, under Lieutenant-Colonel Everett, embarked on the largest of these steamers, the SS. *Messir*, and the two smaller steamers were placed respectively in charge of Lieutenants Cameron and Hon. A. D. Murray.

The regiment spent the night of the 14th at Ibrim island, the 15th at the temple of Aboo Simbel, and the 16th at the village of Eskeh.

On the 17th it arrived at Wady Halfa and disembarked. Here orders were received for the right half battalion and head-quarters to go under canvas, and for the left half battalion, under Lieutenant-Colonel Everett, to proceed to the advanced outposts of Kosheh and Akasheh.

In accordance with these orders "G" and "H" companies, under the command of Major Chalmers, left by train for Akasheh on the 18th of October. From Akasheh they marched on 26 miles to Kosheh fort, which was reached on the 22nd.

Kosheh was a small brick fort 113 miles to the south of Wady Halfa, and was the most advanced British post in the Soudan.

On the 19th of October "E" and "F" companies, under the command of Lieutenant-Colonel Everett, went by train to Akasheh, where he assumed command.

On the 28th, 100 rank and file from the right half battalion were sent as a reinforcement to Akasheh, and 50 of them, under Lieutenant Hon. A. Murray, moved by whale-boat to Kosheh to join Major Chalmers.

On the 2nd of November a draft of 2 sergeants and 156 rank and file, under the command of Lieutenant Scott-Elliot, arrived at Wady Halfa from the depôt at Fort George.

On the 9th of this month "D" company, under Major R. C. Annesley, was sent to Sarras, 37 miles south of Halfa, to protect the railway to Akasheh. From Sarras a party was sent out, under Lieutenant Scott-Elliot, in search of some marauders who had been seen in the vicinity of the railway, and a party of 12 men, under Sergeant Alexander Mackenzie, was placed in a blockhouse at Mohrat Wells, 13 miles from Sarras.

On the 7th of November Lieutenant-Colonel Everett moved with his two companies from Akasheh to Kosheh, where the whole of the left half battalion was now united.

On the 17th of November a camel corps was formed at Wady Halfa; 25 volunteers from the regiment, under Lieutenant Scott-Elliot, joined it, being designated the "Cameron Division of the Camel Corps."

On the 19th of November the head-quarters and right half battalion, under Colonel St. Leger, moved to Akasheh, being joined at Sarras by "D" company. They bivouacked for the night at Akasheh and proceeded the following day by whale-boats to the Dal Cataract, and from thence marched to Firket, eight miles further on.

On the 21st, in pursuance of orders, the head-quarters and right half battalion moved from Firket to Mograkeh, an old Arab fort in

total ruins, which Colonel St. Leger had been directed to place in a state of defence with a view to keeping open the communications between Akasheh and Kosheh.

Work was at once commenced, the old towers were loopholed, the walls cut down, and rendered defensible, and a zeriba was made round the most exposed sides. In the meantime Lieutenant-Colonel Everett and the left half battalion were working hard at the defences of Kosheh, where the trees were felled, the ground cleared, and a large zeriba constructed on the west bank of the Nile.

It was known that the Soudanese army was approaching rapidly and might be expected before Kosheh in a few days.

On the 25th, Brigadier-General Butler, C.B., A.D.C., arrived at Mograkeh, and directed that the right half battalion should move to Kosheh at once, on being relieved by the 3rd battalion of the Egyptian army. "A" company moved that afternoon and "B" company on the following morning, "C" and "D" companies remaining at Mograkeh until the arrival of the Egyptians.

Early the following day news was received that a large body of the enemy had arrived at the pass of Attab, only six miles from Kosheh, and that an attack that night upon the fort was contemplated. Every preparation was made, and the regiment remained under arms throughout the night, but no attack came off.

During the night "D" company was moved from Mograkeh, under Lieutenant D. Davidson, and was conveyed across the river to the zeriba on the west bank of the Nile.

On the 28th the enemy, whose strength was estimated at 7,000 men, showed in great force on the hills above Amara, displaying many banners. In the evening "C" company, under Major Annesley, moved from Mograkeh to Kosheh on the arrival of the 3rd battalion of the Egyptian army. A small signalling party from the Cameron Highlanders was left at Mograkeh.

The garrison of Kosheh now consisted of 1 troop of the 20th Hussars, 1 troop of Mounted Infantry, a few British and Egyptian Artillerymen, the Cameron Highlanders, and 100 men of the 9th Soudan battalion, under Major Archibald Hunter; 150 blacks from the same battalion, under Major Borrow, occupied the zeriba on the west bank. Mograkeh was held by the 3rd battalion of the Egyptian army, under Major Besant, and some of the Egyptian Camel Corps.

The armed steamers *Lotus* and *Shaban* patrolled the river.

On the 29th and 30th of November the mounted troops, under Lieutenant Legge of the 20th Hussars, exchanged shots with the enemy near Giniss, and the *Lotus* hotly engaged him along the banks near Attab. One Egyptian soldier was killed.

On the 1st of December information was received that a force of the enemy had moved round to the rear, had torn up a mile of the railway between Ambigole and Akasheh, and had attacked the fortified post at Ambigole Wells.

On the 3rd of December the Arabs made a reconnaissance to within 700 yards of the fort, but the garrison did not open fire, hoping that they would commit themselves to an attack.

The following day the *Lotus* again moved up stream and engaged the enemy at Giniss; the Arabs returned her fire with musketry and artillery.

In the evening the whole of the mounted troops at Kosheh and Mograkeh were ordered to leave immediately for Akasheh to assist in protecting the railway.

On the 5th of December the enemy advanced on both banks of the river and occupied a ridge of sandhills on the west bank and the village of Absari, which was about 800 yards from Kosheh fort on the east bank. From this date the dervishes kept up an almost ceaseless fire of artillery and musketry upon the fort and zeriba, occasioning many casualties in the garrison. When it became evident that they did not mean to attack in earnest, but to harass and annoy the garrison with their fire, internal defences, traverses, magazines, and covered ways were constructed to protect the men as far as possible. The garrison was also divided into three watches, so that one-third was always available, night and day, to repel any sudden attack and to return the enemy's incessant fire.

On the 9th "C" company, under Major Annesley, with 80 blacks, under Major Hunter, cleared and set fire to the village of Absari.

On the 11th the Cameron Highlanders had Captain Hacket-Thompson and four rank and file wounded.

At daybreak on the morning of the 12th about 3,000 of the enemy suddenly attacked Mograkeh fort. Three companies of the Cameron Highlanders were paraded at once to go to the assistance of the garrison, but their services were not required, as the 3rd battalion of the Egyptian army repulsed the attack with heavy loss to the Arabs. The Cameron Highlanders had two rank and file wounded.

On the 16th of December "F" and "H" companies, under Lieutenant-Colonel Everett, were sent out at 6 a.m. to make a demonstration against the enemy occupying the village of Absari. As the companies approached the dervishes opened a heavy fire from the loopholed houses, which was vigorously replied to. Lieutenant Riach, with Lance-Sergeant Murray, Corporal Macrae, and Privates Gray and King, moving by the bank of the river, attacked a party of the enemy concealed behind some black rocks in the nullah between Kosheh and Absari, and killed fourteen of them. In doing this, Lieutenant Riach had a very narrow escape, as a bullet, fired by a dervish from the top of the rocks, passed through his helmet, removing some of his hair. Corporal Macrae was wounded in the hand.

Having advanced close to the village the companies retired again under cover of the guns in the fort.

In this reconnaissance the Cameron Highlanders had Major Chalmers (severely), Lieutenant W. G. Cameron (fatally), and four rank and file wounded. Major Archibald Hunter, 9th battalion Egyptian army, was also very dangerously wounded.

The enemy kept up a heavy fire upon the fort throughout the day, nine of his shells bursting inside the works.

On the 17th the Cameron Highlanders had one man (Private David McKenzie) killed and one man wounded.

To the great regret of all ranks Lieutenant W. G. Cameron died of his wounds on the 19th, and the following regimental order was published referring to his death:—

"The Officer Commanding feels sure that all ranks will share his deep sorrow at the deaths of Lieutenant Cameron, Private McKenzie, and Private Farrington, of wounds; and will sympathise with their bereaved relatives. In Lieutenant Cameron, the Cameron Highlanders have lost a most promising and gallant young officer, whose zeal and readiness to perform any duty, however difficult or dangerous, will long be remembered by all who have served with him."

The fort was again exposed to artillery fire on the morning of the 20th and the regiment had 1 sergeant (Armourer-Sergeant H. Messenger) and 2 rank and file wounded.

On the 22nd a reconnaissance was made by the mounted troops, who had again arrived at Mograkeh from Akasheh; they were supported by "A" and "G" companies, under Major Hunt and Captain Napier.

On the 24th the Cameron Highlanders had 1 corporal wounded; on the 26th, 2 rank and file killed and 1 wounded; on the 29th, 1 man killed and 1 wounded.

On the 29th of December, 1885, Lieutenant-General Sir Frederick Stephenson arrived at Mograkeh with 4,000 British and Egyptian troops, and the investment of Kosheh, which had lasted 31 days, terminated.

The following morning the Anglo-Egyptian force, under Lieutenant-General Stephenson, attacked and dispersed the dervishes at Giniss.

The Cameron Highlanders and 9th Soudan battalion of the Egyptian army, under the command of Lieutenant-Colonel Everett, took the village of Absari at the point of the bayonet, and afterwards occupied and burnt the village of Giniss. All the enemy's standards, five guns, and his ammunition and nuggars fell into the hands of the British and Egyptians.

In this engagement the Cameron Highlanders had 8 rank and file wounded.

The regiment bivouacked for the night at Giniss, and on the morning of the 31st "D" and "E" companies, under Captains Hacket-Thompson and Urquhart, were sent to dislodge some dervishes who were still holding out in some houses near Kosheh; this they accomplished without loss, returning the same evening to Giniss.

The following is a complete list of casualties incurred by the regiment in the defence of Kosheh and the engagement at Giniss:—

79TH CAMERON HIGHLANDERS.

Major	N. G. Chalmers	Severely wounded
Captain	F. Hacket-Thompson	Wounded
Lieutenant	D. Davidson	Contusion
,,	W. G. Cameron	Died of wounds
Armourer Sergeant	H. Messenger	Severe contusion
Lance-Corporal	D. Macrae	Wounded
,,	J. Reid	Wounded
Drummer	J. Thompson	Dangerously wounded
Private	T. Farrington	Died of wounds
,,	J. Howse	Severely wounded
,,	H. McIntosh	Wounded
,,	D. Mathieson	Dangerously wounded
,,	D. Ramsay	Slightly wounded
,,	C. Gray	Severely wounded
,,	W. Fletcher	Severely wounded
,,	E. Drinkwater	Slightly wounded
,,	J. Stanley	Twice wounded
Lance-Corporal	J. Stewart	Severely wounded
Private	D. Mckenzie	Died of wounds
Pioneer	W. Anderson	Severely wounded
Private	J. McGruer	Contusion
,,	J. Kennedy	Killed.
,,	J. McLaren	Killed
,,	C. Hughes	Dangerously wounded
,,	D. Hogg	Killed
,,	W. Nathan	Severely wounded
,,	J. Smith	Severely wounded
,,	W. Foulks	Severely wounded
,,	J. Charters	Severely wounded
,,	J. McShane	Severely wounded
,,	J. Redfern	Slightly wounded
,,	T. Harris	Slightly wounded
,,	D. Lowe	Severely wounded
Piper	J. McDonald	Died of fever
Private	J. Stevenson	Died of wounds

There were also many casualties in the 9th battalion of the Egyptian army, and amongst the natives employed in the fort.

1886.

On the 1st of January the cavalry pursued the dervishes as far as

Absarat, and the Cameron Highlanders, forming part of the 2nd brigade, under Brigadier-General Huyshe C.B., advanced to Abri, fourteen miles beyond Kosheh. Here Sir Frederick Stephenson's force bivouacked for four days, waiting for orders from the British Government.

On the 7th, all intention of re-occupying Dongola having been abandoned, the army returned to Kosheh, and on the 8th the Cameron Highlanders, having handed over the fort and works to the 106th Durham Light Infantry, resumed their march towards Akasheh.

The regiment bivouacked on the night of the 8th at Sarkamatto, and on the morning of the 9th marched to the north end of Dal Cataract, where they embarked for Akasheh in whale-boats.

On the 11th of January the left half battalion, under the command of Major R. C. Annesley, moved by train from Akasheh to Wady Halfa, being followed the next day by the head-quarters and right half battalion.

At Wady Halfa the regiment was met by a draft of 3 officers (Lieutenants C. Davidson, Findlay, and Lumsden), 1 sergeant, and 194 rank and file, and—after bivouacking for two nights—it moved into the mud huts recently occupied by the South Staffordshire regiment.

For the operations of the Soudan frontier field force, those officers, non-commissioned officers, and men, not already in possession of it, received the Egyptian war medal. Colonel St. Leger, Lieutenant-Colonel Everett, and Major Money were mentioned in Sir Frederick Stephenson's despatches and received the Distinguished Service order, and Sergeant-Major J. Emslie and Sergeant I. Healy (sergeant-major of the 9th Soudan battalion) were awarded the silver medal for distinguished conduct in the field.

The 4th class of the order of the Osmanieh was conferred upon Majors N. G. Chalmers and Money by His Highness the Khedive.

The following officers, non-commissioned officers, and men were brought favourably to the notice of the general officer commanding by Colonels St. Leger and Everett in their official reports:—

Major R. C. Annesley	Colour-Sergeant Ilott
Major N. G. Chalmers	Armourer-Sergeant Henry Messenger
Captain R. F. L. Napier	Lance-Sergeant William Murray
Lieutenant D. Davidson	Corporal Peter Binnie
Lieutenant M. S. Riach	Corporal James Melville
Quarter-Master Howard	Lance-Corporal Colin Hutchison
Lieutenant and Adjutant J. S. Ewart	Lance-Corporal John Wakelen
Rev. J. Robertson	Lance-Corporal David Macrae
Sergeant-Major J. Emslie	Private Joseph Stevenson (died of wounds)
Colour-Sergeant James Morton	Private Thomas Gray
Colour-Sergeant James Keys	Private Robert King
Colour-Sergeant James McNeil	Private John Reilly

On the 12th of February the regiment was inspected by Brigadier-General Butler, C.B., A.D.C., who expressed himself much pleased with its efficient state.

On the 4th of April orders were received for the Cameron Highlanders to be held in readiness to proceed to Cairo, as the British Government had decided to hand over Wady Halfa to the Egyptian authorities, and to withdraw all British troops to Assouan and Cairo.

On the 9th of April the right half battalion, under the command of Captain T. A. Mackenzie, left for Assouan in the stern wheelers *Okmeh*, *Waterlily*, and *Amara*, and, on the return of these steamers to Wady Halfa, the head-quarters and left half battalion embarked.

On the 23rd of April the left half battalion joined the right at Assouan, and the whole regiment went under canvas, with the exception of "E" company, which proceeded on detachment to Assioot, under Captain Mackenzie. The most intense heat prevailed whilst the regiment was at Assouan, and several deaths occurred.

On the 27th of April the regiment embarked for Cairo on board the SS. *Mahmoudieh*, towing two large troop barges. "C" company, under Major Annesley, remained behind for a few days to bring on the officers' horses. The following officers embarked with the regiment :—

Lieutenant-Colonel Everett ; Major Annesley ; Captain Hacket-Thompson ; Lieutenants Findlay, Douglas-Hamilton, Hon. A. D. Murray, W. D. Ewart, Gordon, Lumsden, Hon. J. Forbes-Sempill ; Lieutenant and Adjutant J. S. Ewart ; Quarter-Master Howard ;

Paymaster, Captain Nettleship and Rev. J. Robertson; Warrant Officers, Sergeant-Major J. Emslie and Bandmaster Wakelen.

During the voyage, halts for the night were made at Gebel Silsileh on the 27th, at Salaayeh on the 28th, at the village of Kamuleh on the 29th, at Deshneh on the 30th, at Betianeh on the 1st of May, and at Sohag on the 2nd of May.

On the 3rd of May the Cameron Highlanders disembarked at Assioot, and proceeded the same night to Cairo by train, where they occupied the Kasr-el-Nil barracks, recently vacated by the 42nd Royal Highlanders.

On arrival the regiment was joined by a draft of 1 corporal and 51 rank and file, under the command of Lieutenant Forbes.

"F" and "G" companies were at once sent on detachment to Abdin barracks, as there was not sufficient accommodation in Kasr-el-Nil for the whole regiment.

On the 27th of May the Cameron Highlanders presented a standard on parade to the 9th Soudan battalion of the Egyptian Army, in recollection of the association of the two regiments in the defence of Kosheh. The standard was first trooped by the regiment, and it was then handed over by the Commanding Officer to a Guard of Honour of the 9th battalion. The whole of the Egyptian troops composing the Cairo garrison were present at this interesting ceremony, which took place in Abdin Square.

On the 16th of June a party of invalids of the regiment, under Lieutenant Wolrige Gordon, proceeded to Cyprus for change of air.

On the 13th of July "F" Company, under the command of Major Smith, proceeded to Assioot to relieve "E" company, which returned to Cairo. "F" company remained at this station until relieved by "G" company, under Captain Napier, on the 19th of October.

During the month of July the regimental depôt was moved from Fort George to Inverness, where the new barracks were now completed.

On the 16th of October the Abdin detachment, under Brevet-Major Hunt, re-joined head-quarters at Kasr-el-Nil.

On the 25th of November the regiment moved from Kasr-el-Nil to the Citadel, where it was joined by the company from Assioot.

Whilst at the Citadel it was inspected by Major-General Hales Wilkie, commanding the Cairo brigade, who was much pleased with the smart appearance of the battalion on parade, and with the cleanliness and neatness of the barrack rooms.

On the 7th of December it marched from the Citadel to the camp at Abassiyeh for the annual course of musketry, leaving "E" company (Captain Hacket-Thompson) in charge of the barracks and regimental baggage.

"E" company moved into camp on the 24th of December, on being relieved by "A" company under Major Hunt.

1887.

On the 24th of January the Cameron Highlanders had the honour of being reviewed by His Royal Highness the Prince of Naples, the eldest son of the King of Italy (who was accompanied by Sir Frederick Stephenson and Staff, and many Foreign Officers). After the parade His Royal Highness visited the camp and the officers' mess tent; he expressed himself highly pleased with all he saw.

The regiment returned to the Citadel on the 2nd of February on the completion of the annual course of musketry, and occupied its original quarters.

Whilst the regiment was at Abassiyeh Sergeant-Major John Emslie was presented, on a parade of all the troops in Cairo, with the silver medal for " Distinguished Conduct in the Field," conferred upon him for his gallant behaviour at the defence of Kosheh.

On the 9th of February His Royal Highness the Prince of Naples again honoured the officers of the regiment with his presence at an "At Home" given by them in the Bijou Palace. He remained for some time, and appeared to take great interest in the sword dance and a reel which were performed by Pipe-Major W. McDonald and Pipers D. Campbell, Sharp, and Alan McKenzie, in the large reception room of the Palace.

On the 4th of March the regiment received orders to be ready to embark for England at short notice, and on the 11th of March it left Cairo by train for Alexandria.

Amongst the many friends who came to the station to say farewell to the Cameron Highlanders were His Excellency Tonino Pasha, representing His Highness the Khedive, and the Italian military attaché, who attended to mark the regard felt for the regiment by the Italian community. The same evening the regiment embarked, after a stay of four-and-a-half years in Egypt, on board H.M.S. *Tamar* and sailed at once for Malta. The following officers embarked with it :—

Colonel St. Leger, D.S.O., (commanding); Lieutenant-Colonel Everett, D.S.O. ; Colonel McCausland ; Major Hunt ; Captains Napier, Hacket-Thompson, Mackenzie, Urquhart, and D. Davidson ; Lieutenants Macleod, C. Davidson, Scott-Elliot, Riach, Findlay, McKerrell, Douglas-Hamilton, Hon. A. Murray, W. D. Ewart, Gordon, MacFarlan, Lumsden, Hon. J Forbes-Sempill (Master of Sempill), and Egerton ; Quarter-Master Howard ; Lieutenant and Adjutant J. S. Ewart ; and Captain Nettleship (paymaster) ; Warrant Officers, Sergeant-Major J. Emslie, Bandmaster R. B. Wakelen.

Before the departure of the regiment His Highness the Khedive conferred the 3rd class of the order of the Medjidie upon Lieutenant-Colonel Everett, D.S.O., the 4th class upon Captain Napier, and the 5th class upon Lieutenant and Adjutant Ewart in recognition of their services at the engagement at Giniss.

The regiment landed at Devonport (Millbay Pier) on the 26th of March, 1887, and occupied the South Raglan barracks. On the 1st of April a draft from the depôt at Inverness, consisting of 1 subaltern (Lieutenant Scott), 2 sergeants, and 199 rank and file, under the command of Major A. Y. Leslie, joined the head-quarters at Devonport.

In the beginning of May Sergeant Thomas Healy of the regiment, who had been acting as Sergeant-Major of the 9th Soudan battalion of the Egyptian army, in which capacity he had won the Silver Medal for distinguished conduct in the field at the engagement at Giniss, again greatly distinguished himself in the hand-to-hand fight with the dervishes at Sarras on the Soudan frontier.

On this occasion he killed the celebrated dervish leader Nur

Hamza, and gained possession of his sword and spear, receiving five wounds himself in the course of the action.

Shortly after the arrival of the regiment in England it became known that it was in contemplation to convert the Cameron Highlanders into a 3rd battalion of the Scots Guards.

As such a proposal was tantamount to a total extinction of the regiment, and the loss of its character as a Highland corps, the news was received with the greatest consternation by all ranks, and much indignation was felt and expressed in the town and county of Inverness and in the Highlands generally.

Meetings protesting against the scheme were at once held by the Highland Society of London, the Town Council of Inverness, the Inverness Commissioners of Supply, and other influential bodies, with the result that, on the 17th of May, Lord Lovat was authorised by the Secretary of State for War to state that the proposed change would not take place, and that the question was as dead as if it had never been mooted.

Amongst the many friends of the regiment who on this occasion exerted themselves to avert what was regarded by all interested in the Highland regiments as a calamity, may be mentioned :—

The Marquis of Lorne, Lord Lovat, Lord Archibald Campbell, Mr. Cameron of Lochiel, the Mackintosh of Mackintosh, Mr. Forbes of Culloden, Mr. Grant of Glenmoriston, Mr. Davidson of Cantray, Mr. Macleod of Cadboll, Hon. Ivan Campbell, Mr. Macandrew, Provost of Inverness, Colonel Lumsden, Major Grant, Drumbuie, Major Kenneth Macleay, and almost every one connected with the district to which the regiment belongs.

On the 14th of June the regiment furnished a Guard of Honour, under Captain Napier, consisting of the band, pipers, and 100 rank and file, with the Queen's colour, to receive the Crown Prince and Princess of Portugal on landing at Devonport.

During this month the feelings of goodwill and cordiality prevailing between the two battalions of the Cameron Highlanders were shown in a marked manner by the officers making each other perpetual honorary members of their respective messes.

In the month of July the regiment took part in the Jubilee Review at Aldershot, when 60,000 men marched past Her Majesty the Queen.

The regiment embarked at Devonport on the 6th of July on board H.M.S. *Tamar*, 756 strong of all ranks, and proceeded to Portsmouth, where it landed and moved by train to Aldershot. At Aldershot it went under canvas on Church Plateau, in the North Camp, forming part of the 5th brigade of the 3rd division.

The regiment was the only Highland regiment present at the review in the Long Valley on the 9th of July, and its appearance elicited the loudest applause from the enormous crowds present to see the march past. It returned to Portsmouth on the 11th of July, and re-embarked on board H.M.S. *Tamar*; the next day it disembarked at Devonport and re-occupied its quarters in Raglan barracks.

On the 16th of July Colonel St. Leger, D.S.O., retired from the command of the regiment, being succeeded by Lieutenant-Colonel Everett, D.S.O.

"A" company (Major Hunt) and "B" company (Captain Mackenzie) went on detachment to Fort Staddon on the 13th of July to commence the annual course of musketry.

SUCCESSION OF COLONELS OF THE 79TH CAMERON HIGHLANDERS FROM 1793 TO 1887.

Major Alan Cameron	August 17th, 1793	-	Died March 9th, 1828.
Lieutenant-General Sir Ronald Ferguson, K.C.B.	March 24th, 1828	-	„ April 10th, 1841.
Major-General Honourable J. Ramsay	April 27th, 1841	-	„ June 28th, 1842.
Lieutenant-General Sir James Macdonnell, K.C.B.	July 14th, 1842		Transferred to 71st Highlanders, February 8th, 1849.
Major-General James Hay, C.B.	Feb. 8th, 1849	-	Died Feb. 25th, 1854.
Lieutenant-General W. H. Sewell, C.B.	March 24th, 1854	-	„ 1862.
General Honourable Hugh Arbuthnott, C.B.	March 14th, 1862	-	„ 1868.
General J. F. Glencairn Campbell	July 12th, 1868	-	„ 1870.
Major-General Henry Cooper, C.B.	August 21st, 1870		
General Sir Alfred Horsford, G.C.B.	March 17th, 1876		Transferred to the Rifle Brigade.
General Sir John Douglas, G.C.B.	January 1st, 1879		

SUCCESSION OF LIEUTENANT-COLONELS OF THE 79TH CAMERON HIGHLANDERS.

1st Batt.		Alan Cameron	17th August,	1793.
,,	,,	Honourable A. C. Johnstone	2nd May,	1794.
,,	,,	William Ashton	18th September,	1794.
,,	,,	Patrick Macdowall	1st November,	1796.
,,	,,	William Eden	15th August,	1798.
,,	,,	Archibald McLean	3rd September,	1801.
2nd	,,	Philips Cameron	19th April,	1804.
,,	,,	John Murray	28th May,	1807.
1st	,,	Philips Cameron	11th December,	1806.
,,	,,	John Murray	28th May,	1807.
2nd	,,	Robert Fulton	28th May,	1807.
1st	,,	Robert Fulton	13th May,	1811.
2nd	,,	William Harvey	30th May,	1811.
1st	,,	William Harvey	3rd December,	1812.
2nd	,,	Neil Douuglas	3rd December,	1812.
1st	,,	Neil Douglas	20th February,	1813.
2nd	,,	Nathaniel Cameron	24th June,	1813.
1st	,,	Duncan MacDougall	6th September,	1833.
,,	,,	Robert Ferguson	13th March,	1835.
,,	,,	Andrew Brown	8th June,	1841.
,,	,,	John Carter, K.H.	29th October,	1841.
,,	,,	Honourable Lauderdale Maule	14th June,	1842.
,,	,,	Edmund James Elliot	24th December,	1852.
,,	,,	John Douglas	13th August,	1854.
,,	,,	Richard C. H. Taylor, C.B.	1st August,	1857.
,,	,,	Thomas Bromhead Butt	15th April,	1859.
,,	,,	William C. Hodgson	10th July,	1860.
,,	,,	Richard M. Best	13th September,	1864.
,,	,,	Keith Ramsay Maitland	2nd March,	1872.
,,	,,	George Murray Miller	19th October,	1872.
,,	,,	Edward W. Cuming	6th August,	1879.
,,	,,	John Macdonald Leith	1st July,	1881.
2nd	,,	Simon, Lord Lovat, A.D.C.	1st July,	1881.
1st	,,	Henry Hungerford St. Leger	1st April,	1885.
,,	,,	Edward Everett, D.S.O.	1st July,	1887.

The following officers were serving in the regiment when these records were completed:—

1st Battalion.

Lieutenant-Colonel	E. Everett, D.S.O.
Colonel	W. H. McCausland
Major	A. Y. Leslie
"	O. B. Gordon
"	N. G. Chalmers
"	G. L. C. Money, D.S.O.
"	W. H. Smith
"	J. M. Hunt
Captain	F. S. Chapman
"	K. S. Baynes (Bt.-Major)
"	R. F. L. Napier
"	F. Hacket-Thompson
"	T. A. Mackenzie
"	H. H. L. Malcolm
"	B. C. Urquhart
"	D. F. Davidson
Lieutenant	R. W. Macleod
"	C. F. H. Davidson
"	G. E. Forbes
"	A. Scott-Elliot
"	G. R. Cavaye
"	M. S. Riach
"	C. Findlay
"	A. de S. McKerrell
"	A. F. Douglas-Hamilton
"	Hon. A. D. Murray
"	W. D. Ewart
"	H. G. Wolrige-Gordon
"	F. A. MacFarlan
"	H. R. Lumsden
"	Hon. J. Forbes-Sempill (Master of Sempill)
"	A. F. Egerton
Adjutant	J. S. Ewart (Lieutenant)
Paymaster	A. J. Nettleship (Captain)
Quarter-Master	W. Howard (Lieutenant)
Sergeant-Major	W. Young
"	H. McLean (Depôt)
Bandmaster	R. B. B. Wakelen

2nd Battalion.

Colonel	S. Lord Lovat, A.D.C.
Major	J. A. Macdonald
"	G. A. Duff
Captain	G. R. McKessack
"	H. L. Langford Brooke (Hon. Major)
"	A. D. Mackintosh of Mackintosh (Hon. Major)
"	C. J. Merry
"	H. W. Kemble
"	W. H. Garforth
"	W. G. S. Menzies
"	C. L. McKenzie
"	I. R. J. M. Grant
Lieutenant	C. Aytoun
"	R. A. Paterson
"	J. W. MacGillivray
"	H. E. Boulton
"	A. J. Campbell-Orde
"	C. D. Stewart
"	E. J. Stourton
"	J. H. F. Radcliffe
"	J. H. Younger
"	J. McDonald
"	W. R. D. Mackenzie
2nd Lieutenant	D. J. F. Potts-Chatto
"	K. A. Fraser
Adjutant	K. S. Baynes (Bt.-Major)
Quarter-Master	J. Emslie (Lieutenant)
Medical Officer	D. McFadyen (Surgeon-Major)
Sergeant-Major	A. D. Fraser

SERVICES OF THE OFFICERS.

Compiled from the Annual Army Lists and other authentic sources.

Services of the Officers.

ACKLAND. Robert Innes Ackland. Ensign, 17th of August, 1809; he was placed on half pay of the regiment in September, 1814; afterwards served in the 72nd regiment. He was present with the 79th at Busaco, Fuentes d'Onor, and the Pyrenees.

ADCOCK. Herbert Burrows Adcock. Ensign, 2nd of March, 1855; lieutenant, 17th of February, 1857; exchanged to 6th Foot, 1857.

ADDERLEY. Randolph Ralph Adderley. Exchanged as ensign to 79th from 35th regiment, 21st of May, 1850.

ALLEN. John Edward Allen. Was transferred to the 79th, as lieutenant, from the 92nd Highlanders, 19th of January, 1855. He served with the 79th Highlanders in the Crimea from the 16th of August, 1855, including the siege and fall of Sebastopol, and assault of the 8th of September. (Medal with clasp and Turkish medal.) Served in the Indian campaign of 1858-59, including the siege and capture of Lucknow, attack on the fort at Rooyah, actions at Allygunge, Bareilly, Shahjehanpore, capture of forts Bunniar and Mahomdie, passage of the Gogra at Fyzabad, capture of Rampore Kussia, and subsequent operations in Oude, across the Gogra and Raptee rivers. (Medal with clasp.) Exchanged as major to the 71st Highland Light Infantry.

ALLEYNE. Douglas Alleyne. Ensign, 23rd of February, 1855, served with the 79th Highlanders in the Crimea from the 16th of August until December, 1855, including the siege and fall of Sebastopol, and assault on the Redan on the 8th of September. (Medal with clasp and Turkish medal.) Served also with the 79th in the Indian campaign of 1858-59, including the affair of Secundragunge near Allahabad, siege and capture of Lucknow, attack on the fort of Rooyah, actions of Allygunge, Bareilly, and Shahjehanpore, capture of forts Bunniar and Mahomdie, passage of the Gogra at Fyzabad, and acted as adjutant at the capture of Rampore Kussia, and during the subsequent operations in Oude, across the Gogra and Raptee rivers. (Medal with clasp.) Exchanged to the 37th Foot on the 27th of June, 1860; retired as lieutenant-colonel.

ANDERSON. Allan Meyrick Anderson. Lieutenant, 2nd battalion, 25th of April, 1885.

ANDERSON. Andrew Anderson, M.D. Appointed assistant-surgeon in the 79th on the 4th of February, 1808; was present with the 79th at the battles of Busaco and Fuentes d'Onor; was transferred to the 61st regiment on the 25th of June, 1812, and was present at the battles of Salamanca and Pyrenees (silver medal with clasp), and at the siege of Burgos.

ANDERSON. John Anderson, M.D. Appointed assistant-surgeon in the 79th on the 8th of May, 1840; transferred to the 22nd regiment in the same year. Died at sea. Served with the 22nd regiment at the battle of Meeanee. (Medal.)

ANDERSON. William Anderson. Ensign, 22nd of October, 1799; placed on half pay, 1802. Afterwards served in the 78th Highlanders.

ANGUS. John Angus. Ensign, 1st of March, 1864; lieutenant, 8th of February, 1868; instructor of musketry, 4th of May, 1873. Exchanged to the 7th Fusiliers on the 27th of August, 1873. Served as paymaster of the 4th battalion Rifle Brigade in the Afghan war, in 1878-79. (Medal.)

ANNESLEY. Reginald Carey Annesley. Ensign, 15th of January, 1864; lieutenant, 29th of January, 1867. Served throughout Ashantee campaign, attached to the 42nd Black Watch in 1873-74; was present at the battle of Amoaful (slightly wounded), the capture and destruction of Becquah, battle of Ordahsu, and capture of Coomassie. (Medal and clasp.) Also served throughout the operations of the Soudan Frontier Field Force, 1885-86, with the Cameron Highlanders; was present in Kosheh during its investment by the Arabs, and at the engagement at Giniss. (Medal.) Retired in 1886 with the honorary rank of lieutenant-colonel.

ANYSLEY. James Murray Anysley. Ensign, 21st of October, 1799; placed on half pay, 1802; captain, 26th of June, 1846. Retired, 27th of October, 1848.

ARBUTHNOTT. Honourable Sir Hugh Arbuthnott, K.C.B. General, 20th of June, 1854; colonel of the 79th, 14th of March, 1862. He served in the campaign in Holland in 1799, at the bombardment of Copenhagen in 1801 and 1807, with the expedition to Sweden in 1808, and throughout the Peninsular war. He received a gold medal for Busaco, and a silver medal with two clasps for Corunna and Fuentes d'Onor. He died in 1868.

ARBUTHNOTT. Thomas H. C. Arbuthnott. Ensign, 10th of February, 1843. Retired, 6th of June, 1845.

ARCHER. Anthony Archer. A volunteer from the 94th regiment; ensign, 14th of October, 1812. Died the same year.

ARTHUR. Rev. David Arthur. Was chaplain to the 79th Cameron Highlanders throughout the Egyptian campaign of 1882, and was present at the battle of Tel-el-Kebir. (Medal with clasp, and Khedive's star.) Was also with the regiment during the Nile expedition of 1884-85. (Clasp.)

ASHTON. William Ashton. Lieutenant-colonel, 18th of September, 1794. Died in 1797.

ASSIOTTI. Francis Assiotti. Exchanged from the 45th regiment; lieutenant, 25th of March, 1805; went to the 27th regiment as captain, 15th of May, 1806.

ATKINSON. Agit Atkinson. Appointed assistant-surgeon of the 79th from the Aberdeen Fencibles on the 14th of May, 1803. Served with the 79th in the Peninsula, and was drowned in the river Douro.

AYTOUN. Chadwick Aytoun. Lieutenant in the 2nd battalion, 1st of July, 1881.

AYTOUN. Robinson Aytoun. Appointed assistant-surgeon of the 79th, 1st of May, 1806; transferred to the 13th Foot on the 4th of February, 1808. Had a medal for Martinique.

BAILEY. David Bailey. Ensign, 11th of July, 1811. Died at Elvas, August, 1811, of a wound received at the battle of Albuhera.

BAILLIE. Alexander Peter Baillie. Ensign, 14th of August, 1857; lieutenant, 4th of September, 1860; captain, 11th of June, 1867; half pay, 10th of April, 1869.

BAILLIE. Matthew Baillie, M.D. Appointed assistant-surgeon in the 79th, 18th of January, 1827. Died at Belfast on the 6th of February, 1828.

BALDOCK. John Baldock. Paymaster, 21st of July, 1798. Died in the Walcheren expedition in 1809.

BALFOUR. Jeremiah Balfour. Ensign, 1st of October, 1812; lieutenant, 19th of May, 1814; placed on half pay of the regiment, 25th of March, 1817. Died at Chatham on the 20th of September, 1822.

BALFOUR. William Balfour. Lieutenant in the 79th from half pay, 26th of July, 1839; retired on the 14th of October, 1842.

BANKES. William Meyrick Bankes, younger, of Letterewe. Major, 2nd battalion, 1st of July, 1881. Died in 1884.

BARNES. Sir Edward Barnes, G.C.B. Exchanged as lieutenant-colonel to the 79th from the 99th regiment, 17th of January, 1800, and was appointed to the 46th regiment on the 23rd of April, 1807; major-general, 4th of June, 1813; lieutenant-general, 27th of May, 1825; general, 7th of June, 1831; colonel of the 31st regiment, 10th of October, 1834. Sir Edward served with the 79th in the Egyptian campaign in 1801. (Gold medal from Sultan Selim III.). Was present at the captures of Martinique, Guadaloupe, battles of Vittoria, Pyrenees, Nivelle, Nive, and Orthes. (Gold medal). He was adjutant-general at the battle of Waterloo, where he was very severely wounded. He died in London on the 31st of August, 1848.

BARNEWELL. Bartholemew Barnewell. Lieutenant in the 79th, 22nd of October, 1799. Retired on half pay of the regiment, 1800. Died on the 31st of August, 1848.

BARWICK. James Barwick. Lieutenant, 26th of January, 1804; exchanged to the 14th Foot; became a major in 1830, and died in Canada.

BATEMAN. Robert Bateman. Exchanged to 79th as paymaster, 25th of April, 1824; went on half pay on the 16th of February, 1829. Had previously served in Hanover in 1805, and was shipwrecked and made prisoner in the Texel. He was present at the attack on Buenos Ayres; served in the Peninsula, and was severely wounded at the battle of Vittoria; was also at the battle of Plattsburg, in America, in 1814.

BAYNES. Kenneth Schalch Baynes. Lieutenant, 10th of September, 1876. Served as adjutant of the Cameron Highlanders throughout the Egyptian war of 1882, and was present at the battle of Tel-el-Kebir. (Medal with clasp, and Khedive's star.) Served with the expedition to the Soudan in 1884, as assistant-military-secretary to Sir Gerald Graham, and was present in the engagements at El Teb and Tamaii. (Brought home the despatches, mentioned in despatches, brevet of major, two clasps.) Served in the Nile expedition of 1884-85 as adjutant of the Cameron Highlanders, and staff officer at Korosko. (Clasp.) He also served in the campaign in the eastern Soudan in 1885 as deputy-assistant-adjutant and quartermaster-general, and was present in the engagement at Hasheen and at the destruction of Tamaii. (Mentioned in despatches, clasp.)

BEATTIE. James Forbes Beattie. Appointed assistant-surgeon to the 79th Highlanders, 20th of September, 1864. Transferred to the Army Medical Staff, 16th of December, 1871.

BEATTIE. George Beattie, M.D. Appointed surgeon of the 79th, 1st of March, 1810. Died at Langholm, Dumfries, 18th of August, 1837.

BECKHAM. Thomas Beckham. Exchanged as lieutenant from the 89th Foot, 30th of August, 1820. Placed on half pay of the regiment in 1821. Before joining the 79th Lieutenant Beckham served in the Peninsula with the 43rd regiment.

BEDFORD. R. B. R. Bedford. Ensign, 19th of January, 1855; lieutenant, 9th of September, 1855. Retired from the service, 10th of May, 1861.

BELL. James Bell. Ensign, 3rd of March, 1854; lieutenant, 13th of August, 1854; captain, half pay, 4th of April, 1856. He served with the regiment in the Eastern campaign of 1854-55, including the battle of Balaclava, siege of Sebastopol, and expedition to Kertch and Yenikale. (Medal with two clasps, and Turkish medal.)

BELL. James Nicholas Bell. Appointed assistant-surgeon of the regiment, 1st of April, 1853; transferred to the 93rd Highlanders, 1859. He served with the 79th Highlanders in the

Eastern campaign of 1854-55, including the battle of Balaclava and siege of Sebastopol. (Medal with two clasps, and Turkish medal.)

BERTRAM. Archibald Bertram. Transferred in 1795, as captain, from the 37th regiment; exchanged as major on the 28th of February, 1805, to the 100th regiment. Lost at sea. He served with the 79th in Egypt in 1801.

BEST. Richard Mordesley Best. Exchanged as brevet-colonel to the 79th on the 13th of September, 1864. Served previously in the Punjaub campaign of 1849 in the 10th Foot, and was present at the siege of Mooltan and the battle of Gujerat. (Slightly wounded in the leg. Medal with two clasps.) Became major-general on the 28th of October, 1868, and lieutenant-general on the 1st of July, 1881.

BIRCH. Alexander John Colin Birch. Ensign, 2nd of March, 1855; lieutenant, 3rd of November, 1856. Went to Indian Staff Corps in 1865.

BLACKBURN. Adam Gillies Blackburn. 2nd lieutenant, 13th of August, 1879; lieutenant, 16th of June, 1880. He served with the regiment throughout the Egyptian campaign of 1882, and was present at the battle of Tel-el-Kebir. (Dangerously wounded, mentioned in despatches. Medal with clasp, 5th class of the Medjidie, and Khedive's star.) Retired in consequence of his wounds, which necessitated the amputation of his leg, on the 23rd of February, 1884.

BOOTHBY. Robert Tod Boothby. Ensign, 31st of March, 1848.

BORTHWICK. John Borthwick. Ensign, 6th of October, 1843. Retired, 20th of March, 1844.

BORTHWICK. Robert Macgowan Borthwick. Ensign, 18th of January, 1857; lieutenant, 9th of April, 1861; captain, 2nd of March, 1872. Retired in 1879.

BOULTON. Harold Edwin Boulton. Lieutenant, 2nd battalion, 25th of July 1883.

BOURKE. Sir Richard Bourke, K.C.B. Exchanged from the 46th regiment as brevet major 4th of January, 1810, and re-exchanged to half pay of Lowenstein's late levy on the 22nd of February, 1810. Served previously in the campaign in Holland in 1799; present in the actions of the 27th of August, 10th and 19th of September, and 2nd and 6th of October; at the latter he received a severe wound through both jaws. Served in South America for fifteen months; present at the actions near Monte Video, on the 19th and 20th of January, 1807; served in the expedition against Buenos Ayres in the same year. Became a general on the 11th of November, 1851.

BREBNER. John Brebner. Ensign from the 85th Foot, 15th of November, 1859; lieutenant, 31st of March, 1863. Retired in 1869.

BRITTAIN. Richard Brittain. Appointed paymaster of the 79th on the 1st of January, 1810. Died at Edinburgh on the 22nd of May, 1815.

BROWN. Andrew Brown, C.B. Ensign, 8th of September, 1795; captain, 17th of September, 1803. Served as adjutant of the regiment in the Egyptian campaign in 1801. (Gold medal from Sultan Selim III.). Joined the 1st battalion of the 79th in the Peninsula in 1811; present at the battles of Fuentes d'Onor, Salamanca, Nivelle, Pyrenees, and Toulouse, and at the siege of Burgos. He was severely wounded at the battle of Quatre Bras. He became a lieutenant-colonel in 1830, and died at Derry in 1835.

BROWN. Andrew Brown. Ensign, 26th of October, 1820; lieutenant, 17th of March, 1825; captain, 5th of April, 1831; major, 26th of May, 1838; lieutenant-colonel, 8th of June, 1841. Exchanged to the 1st Foot on the 29th of October, 1841.

BROWN. Charles Brown. Ensign, 2nd of November, 1809; lieutenant, 9th of May, 1811. Lost a leg at the battle of Fuentes d'Onor, and retired upon full pay.

BROWN. James Brown. Ensign, 31st of September, 1803; lieutenant, 22nd of April, 1805; appointed adjutant of the Perth Militia, 27th of February, 1808; afterwards head of the police at Edinburgh, where he died in 1832.

BROWN. James Dudgeon Brown. Exchanged as lieutenant to the 79th from the 3rd West India Regiment, 15th of November, 1821; captain, 29th of July, 1824; was given an unattached majority, 18th of May, 1832. Died at Preston Kirk on the 16th of December, 1851. Before entering the 79th he served in the campaign in Holland in 1814, and was present at the storming of Egmont-op-Zoom.

BROWN. John Brown. Appointed paymaster of the regiment, March, 1884, and served with it in the Nile expedition of 1884-85. (Medal and clasp.) Had previously served with the 17th Lancers throughout the Eastern campaign of 1854-55, including the affairs of Bulganak and Mackenzie's farm, battles of Alma, Balaclava (severely wounded and horse killed), and Tchernaya, and the siege and fall of Sebastopol. (Medal with three clasps, and Turkish medal.) Served in the Central Indian campaign in 1858-59, and was present at the action of Burrode. (Medal.) Served as paymaster of the 17th Lancers in the Zulu war of 1879. (Medal.)

BROWN. James Moray Brown. Ensign from the 84th regiment, 2nd of November, 1866; lieutenant, 28th of October, 1871. Retired in 1881.

BROWN. Thomas Brown. Ensign, 23rd of October, 1806; lieutenant, 15th of December, 1807; captain, 20th of July, 1815; placed on the half pay of the regiment, 25th of February, 1816. He was present with the regiment at the siege of Copenhagen;

served in the Peninsula with the 79th, and was present at the battles of Busaco, Fuentes d'Onor, Salamanca, Pyrenees, Nivelle, Nive, and Toulouse; at the action of Foz d'Aronce, and at the siege of Burgos. He was severely wounded at the battle of Quatre Bras. He received the silver medal with clasps, and the Waterloo medal.

BROWN. Ebenezer Brown, M.D. Appointed assistant-surgeon in the 79th, 24th of December, 1796; transferred to the 30th regiment, April 4th, 1800. Died at Madras in 1828.

BROWNE. Charles Francis Browne. Ensign, 15th of October, 1850.

BRUCE. William Bruce, K. H. Exchanged as lieutenant to the 79th from a veteran battalion, 26th of May, 1808; captain, 14th of March, 1811; exchanged to the 82nd regiment as a captain, 10th of July, 1817. Served in the Peninsula, and was present at the battles of Albuhera, Nivelle, Nive, and Toulouse, the blockade of Pempeluna, and at the investment of Bayonne. He was severely wounded at the battle of Quatre Bras. He had the silver medal and clasps and the Waterloo medal. Retired as a colonel, 11th of December, 1849, and died at the Grosvenor Hotel, London, in 1863.

BUCHANAN. Alexander Buchanan (Powis). Ensign, 26th of May, 1838; lieutenant, 21st of August, 1840. Retired on the 10th of February, 1843.

BUCKNALL. Samuel Charles Lindsay Bucknall. Ensign, 21st of October, 1862; lieutenant, 15th of June, 1866. Retired in 1878.

BURNETT. William Burnett. Transferred as ensign from the 72nd regiment on the 23rd of July, 1803; re-transferred to the 18th Foot on the 19th of October, 1804. Died in 1812.

BURKE. John Burke. Exchanged to the 79th as lieutenant on the 3rd of July, 1799.

BURKE. John Burke. Ensign, 6th of July, 1804; lieutenant, 24th of April, 1805; transferred to the 38th regiment on the 26th of March, 1807. Retired on the 4th of January, 1810.

BUSFIELD. John Busfield. Ensign, 30th of March, 1860; lieutenant, 12th of May, 1863; captain, 16th of June, 1877. Retired in 1880.

BURRELL. William George Burrell. Appointed assistant-surgeon in the 79th on the 14th of December, 1809. Was present with the 79th at the battle of Waterloo. Transferred to the 5th Foot on the 11th of January, 1816. Died in 1820.

BUTLER. Thomas Lewis Butler. Captain, from the 72nd regiment, 2nd of February, 1830. Retired on the 23rd of August, 1834.

BUTT. Thomas Bromhead Butt. Ensign, 3rd of April, 1840; lieutenant, 2nd of August, 1842; captain, 2nd of April, 1847; Major, 17th of July, 1857; lieutenant-colonel, 26th of April, 1859; colonel, 23rd of May, 1864, exchanged to the 86th regiment. He served in the Indian campaign of 1858-59, including the siege and capture of Lucknow, with the 79th Highlanders. (Brevet of lieutenant-colonel. Medal and clasp.)

CALDER. James Calder. Lieutenant, 19th of April, 1804. He served with the 79th in the Peninsular war, and was wounded at the battle of Fuentes d'Onor. He died at Abrantes of fever, on the 25th of July, 1812.

CAMERON. Sir Alan Cameron, K.C.B., of Erracht. Raised the regiment in 1793. Served with and commanded the regiment in the expedition to Holland in 1799, and was wounded at the battle of Egmont-op-Zee. In 1800 he served with the expedition to Ferrol and Cadiz, and afterwards throughout the whole of the Egyptian campaign in 1801. (Gold medal from Sultan Selim III.) In 1807 he served at the capture of Copenhagen, and in the following year he accompanied the expedition to

Sweden, under Sir John Moore, as a brigadier-general; returning to England the same year he was ordered with the 79th to Portugal. He commanded a brigade at the battle of Talavera, where he had two horses shot under him (gold medal); and also at the battle of Busaco. On the 25th of July, 1810, he was promoted to major-general, and at the termination of the war he was nominated a K.C.B. On the 12th of August, 1819, he became a lieutenant-general. He died at Fulham on the 9th of March, 1828.

CAMERON. Allan Cameron. Appointed lieutenant in the 79th, 17th of July, 1801, from the 11th Foot. He served with the 79th in Egypt in 1801, and was wounded at the battle before Alexandria. (Gold medal from Sultan Selim III.). He was transferred to the 8th Garrison battalion in 1806, and retired on half pay. Died at Perth in 1835.

CAMERON. Allan Cameron. Ensign, 19th of April, 1805; lieutenant, 30th of January, 1806; went on half pay in 1808, but was re-appointed to the 79th as paymaster in 1821. He exchanged to half pay of the 5th Foot on the 25th of April, 1824. Died at Clunes on the 13th of April, 1841.

CAMERON. Alexander Cameron. Ensign, 5th of November, 1794; lieutenant, 6th of September, 1795. Served with the 79th in Holland in 1799, and was present at the battle of Egmont-op-Zee; accompanied the regiment to Egypt in 1801, and was present at the battle before Alexandria. (Gold medal from Sultan Selim III.). He served continuously with the 79th in the Peninsula until he was killed at the battle of Busaco in 1810.

CAMERON. Alexander Cameron. Ensign, 29th of December, 1804; lieutenant, 25th of March, 1805; captain, 11th of June, 1807. Retired in 1812, and died at sea whilst returning from the West Indies.

CAMERON. Alexander Cameron. Ensign, 8th of April, 1806; lieutenant, 12th of May, 1807; captain and brevet-major, 21st of

January, 1819. Died at Tobago in 1820. He served with the 79th Highlanders at the bombardment of Copenhagen and throughout the Peninsular war, being wounded at the battles of Fuentes d'Onor and Toulouse; he was also present at the battle of Quatre Bras, and commanded the remnant of the regiment at the close of the battle of Waterloo, where he was slightly wounded. (Brevet of major.) He was a son of Cameron of Scamadale, and nephew of Sir Alan Cameron.

CAMERON. Alexander Cameron. Ensign, 17th of July, 1815; lieutenant, 7th of March, 1822; half pay, 29th of March, 1827. Died in the south of France on the 16th of January, 1832. Before being gazetted to the regiment he served with it as a volunteer at the battle of Quatre Bras, where he was wounded.

CAMERON. Archibald Cameron. Ensign, 13th of January, 1814; lieutenant, 26th of July, 1815; exchanged to the 89th regiment, 15th of February, 1821; half pay, 25th of July, 1821. Died on the 5th of March, 1824. He served with the regiment at the battles of Quatre Bras and Waterloo. He was a brother of Lieutenant Alexander Cameron, who commanded the regiment at the close of Waterloo.

CAMERON. Charles Cameron. Ensign, 9th of April, 1826; lieutenant, 12th of February, 1828; exchanged to the 4th Foot on the 11th of December, 1828; afterwards in the 78th Highlanders. Retired on the 12th of July, 1839.

CAMERON. Donald Cameron. Ensign, 4th of November, 1794; lieutenant, 2nd of September, 1795; captain, 3rd of September, 1801; major, 30th of May, 1811. Retired on the 1st of April, 1812. Died near Maidstone. He served with the regiment in Egypt in 1801, and was present at the battle before Alexandria. (Gold medal from Sultan Selim III.). He afterwards served in the Peninsula with the 79th.

CAMERON. Donald Cameron. Ensign, 10th of April, 1806; lieutenant, 13th of May, 1807. He was present with the regiment at the bombardment of Copenhagen in 1807, and was wounded in the attack on Cadiz on the 12th of February, 1810. He served in the Peninsular war with the 79th, and was severely wounded at Toulouse. He was also present at the battles of Quatre Bras and Waterloo, and died in July, 1815, of wounds received at Waterloo.

CAMERON. Donald Cameron. Ensign, 4th of October, 1815; half pay, 25th of February, 1816. Retired from the service in 1829.

CAMERON. Donald Cameron. Captain, 19th of August, 1793. He was one of the first officers appointed to the regiment by Sir Alan Cameron, K.C.B. Retired in 1796.

CAMERON. Duncan Cameron, C.B. Appointed lieutenant, 2nd of November, 1796; captain, 19th of April, 1804; major, 29th of October, 1812; brevet-lieutenant-colonel, 12th of April, 1814. Retired on the 3rd of June, 1819. Died near Toronto, Upper Canada, on the 14th of October, 1842. He served with the 79th Highlanders in Holland, and was present at the battle of Egmont-op-Zee; accompanied the regiment to Egypt in 1801; and was present at the battle of Alexandria. (Gold medal from Sultan Selim III.) He was at the bombardment of Copenhagen in 1807, and served continuously throughout the Peninsular war. He was made a brevet-lieutenant-colonel for his conduct at the battle of Toulouse. He was very severely wounded at the battle of Quatre Bras, for which battle he was made a Companion of the Bath.

CAMERON. Duncan Cameron. Ensign, 9th of November, 1799; lieutenant, 9th of December, 1802; captain, 25th of March, 1805.

CAMERON. Duncan Cameron. Ensign, 19th of July, 1810; lieutenant, 2nd of April, 1812. He served with the 79th in the Peninsula. Was wounded at the battle of Fuentes d'Onor, and killed at Toulouse.

CAMERON. Ewen **Cameron, youngest** son of Sir Alan. Lieutenant, 25th of March, 1805; captain, 10th of April, 1806. He acted his father's aide-de-camp at the battle of Talavera, and died of fever at Lisbon, brought on by hardships and exposure during the campaign.

CAMERON. Ewen Cameron. Ensign, 7th of April, 1804; lieutenant, 25th of March, 1805; captain, 8th of April, 1811. Died at Erracht in 1813.

CAMERON. Ewen Cameron. Ensign, 20th of May, 1806; lieutenant, 14th of May, 1807.

CAMERON. Ewen Cameron. Ensign, 16th of March, 1809; lieutenant, 29th of May, 1811. Served with the 79th continuously in the Peninsula, and was wounded at the battle of Toulouse. He was present at the battle of Quatre Bras, and was wounded at Waterloo. He died in Ireland in 1822 of brain fever.

CAMERON. Ewen Cameron. Ensign, 26th of July, 1810; lieutenant, 1st of October, 1812. He died of wounds received at the battle of Toulouse, and was buried in the same grave as Captain Purves, Captain John Cameron, and Lieutenant Duncan Cameron, all of the 79th Highlanders, in the citadel at Toulouse.

CAMERON. Ewen Cameron. Appointed lieutenant from the 75th regiment, 31st of July, 1828; captain, 29th of March, 1839. Retired on the 21st of August, 1840.

CAMERON. Ewen Cameron, known as "Eoghainn Mor," a younger brother of Sir Alan's. Was appointed captain and recruiting officer in Lochaber, 17th of August, 1793. He raised the first company of the 79th.

CAMERON. Ewen Cameron. Lieutenant, 7th of June, 1794. Retired in 1796.

CAMERON. Archibald Cameron. Ensign, 22nd of August, 1793. Retired in 1796.

CAMERON. Adam Cameron. Ensign, 6th of November, 1794; lieutenant, 5th of September, 1795. Retired in 1797.

CAMERON. James Cameron. Ensign, 4th of September, 1805.

CAMERON. James Cameron. Appointed lieutenant in the 79th from the 85th regiment, 25th of January, 1813. He was present at the battles of Quatre Bras and Waterloo, and died at Blandecque, France, in 1818.

CAMERON. John Cameron. Ensign, 7th of November, 1794; lieutenant, 5th of September, 1795. He served in Holland in 1799 and was present at the battle of Egmont-op-Zee. He accompanied the 79th to Egypt in 1801, and was at the battle before Alexandria. (Gold medal from Sultan Selim III.).

CAMERON. John Cameron. Ensign, 3rd November, 1799; lieutenant, 8th of December, 1802; exchanged to the 1st Foot as captain, and was killed at the storming of St. Sebastien, July, 1813.

CAMERON. John Cameron. Ensign, 21st of April, 1805; lieutenant, 8th of April, 1806; captain, 13th January, 1814. Was killed at the battle of Toulouse.

CAMERON. John Cameron. Ensign, 23rd of April, 1805; lieutenant, 12th of May, 1806; captain, 1st April, 1812. He served with the regiment in the Peninsula and at Quatre Bras, and was killed at the battle of Waterloo.

CAMERON. John Cameron. Ensign, 8th of April, 1806; lieutenant, 11th of May, 1807; captain, 26th of May, 1814; exchanged to the 92nd Highlanders, and went on half pay, 21st of August, 1835. He died in Jersey on the 2nd of February, 1851. He accompanied the Walcheren expedition and was present at the siege of Flushing. He served with the 79th throughout the Peninsular war and was present at the battles of Corunna,

Busaco, Fuentes d'Onor, Salamanca Pyrenees, Nivelle, Nive, and Toulouse. (Silver medal with eight clasps.)

CAMERON. John Cameron. Ensign, 17th of August, 1806; lieutenant, 13th of August, 1807; exchanged to the 4th Garrison battalion, 26th of May, 1808; half pay, 1815. He was present with the 79th at the bombardment of Copenhagen.

CAMERON. John Campbell Cameron. Ensign, 12th of March, 1801; lieutenant, 29th of November, 1804. Retired on the 13th of June, 1811, and died of consumption in Scotland brought on by exposure. He accompanied the 79th to Egypt in 1801, and was present at the battle before Alexandria. (Gold Medal from Sultan Selim III.). He served in the Peninsula and commanded the detachment of the 79th at the battle of Talavera, where he was taken prisoner by the French—effecting his escape the same night.

CAMERON. Kenneth Cameron, of Clunes, in Lochaber. Ensign, 22nd of April, 1805; lieutenant, 10th of April, 1806; captain, 18th of May, 1814; placed on half pay of the regiment on the 25th of February, 1816, but returned on full pay the following year. Retired as major on the 7th of August, 1835. He served with the 79th Highlanders throughout the Peninsular war, and was present at the battles of Corunna, Busaco, Fuentes d'Onor, Salamanca, Nivelle, Nive, and Toulouse. (Wounded.) He was adjutant of the regiment during the latter part of the war. In the affair of Foz d'Aronce Lieutenant Kenneth Cameron, who was in the light company, captured the colonel of the 39th French Infantry and took him a prisoner to head-quarters. He died in Canada on the 20th of June, 1872, aged 84, and there is a fine monument to his memory in the churchyard of Thorah, Ontario.

CAMERON. Lachlan Maclean Cameron. Ensign, 13th of October, 1812; lieutenant, 20th of May, 1814; half pay, 26th of February, 1829. He served with the regiment in the Peninsular war, and was present at the battles of Pyrenees, Nivelle, Orthes, and Toulouse. (Silver medal with four clasps.) He commanded a party of volunteers during the Canadian rebellion of 1838.

CAMERON. Nathaniel Cameron, second son of Sir Alan. Ensign, 6th of April, 1804; lieutenant, 25th of March, 1805; captain, 9th of April, 1806; major, 1st of April, 1812; lieutenant-colonel, 24th of June, 1813; placed on half pay on the 25th of February, 1816. Retired in July, 1828. He commanded the second battalion of the 79th from the 24th of June, 1813, until placed on half pay.

CAMERON. Philips Cameron, eldest son of Sir Alan. Appointed captain, 6th of June, 1794; major, 3rd of September, 1801; lieutenant-colonel, 19th of April, 1804. Served with the 79th in Holland in 1799, and was present at the battle of Egmont-op-Zee. He accompanied the regiment to Egypt, and was at the battle of Alexandria. (Gold medal from Sultan Selim III.). He was present at the bombardment of Copenhagen, and proceeded with the 79th to Portugal. He commanded the regiment during the disastrous retreat to and at the battle of Corunna. (Gold Medal.) He died of wounds received at the battle of Fuentes d'Onor.

CAMERON. Thomas Cochrane Cameron. Appointed lieutenant in the 79th from half pay, 8th of April, 1825. Placed on half pay again on the 1st of November, 1833.

CAMERON. Nathaniel Cameron. Lieutenant, 8th of June, 1794. Retired in 1796.

CAMERON. William Cameron. Ensign, 18th of April, 1805; lieutenant, 8th of April, 1806; captain, 17th of June, 1813. Placed on half pay on the 25th of February, 1816. He died at Camisky, near Fort William, on the 1st of September, 1834.

CAMERON. O'Kane Cameron. Ensign, 1st of November, 1797. Retired in 1798.

CAMERON. Gordon Cameron. Lieutenant, 5th of November, 1794. Retired in 1797.

CAMERON. William Gordon Cameron. Transferred as lieutenant to the Cameron Highlanders from the 4th Foot. He served with the regiment throughout the Nile expedition of 1884-85. (Medal with clasp.) Died of wounds received during the defence of Kosheh in the Soudan.

CAMERON. Angus Cameron. Served as a sergeant with the 79th during the Peninsular war, and was appointed quarter-master on the 13th of February, 1812. He was present as quarter-master at the battles of Quatre Bras and Waterloo. In 1841 he became paymaster of the Canadian Rifles, and died in Canada in 1845.

CAMPBELL. Archibald Campbell. Ensign, 24th of July, 1800; exchanged to the 60th Rifles on the 12th of March, 1801.

CAMPBELL. David Campbell. Appointed lieutenant in the 79th from the 67th regiment, 25th of March, 1824; transferred to the 91st Foot, 30th of July, 1829.

CAMPBELL. Charles Campbell. Exchanged as a captain from the 94th Foot, 25th of August, 1809; placed on half pay of the regiment on the 12th of November, 1812. Died at Glasgow on the 6th of April, 1836.

CAMPBELL. Donald Campbell. Ensign, 24th of July, 1800; lieutenant, 22nd of October, 1803; captain, 19th of April, 1804; major, 13th of January, 1814; placed on half pay of the regiment on the 25th of February, 1816; brevet-lieutenant-colonel, 22nd of July, 1830. Died at Bonar Bridge, Sutherlandshire, on the 6th of December, 1844. He accompanied the regiment to Egypt in 1801, and was present at the battle before Alexandria. (Gold medal from Sultan Selim III.).

CAMPBELL. Archibald Campbell. Ensign, 24th of June, 1853. Retired in 1854.

CAMPBELL. Donald Campbell. Ensign, 2nd of March, 1815; lieutenant, 26th of October, 1820; exchanged as a lieutenant to the 20th regiment. Died at sea.

CAMPBELL. George Campbell. Ensign, 26th of October, 1806.

CAMPBELL. Henry Wotton Campbell. Ensign, 14th of April, 1843; lieutenant, 4th of July, 1845; captain, 22nd of October, 1852. Retired on the 26th of December, 1856. He served with the regiment in the Eastern campaign of 1854-55, including the battles of Alma and Balaclava, siege and fall of Sebastopol, and the expedition to Kertch and Yenikale. (Medal with clasps and Turkish medal, brevet of major, Knight of the Legion of Honour.)

CAMPBELL. James Campbell. Captain, 5th of September, 1805; brevet-major, 12th of August, 1819; major, 31st of October, 1826. Retired December, 1826; died of consumption. He served with the 79th in the Peninsula, at Quatre Bras, and at Waterloo, being wounded at the battles of Toulouse and Waterloo.

CAMPBELL. James Campbell, K. H. Exchanged as a captain from the 91st Foot, 2nd of July, 1812; major, 3rd of June, 1819; lieutenant-colonel, 10th of July, 1824; exchanged to the 95th regiment on the 27th of September, 1831. Served during the Irish rebellion in 1798-99, wounded in the hand at Wilson's Hospital; expedition to Hanover in 1805; Walcheren expedition in 1809.

CAMPBELL. John Campbell. Ensign, 7th of October, 1807; lieutenant, 9th of November, 1809. Retired in January, 1814. Died at Campbeltown, Argyleshire.

CAMPBELL. John Alexander Gavin Campbell. Ensign, 2nd of August, 1842; lieutenant, 11th of April, 1845; exchanged to the 1st Foot on the 24th of July, 1846. He carried the Queen's Colour of the Breadlalbane Highlanders in 1842, when Her Majesty visited Taymouth. Became Earl of Breadalbane in 1862.

CAMPBELL. James Campbell. Ensign, 19th of May, 1814; appointment cancelled on the 30th of November, 1815.

CAMPBELL. Hon. Ivan Campbell. 2nd lieutenant from the Highland Borderers Militia, 11th of October, 1879; lieutenant, 23rd of June, 1880. Served with the Cameron Highlanders throughout the Egyptian campaign of 1882, and was present at the battle of Tel-el-Kebir. (Medal with clasp and Khedive's star.) Retired on the 22nd of August, 1884.

CAMPBELL. Neil Campbell. Lieutenant, 8th of October, 1794; captain, 1st of November, 1796; half pay, 1800.

CAMPBELL. Neil Campbell. Lieutenant from the 78th Highlanders, 25th of March, 1805; captain, 8th of April, 1806. He served with the 79th in the Peninsula, at Quatre Bras, and at Waterloo. He was slightly wounded at Quatre Bras and mortally at the battle of Waterloo. He died in Brussels in October, 1815.

CAMPBELL. Neil Campbell. Ensign, 22nd of February, 1855; lieutenant, 21st of September, 1855; captain, 30th of November, 1866; brevet-major, 19th of April, 1880. Retired on a pension with the rank of lieutenant-colonel on the 21st of July, 1880. He served with the 79th in the Crimea from the 16th of August, 1855, including the siege and fall of Sebastopol. (Medal with clasp and Turkish medal.) Served in the Indian campaign of 1858-59, including the siege and capture of Lucknow, attack on the fort at Rooyah, actions of Allygunge, Bareilly, and Shahjehanpore, capture of forts Bunniar and Mahomdie, passage of the Gogra at Fyzabad, capture of Rampore Kussia, and subsequent operations in Oude across the Gogra and Raptee rivers. (Medal with clasp.) Served on the north-west frontier of India against the Mohmund tribes, near Peshawur; present at the affairs of Michinie and Shubkudder. (Medal and clasp.)

CAMPBELL. Archibald Campbell. Ensign, 16th of December, 1795. Retired in 1798.

CAMPBELL. James Campbell. Appointed captain, 30th of December, 1795. Retired in 1800. Was wounded at the battle of Egmont-op-Zee, where he commanded the Grenadier company.

CAMPBELL. Walter Douglas Somerset Campbell, (Islay.) Ensign, 15th of June, 1860; lieutenant, 7th of November, 1863; captain, 31st of October, 1877. Retired on the 12th of February, 1881.

CAMPBELL. F. Pemberton Campbell. Ensign, 3rd of November, 1854; lieutenant, 9th of March, 1855; transferred to the 83rd regiment, 1862. He served with the regiment in the Eastern campaign of 1855, including the siege and fall of Sebastopol and assault of the 8th of September. (Medal with clasp and Turkish medal.) Served in the Indian campaign of 1858-59, including the siege and capture of Lucknow. (Medal and clasp.)

CAMPBELL. James Bell Campbell. Ensign from the Ceylon Rifle Regiment, 21st of September, 1855. Retired in 1859.

CAMPBELL. George Campbell. Ensign, 29th of July, 1862. Retired in 1866.

CAMPBELL. John Francis Glencairn Campbell. Major-general, 12th of November, 1860; colonel of the 79th, 12th of July, 1868. He commanded the 91st regiment throughout the whole of the Kaffir war of 1846-47. He died as a lieutenant-general in 1870.

CAMPBELL-ORDE. Arthur J. Campbell-Orde, younger, of Kilmorey. Lieutenant, 2nd battalion, 27th of October, 1883.

CANT. David Cant. Ensign from quarter-master-sergeant, 10th of August, 1854; lieutenant, 8th of December, 1854; paymaster,

24th of June, 1856; major, 10th of August, 1869. Served with the 79th Highlanders throughout the Eastern campaign of 1854-55, including the battles of Alma and Balaclava, the siege of Sebastopol, assault of the 18th of June, and expedition to Kertch and Yenikale. (Medal with three clasps and Turkish medal.) Served with the 79th Highlanders in the Indian campaign of 1858-59, including the siege and capture of Lucknow. (Medal and clasp.)

CARDROSS, Henry. Lord Cardross. Ensign, 16th of March, 1832. Retired on the 27th of July, 1832. Died on the 21st of December, 1836.

CAREY. Robert Carey. Ensign, 24th of November, 1803.

CARMICHAEL. Peter Carmichael. Ensign, 19th of March, 1807.

CARTAN. William Cartan. Ensign, 20th of July, 1815; lieutenant, 12th of December, 1822; captain, 28th of August, 1838. Afterwards staff officer of pensioners at Belfast.

CARTER. N. Carter. Ensign, 30th of May, 1811; exchanged to Staff Corps Cavalry, 13th of October, 1815.

CASTLE. William Castle. Appointed paymaster of the 79th, 16th of February, 1829; left the regiment on the 19th of February, 1836.

CATHCART. Hon. Charles Cathcart. 2nd lieutenant from the 82nd regiment, 12th of April, 1879. Died in London on the 21st of May, 1880.

CAVAYE. George Ross Cavaye. 2nd lieutenant, 23rd of October, 1880; lieutenant, 1st of July, 1881. Served with the Cameron Highlanders throughout the Egyptian war of 1882, and was present at the battle of Tel-el-Kebir. (Medal with clasp and Khedive's star.) He also served throughout the Nile expedition of 1884-85 with the Cameron Highlanders. (Clasp.) Served in the operation of the Soudan Frontier Field Force in 1885-86 with the Cameron Highlanders, and was present at Kosheh during the investment, and in the engagement at Giniss.

CHALMERS. John Snodgrass Chalmers. Ensign, 11th of April, 1845; lieutenant, 10th of April, 1849. Went to 36th regiment.

CHALMERS. Norman Guthrie Chalmers. Ensign, 11th of January, 1867; lieutenant, 28th of October, 1871; captain, 21st of July, 1880; major, 21st of November, 1881. Served with the Cameron Highlanders throughout the Egyptian war of 1882, and was present at the battle of Tel-el-Kebir. (Medal with clasp and Khedive's star.) He also served throughout the Nile expedition of 1884-85 with the Cameron Highlanders. (Clasp.) Served in the operations of the Soudan Frontier Field Force in 1885-86 with the Cameron Highlanders, and was present at Kosheh during its investment, and at the reconnaissance on the 16th of December. (Severely wounded. Mentioned in despatches, and awarded the 4th class of the Osmanieh for active and distinguished service in the field in saving the life of Major Hunter, in doing which he was wounded.)

CHAPMAN. Frederick Stovin Chapman. Exchanged as captain from the 21st Royal Scots Fusiliers, 29th of October, 1881. Served with the Cameron Highlanders in the Egyptian war of 1882 from the landing at Ismailia, and was present at the battle of Tel-el-Kebir. (Medal with clasp and Khedive's star.)

CHEETHAM. Isaac Cheetham. Ensign, 6th of August, 1811; lieutenant, 10th of December, 1812; appointed to the 40th regiment on the 17th of December, 1812. He had previously served in the 29th regiment. He was present at the battles of Roleia, Vimiera, Talavera, Busaco, Albuhera, Salamanca, Vittoria, Pyrenees, Orthes, and Toulouse. (Silver medal with ten clasps.)

CHRISTIE. John Stedman Christie. Lieutenant, 19th of April, 1804; captain, 29th of May, 1811; exchanged to the 42nd Highlanders. Died in Portugal.

CHRISTIE. Napier Turner Christie. Exchanged as ensign from the 93rd Highlanders, 18th of July, 1822; lieutenant, 10th of September, 1825; transferred to the 11th regiment.

CHRISTIE. Robert Christie. Ensign, 20th of August, 1812; lieutenant, 18th of May, 1814; placed on half pay, 16th of April, 1817. Retired in 1830. Served with the 79th in the Peninsula, and was present at the battles of the Pyrenees, Nivelle, Nive, and Toulouse.

CHURCHILL. Charles Henry Churchill. Exchanged as a captain from the 60th regiment on the 26th of July, 1833; appointed a lieutenant-colonel in the British Legion of Spain, 4th of August, 1835. (K. St. F.).

CLAY. Albert Newby Clay. Ensign, 7th of September, 1855; lieutenant, 1st of July, 1859; captain, 15th of June, 1866; major, 4th of June, 1879. Retired on the 13th of April, 1881. He served with the 79th Highlanders in the Indian campaign of 1858-59, including the siege and capture of Lucknow; attack on the fort of Rooyah; actions of Allygunge, Bareilly, and Shahjehanpore; capture of forts Bunniar and Mahomdie; passage of the Gogra at Fyzabad; capture of Rampore Kussia; and subsequent operations in Oude, across the Gogra and Raptee rivers. (Medal and clasp.)

CLEATHER. William B. Gordon Cleather. Ensign, 13th of October, 1854; lieutenant, 9th of January, 1855; captain, 9th of April, 1861; exchanged to the 47th regiment in 1863. He served with the 79th Highlanders in the Eastern campaign of 1855, including the siege and fall of Sebastopol and assault of the 8th of September. (Medal and clasp and Turkish medal.) Also in the Indian campaign of 1858-59, including the siege and capture of Lucknow. (Medal and clasp.)

CLEPHANE. Robert Douglas Clephane. Ensign, 8th of June, 1838; lieutenant, 18th of September, 1840; captain, 11th of April, 1845. He served in the Eastern campaign of 1854—and up to the 25th of June, 1855, with the 79th Highlanders—including the battles of Alma and Balaclava; siege of Sebastopol; assault on the 18th of June; expedition to Kertch and Yenikale. (Medal with three clasps, brevet of lieutenant-colonel, and the Sardinian and Turkish medals.)

COCKBURN. James Cockburn. Ensign, 12th of February, 1828; lieutenant, 23rd of August, 1833; captain, 8th of June, 1838; half pay, 21st of February, 1840.

COCKBURN. Wemyss Thomas Cockburn. Ensign, 21st of August, 1849; exchanged to the 35th regiment in 1850.

COCKELL. George Cockell. Appointed assistant-surgeon to the 79th, 25th of June, 1801; transferred to the 13th regiment in 1808.

COOKSEY. Walter C. Cooksey. Ensign, 7th of August, 1799; lieutenant, 3rd of September, 1801; captain, 30th April, 1807 He served with the 79th Highlanders in the Egyptian campaign of 1801, and was present at the battle of Alexandria. (Gold medal from Sultan Selim III.). Carried the regimental colour at the attack on Ferrol. Served with the 79th in the Peninsula, and was killed on picquet near Almeida in 1811.

COOPER. Henry Cooper. Major-general, 9th of November, 1862; colonel of the 79th, 21st of August, 1870. He served with the 45th regiment in the Kaffir war of 1846-47. (Medal.) Transferred as colonel to the 45th Foot on the 17th of March, 1876.

CORBALLIS. James Frederick Corballis. Lieutenant, 2nd battalion, 18th of October, 1884; appointed to the 18th Royal Irish in 1887.

CORNES. John Cornes. Quarter-master of the 53rd regiment, 25th of June, 1841; paymaster of the 79th Highlanders, 5th of November, 1847. He was present at the battles of Aliwal and Sobraon, and at the action of Buddiwal. (Wounded. Mentioned in despatches.) He served with the 77th regiment in the Eastern campaign of 1854-55, including the battle of Alma and the siege and fall of Sebastopol. (Medal with clasp and Turkish medal.) He went on half pay on the 24th of June, 1856.

COTTER. William Pomeroy Cotter. Ensign, 21st of October, 1799; left the regiment in 1800.

COURTNEY. George Courtney. Ensign, 21st of May, 1814; placed on half pay on the 16th of March, 1816; afterwards in the 97th regiment.

COWAN. Thomas Cowan. Ensign, 19th of October, 1812; lieutenant, 26th of May, 1814; half pay, 1821.

CRAWFORD. John Crawford. Ensign, 25th of June, 1812. Appointment cancelled on the 9th of December, 1812.

CRAWFORD. Alexander Speirs Crawford. Ensign, 18th of May, 1814; lieutenant, 27th of July, 1815. Served with the 79th at the battles of Quatre Bras and Waterloo. (Slightly wounded.) Half pay, 25th of February, 1816.

CRAWFORD. William J. M. Crawford. Ensign, 25th of August, 1854; lieutenant, 9th of February, 1855; captain, 23rd of October, 1860; exchanged to the 24th regiment in 1862. He served with the 79th Highlanders in the Eastern campaign of 1855, including the siege and fall of Sebastopol. (Medal with clasp and Turkish Medal.) Also in the Indian campaign of 1858-59, including the siege and capture of Lucknow. (Medal and clasp.)

CROMBIE. Thomas Crombie. Ensign, 12th of August, 1824; lieutenant, 8th of February, 1826; captain, 18th of May, 1832; exchanged to the 60th regiment.

CROZIER. Burrard Rawson Crozier. Transferred as a captain from the 46th regiment on the 29th June, 1881; exchanged to the Royal Scots Fusiliers on the 29th of October, 1881.

CRUIKSHANK. William Cruikshank, M.D. Appointed assistant-surgeon to the 79th, 26th of October, 1830; left the regiment in 1836.

CRUIKSHANKS. Alexander Cruikshanks. Quarter-master, 12th of October, 1838. Retired on half pay on the 11th of May, 1849. He served with the 79th Highlanders at the bombardment of Copenhagen in 1807; expedition to Sweden in 1808; Walcheren expedition; present at the siege of Flushing; expedition to Cadiz. He served in the Peninsula with the 79th; was taken prisoner by the French at the battle of Fuentes d'Onor, and was wounded at Toulouse. He was present with the regiment at the battles of Quatre Bras and Waterloo. He was in possession of the silver war medal, with clasps for Busaco, Fuentes d'Onor, Nivelle, Nive, and Toulouse.

CRUTCHLEY. Robert J. Logan Crutchley. Captain from the 24th regiment, 1862; went to Indian Staff Corps in 1865.

CUMING. Edward William Cuming. Ensign, 24th of July, 1846; lieutenant, 31st of March, 1848; captain, 8th of October, 1854; major, 2nd of March, 1872; placed on retired pay, 1st of July, 1881. He served with the 79th Highlanders throughout the Eastern campaign of 1854-55, including the battles of Alma and Balaclava; siege and fall of Sebastopol; assaults of the 18th of June and the 8th of September; expedition to Kertch and Yenikale. (Medal with three clasps, 5th class of the Medjidie, and Turkish medal.)

CUNNINGHAME. William Cunninghame. Ensign, 26th of June, 1846; lieutenant, 31st of December, 1847; captain, 13th of August, 1854. Retired in 1857. He served with the 79th Highlanders in the Eastern campaign of 1854 up to the 26th of November, also from January to the 9th of February, 1855, including the battles of Alma and Balaclava and siege of Sebastopol. (Medal with three clasps, and Turkish medal.)

CURRIE. Henry Currie. Captain, from the 74th Highlanders, 10th of March, 1869. Retired as major on half pay on the 8th of December, 1877.

DALZELL. Robert Harris Carnwath Dalzell. Ensign, 15th of June, 1866; lieutenant, 28th of October, 1871; captain, 10th of April, 1880; Major, 21st of November, 1881. Retired in 1886.

DAVIDSON. Charles Frederick Herbert Davidson. 2nd lieutenant, 23rd of October, 1880; lieutenant, 1st of July, 1881. Served with the Cameron Highlanders throughout the Egyptian war of 1882, and was present at the battle of Tel-el-Kebir. (Medal with clasp, and Khedive's star.) Served in the expedition to the Soudan in 1884, with the Gordon Highlanders, and was present at the engagements of El-Teb and Tamaii. (Two clasps.) Also served throughout the Nile expedition of 1884-85, on special service as transport officer, and took part in the operations of the desert column. (Clasp.) Served with the Soudan Frontier Field Force in 1886 with the Cameron Highlanders.

DAVIDSON. Duncan Francis Davidson, younger, of Desswood. 2nd lieutenant, 23rd of October, 1880; lieutenant, 1st of July, 1881; captain, 1st of December, 1886. Served with the Cameron Highlanders throughout the Egyptian war of 1882, and was present at the battle of Tel-el-Kebir. (Medal with clasp, and Khedive's star.) Also served throughout the Nile expedition of 1884-85 with the Cameron Highlanders. (Clasp.) Served throughout the operations of the Soudan Frontier Field Force of 1885-86 with the Cameron Highlanders, and was present at Kosheh during its investment (slightly wounded), at the reconnaissance on the 16th of December, and in the engagement at Giniss. (Mentioned in despatches.)

DAVIDSON. Sinclair Davidson. Ensign, 24th of July, 1800; lieutenant, 31st of March, 1804; Captain, 14th of February, 1811. He served with the 79th in the Egyptian campaign of 1801, and was present at the battle before Alexandria. (Gold medal from Sultan Selim III.). Served throughout the Peninsular war, with the 79th, until he died of wounds received at the battle of Fuentes d'Onor.

DAWSON. John Dawson. Captain, 6th of November, 1801. Drowned on passage from Harwich to Landguard Fort, 18th of April, 1807, with all the detachment under his command.

DEANS. James Deans. Ensign, 13th of October, 1815; exchanged to the 92nd Highlanders in 1820.

DEMPSTER. James Carrol Dempster. Appointed assistant-surgeon to the 79th, 15th of January, 1841. Appointed to the 33rd regiment, 23rd of September, 1845.

DOBIE. William Alexander Dobie. Ensign, 6th of April, 1855; transferred to the 1st West India regiment as lieutenant, 24th of February, 1857.

DOIG. Alexander Doig. Appointed assistant-surgeon, 21st of June, 1864; medical department, 1874.

DORAN. William Doran. Exchanged as Major to the 79th, 22nd of February, 1810. Retired as lieutenant-colonel, 31st of January, 1811.

DOUGAL. S. B. Dougal. Ensign, 14th of September, 1855. He served with the 79th Highlanders in the Indian Mutiny campaign of 1858-59, and was present at the capture of Lucknow. (Medal with clasp.) He was killed in action, 6th of November, 1863, in India, during the Umbeyla campaign, whilst attached to the 71st Highlanders.

DOUGLAS. Charles John Cathcart Douglas. 2nd lieutenant from the 74th Highlanders, 5th of October, 1878; exchanged to the 31st regiment, 6th of December, 1879.

DOUGLAS. John Douglas. Ensign, 25th of June, 1829; lieutenant, 25th of October, 1833; captain, 11th of May, 1839; exchanged to the 11th Light Dragoons.

DOUGLAS. John Douglas. Ensign, 13th of March, 1835; lieutenant, 26th of May, 1838; captain, 15th of June, 1842. Retired the 14th of November, 1842.

DOUGLAS. Sir John Douglas, G. C. B., of Glenfinart, Argyleshire. Ensign, 6th of September, 1833; lieutenant, 18th of July, 1836; captain 8th of June, 1841; major, 24th of December, 1852; lieutenant-colonel, 13th of August, 1854; colonel, 1st of August, 1857; major-general, 23rd of August, 1877; general, 30th of January, 1880; full colonel commanding the 79th Highlanders 1st of January, 1879. He served throughout the Eastern campaign of 1854-55, in command of the 79th Highlanders, including the battles of Alma and Balaclava, siege of Sebastopol, assault of the 18th of June, and expedition to Kertch and Yenikale. (Medal with three clasps, C.B., Sardinian and Turkish medals, and 4th class of the Medjidie.) Served in the Indian campaign of 1857-59; commanded the Infantry in the action of Secundra; commanded a brigade during the siege of Lucknow, taking the Residency, Iron bridge, Great Imambara, and several other important positions; afterwards commanded the Infantry of the Azimghur Field Force, and was present in the action at Tigra, taking of Azimghur, pursuit of Koer Sing, actions at Azimghur, Munnear, Sheoporeghat, and various operations in and around Jugdespore and the jungles, and pursuit to Buxar. On the 15th of June, 1858, he was appointed to command the troops in the Azimghur and Jaunpore districts, and on the 25th of June to the command of the disturbed districts of Behar, Dinapore, Ghazepore, and Shahabad, and was constantly engaged in pursuing the rebels during the hot and wet seasons; took the field after the rains, defeated the rebels at Karisath, and drove them into the jungle; took Judgespore, pursued and drove the rebels into the Kymore hills, killing 1,200; campaign of Kymore hills; and successful night attack at Salya Duhar. On the 15th of January, 1859, appointed to command the troops in Palamow and Chota Nagpore, and was engaged in pursuing the rebels in Palamow. (Frequently mentioned in despatches, thanked by the Governor-General of India, brevet of colonel, K.C.B. medal with clasp.)

DOUGLAS. Sir Neil Douglas, K.C.B., K.C.H. Ensign, 28th of January, 1801; lieutenant, 16th of July, 1802; captain, 19th of April, 1804; major, 31st of January, 1811; lieutenant-colonel, 3rd of December, 1812; colonel and aide-de-camp to the King, 27th of May, 1825; major-general, 10th of January, 1837; governor of Edinburgh Castle, 17th of February, 1837; lieutenant-general, 9th of November, 1846; colonel, 78th Highlanders, 20th of December, 1851. He served with the 79th Highlanders at the bombardment of Copenhagen; expedition to Sweden in 1808; Walcheren expedition and siege of Flushing. He accompanied the expedition to Cadiz. Served with the 79th Highlanders in the Peninsula, succeeding to the command of the regiment, on the 20th of February, 1813. He was present at the battles of Corunna, Busaco, (twice wounded) Pyrenees, Nivelle, Nive, and Toulouse. He commanded the 79th Highlanders in the Waterloo campaign, and was severely wounded at the battle of Quatre Bras. He had the gold medal and clasps for the Pyrenees, Nivelle, Nive, and Toulouse, and the silver war medal and clasps for Corunna and Busaco, He was also in possession of the silver Waterloo medal, cross of the 4th class of the order of St. Vladimir, and cross of Knight Companion of Maria Theresa.

DOUGLAS-HAMILTON. Angus Falconer Douglas-Hamilton. Lieutenant, 23rd of August, 1884. He served with the regiment during the latter part of the Nile expedition in 1885. (Medal with clasp). Served throughout the operations of the Soudan Frontier Field Force in 1885-86, was present at Kosheh during its investment, and at the engagement at Giniss.

DRYSDALE. Andrew Knox Drysdale. Appointed assistant-surgeon, to the 79th, November, 1854; surgeon, 10th of May, 1864. Died 10th of September, 1869 He served with the 79th Highlanders in the Eastern campaign of 1854-55, including the battles of Alma and Balaclava, and the siege of Sebastopol. (Medal with three clasps, and Turkish medal.) Served in the Indian campaign of 1858-59, including the siege and fall of Lucknow. (Medal and clasp.)

DUFF. Alexander Garden Duff, of Hatton Castle. Captain in the 2nd battalion, 1st of July, 1881; major, 28th of May, 1882.

DUFF. Garden Duff. Ensign, 28th of December, 1855; lieutenant, 28th of October, 1859; exchanged to the 70th regiment, 1860. He served with the 79th in the Indian campaign of 1858-59, including the siege and capture of Lucknow. (Medal and clasp.)

DUNDAS. Thomas Dundas. Ensign, 10th of November, 1837; lieutenant, 21st of February, 1840; transferred to the 22nd regiment.

DURANT. Celestine George Durant. Lieutenant from the 94th regiment, 8th of December, 1854. Retired in 1859.

EDEN. William Eden. Appointed major in the regiment, 16th of December, 1795; lieutenant-colonel, 15th of August, 1798; exchanged to the 84th regiment, 11th of December, 1806. He served with the 79th Highlanders in Holland, and was present at the battle of Egmont-op-Zee. Accompanied the 79th Highlanders to Egypt in 1801, and was present at the battle before Alexandria. (Gold medal from Sultan Selim III.).

EGAN. Michael Egan. Appointed surgeon to the 79th, 7th of December, 1797. He served with the regiment in Holland and Egypt, 1801, and was wounded at the battle before Alexandria. (Gold medal from Sultan Selim III.). He died in Belgium.

EGERTON. Arthur Frederick Egerton. Lieutenant, 27th of October, 1886.

ELLIOT. Edmund James Elliot. Ensign, 1831 ; lieutenant, 10th of October, 1834 ; captain, 3rd of April, 1840 ; major, 12th of April, 1844 ; succeeded as lieutenant-colonel to command the regiment 24th of December, 1852. He died of cholera at Givrakla, near Varna, 12th of August, 1854.

ELPHINSTONE. Honourable Y. D. Elphinstone (Master of Elphinstone.) Lieutenant in the 2nd battalion, 22nd of November, 1884. Retired in 1886.

EMSLIE. John Emslie. Quarter-Master, 2nd battalion, 13th of April, 1887. He served with the Cameron Highlanders throughout the Egyptian campaign of 1882, and was present at the battle of Tel-el-Kebir ; (Medal with clasp, and Khedive's star) also throughout the Nile expedition of 1884-85. (Clasp.) He served with the regiment throughout the operations of the Soudan Frontier Field Force of 1885-86, was present at Kosheh during its investment, and at the engagement at Giniss. (Mentioned in despatches, silver medal for distinguished conduct in the field.)

EVERETT. Edward Everett. Ensign, 1st of March, 1855 ; lieutenant, 14th of September, 1855 ; captain, 2nd of May, 1865 ; major, 1st of July, 1881 ; lieutenant-colonel, 15th of June, 1885. Served in the Crimea with the 79th Highlanders after the fall of Sebastopol. Served with the 79th Highlanders in the Indian campaign of 1858-59, including the siege and capture of Lucknow, attack on the fort of Rooyah, actions of Allygunge, Bareilly, and Shahjehanpore, capture of Forts Bunniar and Mahomdie, passage of the Gogra at Fyzabad, capture of Rampore Kussia, and subsequent operations in Oude across the Gogra and Raptee rivers. (Mentioned in despatches, medal and clasp.) Served throughout the Nile expedition of 1884-85 with the Cameron Highlanders. (Mentioned in despatches, brevet of lieutenant-colonel, medal and clasp.) Served throughout the operations of the Soudan Frontier Field

Force in 1885-86, and was present in Kosheh during its investment, commanded the reconnaissance of the 16th of December, and the right attack, consisting of the Cameron Highlanders and the 9th Soudanese, on the village of Kosheh in the engagement at Giniss. (D.S.O., mentioned in despatches, 3rd class of the Medjidie.) Lieutenant-Colonel commanding the regiment, July 1st, 1887.

EWART. John Spencer Ewart. Lieutenant, 22nd of October, 1881. Served with the Cameron Highlanders throughout the Egyptian war of 1882, and was present at the battle of Tel-el-Kebir. (Medal with clasp, and Khedive's star.) Also served throughout the Nile expedition of 1884-85 with the Cameron Highlanders. (Clasp.) Served throughout the operations of the Soudan Frontier Field Force in 1885-86 as adjutant of the Cameron Highlanders, was staff-officer at Kosheh during its investment, and was present at the engagement at Giniss. (Mentioned in despatches, 5th class of the Medjidie.)

EWART. Walter Douglas Ewart. Lieutenant, 7th of February, 1885. Served throughout the operations of the Soudan Frontier Field Force in 1885-86 with the Cameron Highlanders, was present in Kosheh during its investment, and the engagement at Giniss. (Medal.)

FAIRRIE. William McCormick Fairrie. Ensign, 30th of May, 1845; lieutenant, 9th of June, 1846. Retired in 1846.

FERGUSON. Charles Robert Kennett Ferguson. Ensign, 14th of January, 1862; lieutenant, 22nd of August, 1865. Retired the 12th of May, 1875.

FERGUSON. Arthur George Ferguson. Lieutenant, 2nd battalion, 1st of July, 1881; appointed to the Rifle Brigade, 16th of May, 1883.

FERGUSON. James Ferguson. Ensign, 22nd of July, 1832; lieutenant, 7th of August, 1835; captain, 18th of September, 1840; major, 25th of August, 1846. Died at Givrakla, near Varna, Turkey, 1854.

FERGUSON. Robert Ferguson, of Raith. Ensign, 24th of February, 1820, in the 43rd regiment; exchanged as major to the 79th, 23rd of March, 1827; lieutenant-colonel, 13th of March, 1835. Retired the 8th of June, 1841.

FERGUSON. Robert Ferguson. Ensign, 25th of October, 1833; lieutenant, 8th of July, 1837; captain, 28th of December, 1841. Died in 1847.

FERGUSON. Sir Ronald Crawford Ferguson, G. C. B., of Raith. Ensign, 53rd regiment, 3rd of April, 1790; general, 22nd of July, 1830; appointed full colonel of the 79th, 24th of March, 1828. Died the 10th of April, 1841. He served in Flanders in 1793, and was present at the siege of Valenciennes and Dunkirk, and at the defence of Newport. (Severely wounded.) In 1796 he accompanied the expedition for the capture of the Cape of Good Hope, and in 1800 served with the force sent under Sir James Palt for the purpose of attacking Ferrol and Cadiz. In 1805 he was appointed to the command of the Highland Brigade in the expedition of Sir David Baird, for the re-capture of the Cape of Good Hope, in which service he highly distinguished himself. In 1808 he was promoted to major-general, and commanded a brigade in the Peninsula at the battles of Roleia and Vimiera. (Thanked by both Houses of Parliament, and granted a gold medal by George III.). In 1815 he was nominated a K.C.B., and subsequently given the Grand Cross of the Order.

FERGUSSON. Archibald Fergusson. Ensign, 6th of June, 1845; lieutenant, 26th of June, 1846; exchanged to the 16th regiment.

FERGUSSON. James Fergusson, C.B. Appointed as a major to the 79th from the 43rd regiment, 3rd of December, 1812. Appointed to the 85th regiment, 25th of January, 1813. Had previously served in the 18th regiment. He served in the Walcheren expedition in 1809 and throughout the Peninsular war. He was present at the battles of Vimiera, Corunna, Busaco, Fuentes d'Onor; sieges of Ciudad Rodrigo and Badajoz; battles of Salamanca, Nivelle, Nive; passage of the Bidassoa; and actions at Pombal, Redinha, Miranda de Corvo, Foz d'Aronce, Sabugal, and San Munoz. He was five times wounded. (Gold medal for Badajoz, and the silver war medal with eight clasps.)

FINDLAY. Charles Findlay. Lieutenant, 12th of March, 1884, from the Gordon Highlanders. Served throughout the Nile expedition of 1884-85 with the Cameron Highlanders. (Medal with clasp.) Also served with the Soudan Frontier Field Force in 1886.

FITZGERALD. Massey FitzGerald. Ensign, 30th of June, 1823; lieutenant, 25th of June, 1829; half pay, 7th of July, 1837.

FORBES. Alexander Forbes. Ensign, 28th of September, 1809; lieutenant, 8th of August, 1811; captain, 18th of March, 1825; major, 7th of August, 1835; half pay, 25th of May, 1838. Died in Canada, 30th of March, 1851. He served with the 79th in the Peninsula, and was present at the battles of Nivelle and Nive, also throughout the Waterloo campaign, being slightly wounded at Waterloo. He had the silver war medal with two clasps.

FORBES. Granville Eardley Forbes. 2nd lieutenant, 23rd of October, 1880; lieutenant, 1st of July, 1881. Served throughout the Nile expedition in 1884-85 with the Cameron Highlanders. (Medal with clasp.)

FORBES. Hon. John Forbes. Exchanged as a lieutenant to the 79th 1st of November, 1833, and died two years afterwards.

FORBES. Michie Forbes. Ensign, 31st of December, 1830; exchanged to the 35th regiment, 18th of May, 1833.

FORBES. Peter Forbes. Quarter-master, 2nd battalion, 1st of July, 1881. Retired in 1887. Served with the 71st Highlanders in the Eastern campaign of 1855, including the siege and fall of

Sebastopol and expedition to Kertch. (Medal with clasp and Turkish medal.) Served also in the Indian campaign of 1858, including the actions of Kooneh, Deapoza, and Gowlowlee, and capture of Galpee and Gwalior. (Medal with clasp.) Served in the Umbeyla campaign with the 71st Highlanders. (Medal and clasp.)

FORBES-GORDON. Arthur Newton Forbes-Gordon, of Rayne. Ensign, 12th of May, 1863; lieutenant, 11th of January, 1867; captain, 13th of July, 1878. Retired, 15th of March, 1879. Adjutant, from the 26th of July, 1876, to the 13th of July, 1878.

FORBES-SEMPILL. Hon. John Forbes-Sempill, Master of Sempill. Lieutenant, 6th of January, 1886. Served in the operations of the Soudan Frontier Field Force in 1886 with the Cameron Highlanders.

FORD. John Ford, Ensign, 25th of May, 1809; lieutenant, 30th of May, 1811; exchanged to the 3rd West India Regiment, 15th of November, 1821. He served in the expeditions to Walcheren and Cadiz; also with the 79th Highlanders in the Peninsula, being present at the battles of Fuentes d'Onor, Nivelle, Nive, and Toulouse. (Silver medal with four clasps.)

FORREST. William Forrest (now Sir William Forrest, Bart., of Comiston). Ensign, 14th of October, 1842; lieutenant, 30th of May, 1845. Retired, 1st of October, 1850.

FOWLER. Henry Day Fowler. Appointed assistant-surgeon, 19th of December, 1845; exchanged to the 8th regiment in 1850.

FRASER. Archibald Fraser. Ensign, 24th of April, 1805; lieutenant, 23rd of October, 1806. Served with the 79th Highlanders in the Peninsula, and was wounded at the battle of Fuentes d'Onor. He died of fever at Castel Branco, Portugal, 15th of September, 1811.

FRASER. James Fraser. Ensign, 30th of April, 1807; lieutenant, 16th of March. 1809; captain, 3rd of June, 1819. Retired on the 2nd of February, 1830. Died on the 29th of May, 1849. He served with the 79th Highlanders throughout the Peninsular and Waterloo campaigns, being severely wounded at the battles of Toulouse and Quatre Bras.

FRASER. Malcolm Fraser. Ensign, 24th of July, 1800; lieutenant, 9th of February, 1804: captain, 29th of November, 1810. Died in 1822. He served with the 79th Highlanders throughout the Peninsular and Waterloo campaigns. He was slightly wounded at the battle of Fuentes d'Onor, and severely at the battle of Quatre Bras.

FRASER. William Wemyss Fraser. Ensign, 29th of November, 1815; half pay, 25th of February, 1816.

FRASER. Keith Fraser. 2nd lieutenant in the 2nd battalion, 12th of February, 1887.

FRASER-TYTLER. Edward Fraser-Tytler, of Aldourie. Lieutenant, 2nd battalion, 1st of July, 1881; captain, 24th of August, 1882. Retired in 1887.

FRASER-TYTLER. William Fraser-Tytler. Lieutenant, 1st of July, 1881. Retired in 1884.

FREME. James Herbert Freme. Ensign, 19th of October, 1849; lieutenant, 3rd of March, 1854; captain, 29th of December, 1854. Retired in 1856. He served with the regiment in the Eastern campaign of 1854-55, including the battles of Alma and Balaclava and the siege of Sebastopol. (Medal with three clasps, and Turkish medal.)

FULTON. Robert Fulton. Appointed captain in the 79th, 10th of July, 1800; major, 25th of March, 1805; lieutenant-colonel, 28th of May, 1807. Retired on the 3rd of December, 1812. Died near Lochwinnoch, Ayrshire, in 1851. He served with the 79th Highlanders in the expedition to Egypt in 1801. (Gold medal from Sultan Selim III.). Was present at the bombardment of Copenhagen; commanded the 79th Highlanders in the Peninsula from the 2nd of September, 1811, until the 20th of February, 1813, including the battle of Salamanca, for which he was granted a gold medal.

FULTON. Robert Fulton. Ensign, 12th of February, 1825; lieutenant, 9th of December, 1826; captain, 16th of March, 1832. Died at Paisley.

GAISFORD. Thomas Gaisford. Appointed lieutenant from the 22nd regiment on the 4th of January, 1841; captain, 4th of July, 1845. Retired in 1846.

GARFORTH. William H. Garforth. Captain, 2nd battalion, 1st of July, 1881.

GARSIA. Christopher Garsia. Ensign, 23rd of March, 1858; lieutenant, 11th of October, 1859; exchanged to the 89th regiment in 1864.

GAWNE. Edward Gawne. Ensign, 16th of January, 1855; lieutenant, 9th of March, 1855. Retired in 1859.

GORDON. C. Van R. Conway Gordon. Ensign, 12th of January, 1855; lieutenant, 4th of May, 1855; captain, 3rd of April, 1860; went to the Bengal Staff Corps on the 22nd of March, 1869.

GORDON. Lawrence Gordon. Ensign, 29th of May, 1818; exchanged to the 89th regiment on the 13th of December, 1821.

GORDON. John Henry Gordon. Ensign, 28th of December, 1841. Retired on the 13th of October, 1843.

GORDON. George James Gordon. Ensign, 2nd of February, 1830; lieutenant, 18th of July, 1834; captain, 21st of February, 1840. Retired on the 29th of January, 1841.

GORDON. Orr Boswell Gordon. Ensign, 4th of July, 1865; lieutenant, 17th of February, 1869; captain, 19th of October, 1879; major, 1st of July, 1881; adjutant from the 13th of July, 1878, to 18th of October, 1879. Served with the Cameron Highlanders in the Egyptian war of 1882, and, as divisional baggage-master on the staff of Lieutenant-General Hamley from Ismailia to Cairo. Was present at the battle of Tel-el-Kebir. (Medal with clasp and Khedive's star.)

GRAEME. Patrick James Frederick Graeme, of Inchbrakie. Ensign, 19th of February, 1870; lieutenant, 28th of October, 1871. Retired in 1875.

GRAHAM. John Graham. Lieutenant, 6th of June, 1794. Retired in 1797.

GRAHAM. William Graham. Ensign, 24th of August, 1793; lieutenant, 24th of June, 1795. Retired in 1799.

GRAHAM. Archibald Graham. Lieutenant, 24th of August, 1795. Retired in 1795.

GRAHAM. Oliver Graham. Ensign, 12th of April, 1844; lieutenant, 14th of November, 1845. Retired in 1850.

GRANT. Charles Irwin Grant. Ensign, 18th of July, 1834; exchanged to the 50th regiment, 10th of November, 1837.

GRANT. Ewen Grant. Lieutenant, 2nd battalion, 1st of July, 1881. Retired in 1883.

GRANT. Francis Augustus Grant. Ensign, 11th of June, 1847; lieutenant, 26th of July, 1850. Died of cholera before Sebastopol, October, 1854.

GRANT. Hugh Grant. Ensign, 5th of September, 1805; lieutenant, 30th of April, 1807. Served with the 79th Highlanders in the Peninsula, and died of wounds received at the siege of Burgos in 1812.

GRANT. Ian Robert James Murray Grant, of Glenmoriston and Moy. 2nd lieutenant, 17th of April, 1880; lieutenant, 1st of July, 1881; resigned his commission on the 6th of October, 1886. Served with the Cameron Highlanders throughout the Egyptian war of 1882, and was present at the battle of Tel-el-Kebir. (Medal with clasp and Khedive's star.) Served with the Nile expedition in 1884. Is now a captain in the 2nd battalion.

GRANT. John Grant. Appointed surgeon, 10th of July, 1846.

GRANT. Robert W. E. Grant, of Kincorth. Lieutenant, 2nd battalion, 1st of July, 1881. Retired in 1884.

GRANT. William Grant. Appointed assistant-surgeon, 25th of December, 1825; exchanged to the 10th regiment in 1826.

GRAVES. William Graves. Ensign, 7th of December, 1809. Retired in 1810.

GREENHILL-GARDYNE. Norman Charles Greenhill-Gardyne. Lieutenant, 2nd battalion, 1st of July, 1881. Appointed to the Gordon Highlanders in 1885.

GUNNING. Matthew Gunning. Ensign, 8th of August, 1799; lieutenant, 4th of September, 1801; exchanged to the 92nd Highlanders the same year. He served with the 79th Highlanders in the expedition to Ferrol in 1800, and accompanied the 92nd Highlanders to Egypt in 1801.

HALKETT. Wedderburn Conway Halkett (eldest son of Sir Arthur Halkett, Bart., of Pitfirrane, Fife). 2nd lieutenant, 16th of February, 1878; lieutenant, 17th of December, 1879; captain, 20th of February, 1884. He served with the Cameron Highlanders during the Nile expedition of 1884-85. Was invalided, and died on the 23rd of August, 1885.

HALL. James Hall. Ensign, 21st of February, 1811; lieutenant, 14th of October, 1812; half pay, March, 1815.

HAMILTON. Andrew Hamilton. Joined the 79th from the Canadian Fencibles as lieutenant, 25th of March, 1805; exchanged to the 72nd regiment on the 26th of December, 1805. He was afterwards in the Peninsula with the 23rd Light Dragoons.

HAMILTON. Peter D. Hamilton. Exchanged to the 79th, as captain, from the 39th regiment, 14th of February, 1799. He left the regiment in 1800.

HAMILTON. Robert Hamilton. Lieutenant, 29th of April, 1795; captain, 24th of May, 1799; major, 25th of April, 1805; exchanged to the 78th Highlanders, 21st of April, 1808. Died in Canada. He served with the 79th Highlanders in Egypt in 1801, and was present at the battle before Alexandria. (Gold medal from Sultan Selim III.).

HAMILTON. William Finlay Hamilton. Ensign, 21st of August, 1840; lieutenant, 14th of October, 1842. Retired on the 30th of May, 1845.

HAMILTON. T. A. Hamilton. Quarter-master, 14th of March, 1811. Died in Portugal, 28th of December, 1812.

HANBURY. John M. Hanbury. Lieutenant, 2nd battalion, 1st of July, 1881. Retired in 1883.

HARKNESS. Thomas Harkness. Ensign, 6th of June, 1811; lieutenant, 25th of June, 1812. Died same year.

HARRISSON. Charles Milne Harrisson. Ensign, 3rd of November, 1846; lieutenant, 29th of October, 1848. Retired in 1855.

HARRISON. Francis Joseph Harrison. Ensign, 30th of July, 1847; lieutenant, 1st of October, 1850. Died in the Crimea.

HARRISON. George Alexander Harrison. Ensign, 23rd of November, 1852; lieutenant, 8th of August, 1854; captain, 13th of July, 1855; placed on half pay on the 10th of November, 1856; reappointed to the regiment, and retired in 1866.

HARRISON. George Harrison. Ensign, 10th of December, 1812; lieutenant, 2nd of March, 1815; half pay, 25th of March, 1817. Drowned at sea, 1819. Served with the 79th in the Peninsula and at the battles of Waterloo and Quatre Bras.

HART. William Neville Hart. Appointed captain in the 79th Highlanders, 17th of September, 1794. Left the regiment in 1796.

HARVEY. William Maundy Harvey. Appointed major in the 79th Highlanders from the 1st West India Regiment, 27th of February, 1806; lieutenant-colonel, 30th of May, 1811; colonel, 1st of January, 1812. He died on passage home from the Peninsula, 10th of June, 1813. He was present at the battle of Albuhera and at the storming of Badajos.

HAY. James Hay, C.B. Major-general, 23rd of November, 1841; Colonel of the 79th, 8th of January, 1849. He served with the 16th Lancers in the Peninsula, and was present at the passage of the Douro, battles of Talavera, Fuentes d'Onor, Vittoria, and Nive, the siege of Burgos, and actions of Sabugal, Rediuha, and Foz d'Aronce. (Gold medal for Nive.) He commanded the 16th Lancers at the battle of Waterloo. (Very severely wounded, C.B., and silver medal.) Died in 1855.

HAYWARD. George J. Whitaker Hayward. Ensign, 12th of January, 1859; lieutenant, 24th of March, 1863. Retired in 1865. Murdered in Cashmere.

HICKS. Raymond Hicks. Appointed lieutenant, 12th of March, 1796. Left the regiment in 1798.

HILL. Andrew Hill. Ensign, 31st of December, 1847; exchanged to the 22nd regiment.

HODGSON. William Chauval Hodgson. Ensign, 18th of September, 1840; lieutenant, 10th of February, 1843; captain, 11th of June, 1847; major, 2nd of August, 1857; lieutenant-colonel, 10th of July, 1860; colonel, 10th of July, 1865. He served

with the Cameron Highlanders in the Eastern campaign of
1854-55, including the battles of Alma and Balaclava ; expedition to Kertch and Yenikale ; siege and fall of Sebastopol ;
and assaults of the 18th of June and 8th of September. (Medal
with three clasps, brevet of major, Knight of the Legion of
Honour, 5th class of the Medjidie, and Turkish medal.)
Served in the Indian campaign of 1858-59, including the siege
and capture of Lucknow ; attack on the fort at Rooyah ; actions
at Allygunge, Bareilly, and Shahjehanpore ; capture of forts
Bunniar and Mahomdie ; passage of the Gogra at Fyzabad ;
capture of Rampore Kussia ; and subsequent operations in
Oude, across the Gogra and Raptee rivers. (Medal with clasp.)
Died at Parkhurst in 1873, whilst in command of the regiment.

HOLE. George Hole. Ensign, 5th of September, 1795. Left the regiment in 1798.

HOLFORD. Henry Price Holford. Ensign, 7th of March, 1856 ; went to the 10th Hussars in 1859. He served with the 79th Highlanders in the Indian campaign of 1858, including the siege and capture of Lucknow. (Medal and clasp.)

HOLMES. Arthur L'Estrange Holmes. Lieutenant from the 7th Hussars, 18th of September, 1865 ; captain, 15th of December, 1869 ; transferred to Bengal Staff Corps, 26th of July, 1870.

HORSFORD. Sir Alfred Horsford, G.C.B. Colonel commanding the 79th, 17th of March, 1876 ; general, 1st of October, 1877 ; colonel commanding the rifle brigade, 21st of November, 1880. Served with the rifle brigade in the Kaffir war of 1846-47, and commanded the 1st battalion in that of 1852-53. (Medal and brevet of lieutenant-colonel.) Also commanded the 1st bat-talion in the Eastern campaign of 1854, including the battles of Alma, Balaclava, and Inkerman, and siege of Sebastopol. (Medal with four clasps, C.B., Sardinian and Turkish medals, and 5th class of the Medjidie.) Served in the Indian campaign of 1857-59 ; commanded 3rd battalion rifle brigade at the battle of Cawnpore on the 6th of December, 1857 (wounded); commanded a brigade from February, 1858, to the end of the war, and was present throughout the Oude campaign; commanded the infantry at the battle of Nawabgunge; in February, 1859, was left in command of the Oude and Nepaul frontier, and on one occasion took sixteen guns in an engagement in Nepaul against the rebels. (Medal with clasp, and K.C.B.)

HOWARD. William Howard. Quarter-master, 20th of April, 1878. He served with the regiment in the latter part of the Indian Mutiny campaign. Served throughout the Egyptian war of 1882 with the Cameron Highlanders, and was present at the battle of Tel-el-Kebir. (Medal with clasp and Khedive's star). Also served throughout the Nile expedition of 1884-85. (Clasp.) Served throughout the operations of the Soudan Frontier Field Force with the Cameron Highlanders in 1885-86, and was present in Kosheh during its investment, and at the engagement at Giniss.

HOWKINS. Theophilus Robert Howkins. Ensign, 28th of February, 1855; lieutenant, 7th of December, 1865. He served with the regiment in the Eastern campaign in 1855, including the siege and fall of Sebastopol. (Medal with clasp and Turkish medal.)

HUGHES. Paul Hughes. Ensign, 12th of March, 1818: exchanged to the 93rd Highlanders, 18th of July, 1822.

HUME. Arthur Hume. Ensign, 29th of July, 1859; lieutenant, 29th of July, 1862; captain, 29th of July, 1871; half pay, 31st of October, 1874. He was adjutant from 1862 to 1871

HUME. J. Robert Hume, M.D., C.B. Appointed surgeon of the 79th, 25th of March, 1805; staff-surgeon, 17th of August, 1809. Served with the 79th Highlanders in the Peninsula, and was present at the battles of Corunna, Barrosa, Salamanca, Vittoria, Pyrenees, Nivelle, Nive, Orthes, and Toulouse. (Medal with ten clasps.) He was also present as deputy-inspector of hospitals at the battles of Quatre Bras and Waterloo. (Medal.)

HUNT. Andrew Hunt. Ensign, 22nd of February, 1840; lieutenant, 15th of June, 1842; captain, 25th of August, 1846; major, 12th of December, 1854; half pay, 7th of September, 1855. He served with the regiment in the Eastern campaign of 1854-55, including the battle of Alma, expedition to Kertch and Yenikale, and siege of Sebastopol. (Medal with two clasps, 5th class of the Medjidie, and Turkish medal.)

HUNT. James Maitland Hunt. Sub-lieutenant, 12th of January, 1873; lieutenant, 12th of February, 1874; captain, 12th of February, 1881; brevet-major, 18th of November, 1882; major, 1st of December, 1886. He served with the Cameron Highlanders throughout the Egyptian war of 1882, and was present at the battle of Tel-el-Kebir. (Mentioned in despatches, brevet of major, medal with clasp, 4th class of the Medjidie, and Khedive's star.) Also served throughout the Nile expedition of 1884-85. (Clasp.) Served throughout the operations of the Soudan Frontier Field Force in 1885-86 with the Cameron Highlanders, and was present at Kosheh during its investment, and at the engagement at Giniss.

HUTTON. Alfred Hutton. Ensign, 31st of May, 1859; lieutenant, 14th of January, 1862; went to 7th Hussars in 1864.

IMLACH. James Imlach. Ensign, 2nd of April, 1806; lieutenant, 10th of May, 1807; exchanged to a Cape regiment in 1808.

IMLACH. William Imlach. Ensign, 20th of February 1796; lieutenant, 3rd of October, 1799; Captain, 14th of April, 1805. He served with the 79th Highlanders in Holland in 1799, and was present at Egmont-op-Zee. He accompanied the regiment to Egypt in 1801, and was at the battle before Alexandria. (Gold Medal from Sultan Selim III.). He was present with the regiment at the bombardment of Copenhagen in 1807, and served with it in the Peninsula. He was killed at the battle of Fuentes d'Onor on the 3rd of May, 1811.

INNES. Peter Innes. Lieutenant from the 42nd Highlanders, 9th of July, 1803; captain 4th of September, 1805. Half pay 20th of November, 1816. He served with the 79th Highlanders in the Peninsula, being wounded at Toulouse, and at the battles of Quatre Bras and Waterloo. He died at Tunnach, near Wick, on the 19th of April, 1822.

ISHAM. Thomas Isham. Ensign, 1st of August, 1826; lieutenant, 16th of March, 1832; captain, 26th of May, 1838; major 14th of June, 1842. Retired on the 12th of April, 1844.

JAMESON. Robert Jameson. Quarter-master, 11th of May, 1849. He served with the regiment in the Eastern campaign of 1854-55, including the battles of Alma and Balaclava, expedition to Kertch and Yenikale, siege and fall of Sebastopol, and assaults of the 18th of June and the 8th of September. (Medal with three clasps, Sardinian and Turkish Medals.) Appointed quarter-master, Depôt Battalion, Fort George, 1857.

JAMIESON. Lachlan Foster Jamieson. Ensign, 2nd December, 1859; lieutenant, 28th of October, 1864; went to the 7th Hussars in 1865.

JOHNSON. William Johnson. Appointed captain, 13th of May, 1795. He left the regiment in 1799.

JOHNSTON. George Johnston. Lieutenant from the 68th regiment, 27th of April, 1827; captain, 10th of October, 1834.

JOHNSTONE. Hon. A. C. Johnstone. Lieutenant-colonel, 2nd of May, 1794. He left the regiment in 1798.

JOHNSTONE. Charles Johnstone. Ensign, 14th of September, 1820; exchanged to the 69th regiment in 1823.

JOHNSTONE. John Johnstone. Appointed captain, 7th of June, 1794. He left the regiment in 1796.

JONES. Thomas Sheridan Gore Jones. Lieutenant from the 37th regiment, 1860. He was killed in action in 1863 in the Umbeyla campaign, whilst doing duty as a Volunteer with the 71st Highlanders. He had previously served with the 37th in the Indian campaign of 1857-58. (Medal.)

KEMBLE. Horace William Kemble. Captain, 2nd battalion, 1st of July, 1881.

KENNEDY. Ewen Kennedy. Ensign 3rd of October, 1811; lieutenant, 25th of February, 1813. He served with the regiment at Quatre Bras, and was killed at Waterloo.

KENNEDY. James Frederick Shaw Kennedy. Ensign, 1st of February, 1869; lieutenant, 28th of October, 1871. Retired on the 1st of February, 1873.

KERR. William James Kerr. Ensign, 15th of May, 1857. Resigned his commission in 1859.

KILGOUR. Patrick Kilgour. Appointed assistant-surgeon, 17th of January, 1855. He served with the 79th in the Indian campaign of 1858, including the siege and capture of Lucknow. (Medal and clasp.)

KYNOCK. John Kynock. Ensign, 15th of November, 1810; lieutenant, 13th of June, 1811. He served with the 79th Highlanders in the Peninsula, being wounded at Toulouse. He became adjutant of the regiment, and was killed at the battle of Quatre Bras.

LANCE. William Henry Lance. Ensign, 7th of July, 1825; lieutenant, 2nd of February, 1830; captain, 7th of August, 1835. Retired on the 18th of September, 1840.

LANGFORD-BROOKE. H. L. B. Langford-Brooke. Captain, 2nd battalion, 1st of July, 1881; honorary major, 11th of August, 1882. Formerly served in the 60th Rifles.

LANGLEY. Frederick Langley. Exchanged as a captain from the 82nd regiment, 10th of July, 1817. Half pay on the 17th of June, 1819.

LAWRIE. Andrew Lawrie. Captain from the 61st regiment, 19th of April, 1804; major, 4th of October, 1810. He served with the 79th Highlanders in the Peninsula, and was killed at the siege of Burgos on the 22nd of September, 1812.

LAWRIE. Francis R. Hastings Lawrie. Exchanged as captain to the 79th, from the 11th Light Dragoons, 15th of November, 1839.

LEADER. Thomas Leonard Leader. Exchanged from the 1st Foot as captain, 24th July, 1846. Retired on half pay in 1848. Served in the campaign of 1844-45 in the Southern Concan Country.

LEAPER. William Leaper. Ensign, 29th of April, 1807; lieutenant, 15th of December, 1808; captain, 12th of December, 1822. Half pay on the 6th of October, 1825. Died in 1835. He served with the 79th Highlanders in the Waterloo campaign, and was severely wounded at the battle of Quatre Bras.

LEITH. John Macdonald Leith. Ensign, 17th of March, 1854; lieutenant, 6th of October, 1854; captain, 15th of May, 1857; major, 31st of October, 1877; brevet-lieutenant-colonel, 30th of December, 1878; lieutenant-colonel, 1st July, 1881; colonel, 31st of December, 1882. Placed on half pay on the 30th of June, 1885. He served in the Eastern campaign of 1854-55 with the 79th Highlanders, including the battle of Balaclava, siege and fall of Sebastopol, assaults of the 18th of June and the 8th of September, and expedition to Kertch and Yenikale. (Medal with two clasps, 5th class of the Medjidie, and Turkish medal.) Served in the Indian campaign of 1858-59 with the regiment, including the siege and capture of Lucknow, attack on the Fort of Rooyah, actions of Allygunge, Bareilly, and Shahjehanpore, capture of Forts Bunniar and Mahomdie, passage of the Gogra at Fyzabad, capture of Rampore Kussia, and subsequent operations in Oude, across the Gogra and Raptee rivers. (Medal with clasp.) Commanded the Cameron Highlanders throughout the Egyptian war of 1882, and was present at the battle of Tel-el-Kebir. (Mentioned in despatches, C.B., Medal with clasp, 3rd class of the Medjidie, and Khedive's star.) He commanded the Cameron Highlanders throughout the Nile expedition of 1884-85 (clasp), and was assistant-adjutant-general of the Force in the Eastern Soudan in 1885. (Clasp).

LENON. Arthur Lenon. Ensign, 2nd of July, 1861. Retired in 1864.

LESLIE. Archibald Young Leslie, of Kininvie. Transferred as captain from the 23rd Fusiliers on the 18th of December, 1875; major, 1st of July, 1881.

LESLIE. Kewan Izod Leslie. Ensign, 21st of March, 1811; lieutenant, 1st of April, 1812; captain, 18th of October, 1815; half pay on the 25th of March, 1817. He served with the 79th Highlanders in the Peninsula and Waterloo campaigns, and was wounded at the siege of Burgos. (Silver medal for Peninsula and Waterloo.)

LINDSAY. S. Charles Lindsay. Ensign, 21st of October, 1862. Retired in 1863.

LITHGOW. Stewart Aaron Lithgow, C.B., M.D., D.S.O. Appointed surgeon to the 79th Highlanders on the 20th of October, 1869. Surgeon-major in the army, 1st of March, 1873. He served with the 75th regiment during the Indian campaign of 1857-59, and was present at the action of Budleekeserai; siege and capture of Delhi; actions of Bolunshuhur, Agra, Allygur, Akrabad, and Kanoy; relief of Lucknow by Lord Clyde, and affairs at Dilkoosha and Alumbagh. (Medal with two clasps.) Served throughout the Nile expedition in 1884-85, as principal medical officer on the lines of communication. (Mentioned in despatches, C.B., Medal with clasp.) Also served with the Soudan Frontier Field Force in 1885-86, including the engagement at Giniss. (Mentioned in despatches, D.S.O.).

LOUTH. Randal P. O., Lord Louth. Ensign, 12th of December, 1851; lieutenant, 17th of June, 1858; exchanged to the 24th regiment in 1861.

LOVAT. Simon, Lord Lovat, A.D.C. Lieutenant-colonel-commandant of the Highland Light Infantry Militia, 10th of December, 1855; colonel commanding the 2nd battalion Cameron Highlanders, 1st of July, 1881.

LUMSDEN. Hugh Robert Lumsden, younger, of Pitcaple. Lieutenant, 18th of November, 1885. Served with the Cameron Highlanders in the operations of the Soudan Frontier Field Force in 1886. (Medal.)

LUNDY. Edward Louis Lundy. Appointed assistant-surgeon in the 79th, 7th of April, 1854; went to the 64th regiment in 1855. He served with the regiment during the Eastern campaign of 1854-55, including the battles of Alma and Balaclava, siege of Sebastopol (wounded in the trenches on the 29th of July, 1855), and expedition to Kertch and Yenikale. (Medal with three clasps, and Turkish medal.)

MACANDREW. Henry Y. M. Macandrew. Lieutenant, 2nd battalion, 6th of August, 1884.

MACBEAN. Charles MacBean. Lieutenant, 7th of October, 1807.

MACDONALD. James Macdonald. Lieutenant from the 21st Foot, 29th of March, 1827; captain, 6th of December, 1833. Retired on the 29th of December, 1837.

MACDONALD. John Andrew Macdonald, of Glenaladale. Major, 2nd battalion, 1st of July, 1881.

MACDONELL. Sir James Macdonell, K.C.B., K.C.H. Ensign, 25th of January, 1796. Became lieutenant-general, 23rd of November, 1841; colonel of the 79th Highlanders, 14th of July, 1842. He was present at the battles of Maida, Salamanca, Vittoria, Nivelle, and Nive. (Silver medal with 4 clasps.) He commanded the Coldstream Guards at Waterloo, and was celebrated for having, with the assistance of Sergeant Graham of that regiment, closed the gates of Huguomont upon the French. He was selected by the Duke of Wellington to receive a legacy of £500, left by the Rev. Mr. Norcross of Framlingham, Suffolk, "to the bravest man in England," which legacy was shared, at his own request, with Sergeant Graham.

MACDONELL. Ronald T. Macdonell. Lieutenant, 2nd battalion, 28th of October, 1882.

MACDONNELL. Allan Macdonnell. Ensign, 2nd of April, 1812; lieutenant, 6th of January, 1814; captain, 26th of November, 1830. Retired on the 18th of July, 1834. He served with the regiment in the Peninsula, and was present at the battles of the Pyrenees, Nivelle, Nive, and Toulouse. (Wounded.)

MACDONNELL. Alexander Michael Macdonnell. Ensign, 28th of May, 1812; lieutenant, 13th of January, 1814. Retired on the 26th of July, 1815.

MACDOUGALL. Colin Macdougall. Captain from the 42nd Highlanders, 7th of September, 1815; half pay on the 25th of February, 1816.

MACDOUGALL. Patrick Leonard MacDougall (now General Sir Patrick Leonard MacDougall, K.C.M.G.) Ensign, 8th of July, 1836; lieutenant, 11th of May, 1839; exchanged to the 36th regiment. He was employed on particular service in the Crimea, acting on the Quarter-Master-General's staff to the Kertch expedition, and at the siege of Sebastopol. (Medal with clasp, and Turkish medal.)

MacDougall. Sir Duncan MacDougall, K.C.B. Major from the 85th regiment, 16th of July, 1830; lieutenant-colonel, 6th of September, 1833. Retired on the 13th of March, 1835; colonel of the 9th regiment of the British Legion in Spain, in 1835. Retired from Spanish service in 1836. Sir Duncan served in the Peninsula, and was present at the battles of Salamanca, (severely wounded,) Nivelle, and Nive, and at the assault on St. Sebastien. (Medal and four clasps.) He was also in possession of a war medal for service with the Legion of Spain.

MacFadyen. Duncan MacFadyen. Surgeon, 2nd battalion, 1st of July, 1881.

MacFarlan. Frederick Alexander MacFarlan. Lieutenant, 20th of May, 1885. He served with the regiment throughout the operations of the Soudan Frontier Field Force in 1885-86, and was present at Kosheh during its investment, at the reconnaissance on the 16th of December, and at the engagement at Giniss. (Medal.)

MacGillivray. John William MacGillivray, of Dunmaglass. Lieutenant, 2nd battalion, 1st of July, 1881.

Macintosh. Alexander Fisher Macintosh, K.H. Exchanged as a captain to the 79th from the 60th regiment, 17th June, 1819; went on half pay, October, 1821. He was afterwards from half pay in the 93rd Highlanders. He had served in the Peninsula from 1812 to 1814, including the retreat from Madrid to Salamanca, actions at Alba-de-Formes and San Munos, action at Hormasa before Burgos, investment of Pampeluna, and action at Tarbes.

Mackay. Henry Mackay. Ensign, 18th of June, 1841; lieutenant, 11th of April, 1844; adjutant, 19th of June, 1851. Retired on half pay in 1854.

MACKAY. Robert Mackay. Ensign, 24th of July, 1800; appointed to a reserve battalion on the 24th of November, 1803. He accompanied the 79th Highlanders to Egypt in 1801, and was present at the battle before Alexandria. (Gold medal from Sultan Selim III.).

MACKAY. Robert Mackay. Ensign, 8th of June, 1807; lieutenant, 11th of May, 1809; captain, 2nd of April, 1812; half pay on the 9th of October, 1817. Died in 1826. He served with the regiment in the South of France in 1814, and during the Waterloo campaign, being wounded at Quatre Bras.

MACKENZIE. Alexander Mackenzie. Ensign, 30th of November, 1815; half pay on the 25th of February, 1816.

MACKENZIE. Colin Charles Mackenzie, younger, of Kilcoy. Ensign from the 78th Highlanders, 16th of September, 1868; lieutenant, 28th of October, 1871. He died at Gibraltar, 1880.

MACKENZIE. John Mackenzie. Ensign, 24th of December, 1812; lieutenant, 16th of July, 1815. Half pay on the 26th of March, 1817.

MACKENZIE. James Dixon Mackenzie (now Sir James Mackenzie, Bart., of Findon.) Ensign, 10th of April, 1855; promoted lieutenant of the 1st West India regiment, 7th of November, 1856.

MACKENZIE. Poynty Mackenzie. Ensign, 8th of April, 1825. Retired in September, 1830.

MACKENZIE. Dr. R. J. Mackenzie. Proceeded to Turkey and the Crimea as a volunteer in 1854, and was attached to the 79th Highlanders, being present with the regiment at the battle of Alma. He died of cholera on the heights of the Belbec, on the 25th of September, 1854.

MACKENZIE. Thomas Arthur Mackenzie, younger, of Ord. Lieutenant from the 42nd Highlanders, 18th of August, 1880; captain, 16th of January, 1885. He served with the Cameron Highlanders throughout the Egyptian war of 1882, and was present at the battle of Tel-el-Kebir. (Medal with clasp, and Khedive's star.) He served with the Cameron Highlanders with the Soudan Frontier Field Force in 1886.

MACKENZIE. William R. Dalziel Mackenzie. Lieutenant in the 2nd battalion, 10th of April, 1886.

MACKESSACK. George Ross Mackessack. Captain in the 2nd battalion, 1st of July, 1881.

MACKESY. William Henry Mackesy. Ensign, 11th of August, 1854; lieutenant, 8th of December, 1854; captain, 6th of December, 1859. Went to Indian Staff Corps, 1st October, 1860. He served with the regiment in the Eastern campaign from July, 1855, including the siege and fall of Sebastopol and assault of the 8th of September. Acted as assistant engineer to the Highland Brigade. (Medal with clasp, and Turkish medal.) Also acted as assistant field engineer in the Indian campaign of 1858-59, including the siege and capture of Lucknow. (Medal and clasp.)

MACKINTOSH. Alford D. Mackintosh, of Mackintosh. Captain, 2nd battalion, 1st of July, 1881. Was formerly adjutant of the 71st Highlanders.

MACLACHLAN. Daniel Maclachlan, M.D. Assistant surgeon, 21st of February, 1828; half pay on the 8th of May, 1840.

MACLAINE. John Maclaine. Ensign, 25th of November, 1808. transferred to the 73rd regiment on the 10th of January, 1809.

MACLEAN. John Maclean. The first surgeon of the regiment. Appointed on the 17th of August, 1793. He retired from the regiment in 1798.

MACLEAN. John Maclean. Ensign, 9th of April, 1806. He left the regiment the same year.

MACLEAN. John Maclean. Ensign, 11th of December, 1806; lieutenant, 17th of December, 1807. Retired on the 28th of July, 1814.

MACLEOD. Hugh Tilgham Macleod. Ensign, 26th of June, 1867; lieutenant, 1st of November, 1871. Retired on the 14th of February, 1872.

MACLEOD. Roderick Willoughby Macleod, younger, of Cadboll. 2nd lieutenant, 25th of October, 1880; lieutenant, 1st of July, 1881. He served with the regiment throughout the Egyptian campaign of 1882, and was present at the battle of Tel-el-Kebir. (Medal with clasp, and Khedive's star.) Served in the operations of the Soudan Frontier Field Force in 1885-86 with the Cameron Highlanders; was present at Kosheh during its investment, and at the engagement at Giniss.

MACNEAL. Hector MacNeal. Ensign, 14th of September, 1838; lieutenant, 29th of January, 1841; captain, 11th of November, 1845. Retired on the 2nd of April, 1847.

MACNEILL. Malcolm MacNeill. Lieutenant, 2nd battalion, 11th of February, 1882. Appointed to the 5th Lancers on the 5th of December, 1883.

MACPHERSON. Evan MacPherson. Major from the 92nd Highlanders, 24th of June, 1813; half pay on the 25th of February, 1816.

MACRA. Sir John Macra, K.C.B. Ensign, 17th of April, 1805; lieutenant, 5th of September, 1805; exchanged to the 27th regiment on the 23rd of December, 1812; became colonel in 1837; and died at Bruiach, Inverness-shire, in 1847. He served with the 79th at the bombardment of Copenhagen, expedition to Sweden under Sir John Moore, in the retreat to and battle at Corunna, in the expedition to Walcheren, and at the siege of Flushing. He was also in the Mahratta wars, 1817-19.

MADDOCK. William Maddock. Lieutenant from the 29th regiment, 21st of April, 1808; captain, 12th of October, 1815. Died in 1814, while on half pay. He served with the regiment in the Waterloo campaign and was severely wounded at Quatre Bras.

MAINWARING. William Arthur Mainwaring. Ensign, 14th of June, 1842; lieutenant, 12th of April, 1844; captain, 27th of October, 1848. Retired in 1852.

MAITLAND. Adam Maitland. Ensign, 9th of June, 1846; lieutenant, 11th of June, 1847. He died in the Crimea.

MAITLAND. Sir Alexander G. Maitland, Bart. Ensign, 8th of July, 1838. Retired on the 22nd of February, 1840.

MAITLAND. Keith Ramsay Maitland. Ensign, 4th of July, 1845; lieutenant, 25th of August, 1846; captain, 24th of December, 1852; major, 16th of March, 1860; lieutenant-colonel, 2nd of March, 1872; half pay on the 19th of October, 1872. He served in the Eastern campaign of 1854-55 with the regiment, including the battles of Alma and Balaclava, and siege and fall of Sebastopol (medal with three clasps and Turkish medal). Served in the Indian campaign of 1858-59, including the siege and capture of Lucknow, attack on the fort at Rooyah, actions at Allygunge, Bareilly, and Shahjehanpore, capture of forts Bunniar and Mahomdie, passage of the Gogra at Fyzabad, capture of Rampore Kussia, and subsequent operations in Oude, across the Gogra and Raptee rivers, (medal with clasp, brevet of major). Served with the Sikhim field force in 1861 (mentioned in despatches.)

MAITLAND. Pelham Maitland. Ensign, 18th of July, 1815; half pay, 11th of July, 1816.

MAITLAND. Thomas Maitland. Ensign, 23rd of August, 1844; retired, 27th of June, 1845.

MALCOLM. Henry Huntly Leith Malcolm. Lieutenant from the 42nd Highlanders, 29th of September, 1880; Captain, 24th of May, 1885. He served with the regiment throughout the Egyptian campaign of 1882 and was present at the battle of Tel-el-Kebir—wounded (medal with clasp and Khedive's star.) Served throughout the Nile expedition in 1884-85 on special service as staff-captain (clasp.)

MALL. Alexander Mall. Appointed captain, 3rd of June, 1795; retired 1797.

MANNERS. Robert Manners. Ensign, 11th of August, 1825; transferred to 50th regiment, 31st of December, 1830. Rejoined 79th in 1831; captain, 8th of July, 1837. Retired on the 3rd of April, 1840.

MARJORIBANKS. Coutts Marjoribanks. Lieutenant, 2nd battalion, 1st of July, 1881. Retired in 1883.

MARSHALL. John Marshall. Exchanged as captain from the 91st regiment on the 6th of October, 1825. Retired on half pay on the 15th of January, 1829. He had served with the 91st at the action of Lugo, the battles of Vimiera and Corunna, expedition to Walcheren, battles of Pyrenees, Nivelle, Nive, and Orthes (severely wounded), investment of Bayonne, and siege of Pampeluna. (Wounded. Medal with seven clasps.)

MARSHALL. William Marshall. Ensign, 7th of November, 1799; lieutenant, 25th of June, 1803; captain, 19th of July, 1810; major, 29th of July, 1824; lieutenant-colonel, 1st of January, 1838. Retired on the 17th of September, 1839. He accompanied the regiment to Egypt in 1801, and was present at the battle before Alexandria. (Gold medal from Sultan Selim III.). He served throughout the Peninsular war, and was present at the battles of Corunna, Busaco, Fuentes d'Onor, Salamanca, Nivelle, Nive, and Toulouse. (Wounded. Silver war medal and eight clasps.) Also served throughout the Waterloo campaign and was severely wounded at the battle of Quarte Bras. (Right arm amputated. Waterloo medal.)

MATHIESON. David Mathieson. Ensign, 28th of July, 1814; lieutenant, 12th of March, 1818; Retired on half pay on the 28th of June, 1836.

MAULE. Honourable Fox Maule. Ensign, 3rd of June, 1819; lieutenant, 29th of July, 1824; captain, 8th of April, 1826. Retired on the 5th of April, 1831.

MAULE. Honourable Lauderdale Maule. Captain from the 95th regiment, 21st of August, 1835; major, 11th of May, 1839; lieutenant-colonel, 14th of June, 1842. He commanded the regiment from the 14th of June, 1842, to the 24th of December, 1852. He died in Turkey in 1854, whilst on the staff of the Eastern army as assistant-adjutant-general.

MAXWELL. William Craig Maxwell. Ensign, 18th of May, 1832; lieutenant, 13th of March, 1835; captain, 21st of August, 1840; exchanged the same year to the 95th regiment.

MCARTHUR. Charles McArthur. Ensign, 9th of November, 1809; lieutenant, 17th of October, 1811; appointed to second veteran battalion, 24th of February, 1820. Died at Inverness on the 25th of November, 1846. He served with the 79th Highlanders in the Walcheren expedition as a Volunteer. Served with the regiment in the Peninsula, being present at the battles of Nivelle, Nive, and Toulouse (wounded). He also served with the 79th at Quatre Bras and Waterloo (wounded.)

MCARTHUR. John McArthur. Ensign, 26th of May, 1814; lieutenant, 30th of November, 1815. Drowned on passage from Dover to Calais, 17th of December, 1817, whilst proceeding to join the army of occupation in France.

McArthur. John McArthur. Quarter-master, 20th of June, 1799; paymaster, 21st of November, 1811; left the regiment, 16th of July, 1821. Died at Perth. He served with the 79th Highlanders at the battles of Waterloo and Quatre Bras.

McBarnet. Alexander Cockburn McBarnet, of Torridon. Lieutenant from the 16th Foot, 20th of October, 1846; captain, 10th of March, 1854; major, 20th of July, 1858. He served with the 79th Highlanders throughout the Eastern campaign of 1854-55, including the battles of Alma and Balaclava, siege and fall of Sebastopol, assault of the 18th of June and 8th of September, expedition to Kertch and Yenikale. (Medal with three clasps, 5th class of the Medjidie, and Turkish Medal.) Served in the Indian campaign of 1858-59, including the siege and capture of Lucknow. (Brevet of Major. Medal with clasp.) Lieutenant-colonel, unattached, 25th of April, 1865.

McBarnet. Donald Hay McBarnet. Ensign, 21st of January, 1853; lieutenant, 11th of August, 1854; captain, 7th of September, 1855; half pay on the 10th of November, 1856. He served with the regiment during the Eastern campaign of 1855, including the siege and fall of Sebastopol, assaults of the 18th of June and the 8th of September, and expedition to Kertch and Yenikale, wounded on the 24th of August in the trenches. (Medal and clasp, and Turkish medal.)

McBarnet. William McBarnet. Ensign, 24th of April, 1805; lieutenant, 1st of January, 1807; captain, 19th of May, 1813. He served with the 79th Highlanders in the Peninsula, and died on the 17th of April, 1814, of wounds received at the battle of Toulouse.

McBean. William McBean. Ensign, 19th of July, 1815; half pay on the 28th of May, 1818.

McBeath. George McBeath. Ensign, 24th of July, 1800; transferred to the 89th regiment in 1801.

McCall. William McCall. Ensign, 29th of March, 1839; lieutenant, 8th of June, 1841; captain, 14th of November, 1841; major, 12th of December, 1845; brevet-lieutenant-colonel, 2nd of November, 1855; half pay on the 5th of August, 1857; He served with the regiment in the Eastern campaign of 1854-55, including the battles of Alma and Balaclava, expedition to Kertch and Yenikale, siege and fall of Sebastopol, and assaults of the 18th of June and the 8th of September. (Medal with three clasps, brevet of lieutenant-colonel, Knight of the Legion of Honour, 5th class of the Medjidie, and Turkish Medal.)

McCallum. James Dalgleish Kellie McCallum. Ensign, 26th of May, 1865; lieutenant, 7th of May, 1868; adjutant, 11th of August, 1874. Retired in 1876. He served throughout the second phase of the Ashantee war in 1874, attached to the 42nd Highlanders, and was present at the battle of Amoaful, capture of Becquah, battle of Ordahsu, and capture of Coomassie. (Medal and clasp.)

McCausland. William Henry McCausland. Ensign, 24th of February, 1857; lieutenant, 16th of March, 1860; captain, 29th of January, 1867; major, 1st July, 1881; brevet lieutenant-colonel, 18th of November, 1882; colonel, 18th of November, 1886. He served with the regiment in the Indian campaign in 1858-59, including the siege and capture of Lucknow, attack on the Fort of Rooyah, actions of Allygunge, Bareilly, Shahjehanpore, capture of Forts Bunniar and Mahomdie, passage of the Gogra at Fyzabad, capture of Rampore Kussia, and subsequent operations in Oude, across the Gogra and Raptee rivers. (Medal with clasp.) Served with the regiment throughout the Egyptian war of 1882, and was present at the battle of Tel-el-Kebir. (Mentioned in despatches, brevet of lieutenant-colonel, medal with clasp, 4th class of the Osmanieh, and Khedive's star.)

McCleverty. Robert McCleverty. Captain, from the 94th regiment, 15th of December, 1840. Died on the 6th of March, 1845.

McCraw. Donald McCraw. Ensign, 16th of December, 1795. He left the regiment in 1799.

McCrummen. Patrick McCrummen. Lieutenant from the Canadian Fencibles, 21st of January, 1804 ; captain, 30th of May, 1811 ; half pay in 1815. He served with the 79th Highlanders in the Peninsular war, and was wounded at Cadiz in 1810.

McDonagh. Matthew McDonagh. Ensign, 5th of October, 1815 ; half pay on the 25th of February, 1816.

McDonald. Angus McDonald. Ensign, 1st of January, 1807 ; lieutenant, 17th of March, 1808. He served with the 79th Highlanders in the Peninsula, and died of wounds received at the siege of Burgos.

McDonald. Colin McDonald. Ensign, 20th of April, 1796. He left the regiment in 1799. He served with the regiment in Holland, and was wounded at the battle of Egmont-op-Zee.

McDonald. Donald McDonald. Ensign, 6th of June, 1854 ; lieutenant, 1st of December, 1854 ; captain, 17th of July, 1857. Died in India in 1871. He served with the regiment in the Eastern campaign of 1854-55, including the siege and fall of Sebastopol, and assault of the 8th of September. (Medal and clasp, and Turkish medal.) Served also in the Indian campaign of 1858-59, including the siege and capture of Lucknow. (Medal and clasp.)

McDonald. John McDonald. Lieutenant, 2nd battalion, 11th of July, 1885.

McDonnell. Alexander McDonnell. Lieutenant, 18th of August, 1793. He left the regiment in 1795.

McDougall. Duncan McDougall. Ensign, 16th of July, 1816 ; lieutenant, 3rd of June, 1819 ; captain, 8th of July, 1834. Retired on the 28th of September, 1841.

McDowall. Patrick McDowall. He was appointed captain in the 79th, 18th of August, 1793; major, 31st of January, 1794; lieutenant-colonel, 1st of November, 1796. He accompanied the regiment to Holland in 1799, and was present at the battle of Egmont-op-Zee. He died at Rosetta in 1801 of wounds received at the battle before Alexandria on the 13th of March.

McDowall. Samuel McDowall. Appointed lieutenant, 28th of October, 1795; captain, 3rd of October, 1799; retired on the 8th of June, 1809. He served with the 79th Highlanders in Holland in 1799, and was present at the battle of Egmont-op-Zee. He accompanied the regiment to Egypt in 1801, and was present at the battle before Alexandria, and at the engagement at Rhamaneih. (Wounded. Gold medal from Sultan Selim III.). He was present with the regiment at the bombardment of Copenhagen. He died in 1819 in the West Indies.

McGibbon. Colin McGibbon. Ensign, 7th of August, 1811; lieutenant, 24th of December, 1812. He died in 1815, whilst still serving with the regiment.

McGill. William McGill. Ensign, 5th of November, 1854; lieutenant, 9th of March, 1855; quarter-master, 14th of November, 1856. He served in the Eastern campaign of 1854-55, including the battles of Alma and Balaclava, siege and fall of Sebastopol, assaults of the 18th of June and the 8th of September, and expedition to Kertch and Yenikale. (Medal with three clasps, 5th class of the Medjidie, and Turkish medal.) He served in the Indian campaign of 1858-59 with the regiment, including the siege and capture of Lucknow (medal and clasp); placed on half pay on the 16th of March, 1867. Died in 1886.

McGillivray. William McGillivray. Assistant surgeon, 8th of December, 1804; half pay in 1805.

McGregor. Hugh McGregor. Ensign, 9th February, 1804; lieutenant, 25th of March, 1805; captain, 17th of August, 1806;

exchanged to the 91st regiment in 1812. He served with the 79th Highlanders in the Peninsula, and was present at the battle of Salamanca. (Silver medal with clasp.)

McGwire. Armoric Russell McGwire. Ensign, 11th of May, 1855; resigned his commission in 1859.

McIntosh. Æneas McIntosh. Lieutenant-colonel from the 85th regiment, 30th of May, 1811. He died at Ardgowan, 5th of January, 1814. He served with the 79th Highlanders in the Peninsula, and was present at the battle of Fuentes d'Onor.

McIntyre. Alexander McIntyre. Ensign, 26th of October, 1804; lieutenant, 25th of April, 1805; captain, 12th of November, 1812; half pay, 15th of May, 1817.

McIntyre. David McIntyre. Ensign, 3rd of September, 1805; exchanged to the 91st regiment, and was killed at the battle of Nivelle.

McIntyre. Duncan McIntyre. Served in the regiment during the year 1807.

McIntyre. Peter McIntyre. Quarter-master, 22nd of May, 1806; half pay, 14th of March, 1811. Died at Fort William.

McKenzie. Colin L. McKenzie, of Braelangwell and St. Martin's. Lieutenant, 2nd battalion, 1st of July, 1881; captain, 26th of August, 1882.

McKerrell. Augustus de Segur McKerrell. Lieutenant, 23rd of August, 1884. He served with the regiment throughout the Nile expedition of 1884-85. (Medal with clasp.) Served throughout the operations of the Soudan Frontier Field Force in 1885-86; was present at Kosheh during its investment, at the reconnaissance on the 16th of December, and in the engagement at Giniss.

McKINNON. John McKinnon. Quarter-master, 25th of March, 1805; half pay, 21st of May, 1806.

McLEAN. Alan McLean. Ensign, 9th of December, 1812; lieutenant, 28th of July, 1814; half pay, 25th of March, 1817. He served with the regiment in the Peninsula, and was wounded at the battle of Toulouse. Died about 1820.

McLEAN. Alexander McLean. Ensign, 31st of December, 1803; lieutenant, 23rd of April, 1805; captain, 15th of October, 1812; half pay, 1816. Died in South Uist in 1843.

McLEAN. Archibald McLean. Captain from the Argyle Highlanders, 5th of June, 1794; major, 1st of November, 1796; lieutenant-colonel, 3rd of November, 1801. Retired in 1807 He served as second in command of the regiment in the campaign in Holland in 1799, and was present at the battle of Egmont-op-Zee. He accompanied the regiment to Egypt in 1801, and was present at the battle before Alexandria. (Gold Medal from Sultan Selim III.).

McLEAN. Archibald McLean. Captain-lieutenant and first adjutant of the regiment, 17th of August, 1793. He left the regiment in 1794.

McLEAN. Archibald McLean. Lieutenant, 17th of August, 1793; captain-lieutenant, 8th of October, 1794. He left the regiment the same year.

McLEAN. Donald McLean. Ensign, 21st of August, 1793; lieutenant, 1st of December, 1794. He left the regiment in 1797.

McLEAN. Charles James McLean. Ensign, 17th of June, 1813; lieutenant, 18th of July, 1815; half pay, 11th of July, 1816. He was present with the regiment at the battles of Quatre Bras and Waterloo.

McLEAN. Colin McLean. Ensign, 20th of August, 1793. He left the regiment in 1795.

McLeod. Martin McLeod. Lieutenant from the 27th regiment, 18th of September, 1816; half pay, 25th of March, 1817. He had served at the battles of Nivelle, Nive, Orthes, and Toulouse with the 27th regiment. (Silver medal with four clasps.)

McLeod. Norman McLeod. Ensign, 27th of July, 1815; half pay, 8th of March, 1821.

McMunn. Robert Andrew McMunn, M.D. Appointed surgeon to the 79th, 18th of September, 1840. He left the regiment on the 7th of July, 1846. He served at the bombardment of Antwerp.

McMurdo. Charles Edward McMurdo. Ensign, 17th of November, 1854; lieutenant, 9th of March, 1855; captain, 1st of December, 1865. He served with the regiment in the Eastern campaign of 1855, including the siege and fall of Sebastopol, and the assault of the 8th of September. (Medal and clasp and Turkish medal.) He served in the Indian campaign of 1858-59, including the siege and capture of Lucknow. (Medal and clasp.) Went to the Royal Canadian Rifles.

McNair. John Miller McNair. Ensign, 18th of August, 1854; lieutenant, 9th of February, 1855; captain, 10th of July, 1860; exchanged to the 5th Lancers, but returned to the regiment as paymaster. He served in the Eastern campaign with the 79th Highlanders from the 16th of August, 1855, including the siege and fall of Sebastopol, and the assault of the 8th of September. (Medal with clasp and Turkish medal). He also served in the Indian campaign of 1858-59, including the siege and capture of Lucknow, attack on the fort at Rooyah, actions of Allygunge, Bareilly, and Shahjehanpore, capture of forts Bunniar and Mahomdie, passage of the Gogra at Fyzabad, capture of Rampore Kussia, and subsequent operations in Oude across the Gogra and Raptee rivers. (Medal with clasp). He accompanied the Cameron Highlanders to Egypt in 1882 as paymaster. (Medal and Khedive's star.)

McNeil. David McNeil. Ensign, 1799. Retired in 1800.

McNEIL. Donald McNeil. Ensign, 16th of December, 1795; lieutenant, 14th of November, 1796; captain, 10th of March, 1804; major, 25th of July, 1811. He joined the Portuguese army in 1813. He accompanied the 79th to Holland in 1799, and was wounded at the battle of Egmont-op-Zee. He served with the regiment in Egypt in 1801, and was present at the battle before Alexandria. (Gold medal from Sultan Selim III.). Was present at the bombardment of Copenhagen, and took part in the expedition to Sweden under Sir John Moore. He served throughout the Peninsular war, and was present at the battles of Corunna, Vittoria, Pyrenees, Nivelle, Nive, Orthes, and Toulouse. (Medal with seven clasps.)

McNEILL. John McNeill. Lieutenant, 23rd of April, 1805; captain, 29th of October, 1812. Died in 1825.

McPHEE. Donald McPhee. Ensign, 15th of December, 1808; lieutenant, 29th of November, 1810; half pay on the 2nd of June, 1819. He served in the regiment at the bombardment of Copenhagen, with the expedition to Walcheren, and in the Peninsular and Waterloo campaigns. He was present at the battles of Corunna, Pyrenees, Nivelle, Nive, and Toulouse, and was wounded at Quatre Bras.

McPHEE. Alexander McPhee. Ensign, 30th of November, 1815; half pay on the 25th of February, 1816.

McPHERSON. Duncan McPherson. Ensign, 8th of October, 1807; lieutenant, 19th of July 1810. He served with the regiment in the Peninsula, was wounded at Toulouse, and was killed at the battle of Waterloo.

McVICAR. Charles McVicar. Lieutenant, 27th of March, 1794; left the regiment in 1795.

MENZIES. William G. S. Menzies, of Culdares. Captain, 2nd battation, 1st of July, 1881.

MERRY. Charles James Merry. Captain, 2nd battalion, 1st of July, 1881.

METCALFE. Thomas Levet Metcalfe. Ensign, 5th of August, 1799; lieutenant, 23rd of May, 1800; captain, 25th of April, 1805; appointed to the 6th Veteran Battalion, 22nd of April, 1813. He accompanied the regiment to Egypt in 1801, and was present at the battle before Alexandria. (Gold medal from Sultan Selim III.).

METHUEN. Charles Lucas Methuen. Ensign, 1st of April, 1863; lieutenant, 30th November, 1866. Retired on the 16th of July, 1873.

MIERS. Capel Henry Miers. Captain from the Canadian Rifles, 5th of May, 1869; major, 1st of July, 1881. Retired on the 15th of August, 1883.

MILLBANK. Frederick Millbank. Ensign, 29th of December, 1837; lieutenant, 3rd of April, 1840. Retired on the 2nd of August, 1842.

MILLER. George Murray Miller, C.B. Ensign, 30th of January, 1846; lieutenant, 2nd of April, 1847; captain, 4th of August, 1854; major, 2nd of May, 1865; lieutenant-colonel, 4th of June, 1870. He is now a major-general. He commanded the regiment from 1873 to 1878. He served in the Eastern campaign of 1854-55, including the battles of Alma and Balaclava, and siege of Sebastopol. (Medal with three clasps, and Turkish medal.) Also served in the Indian campaign of 1858-59, including the siege and capture of Lucknow. (Severely wounded through the body.) Present also at the capture of Rampore Kussia and subsequent operations in Oude, across the Gogra and Raptee rivers. (Mentioned in despatches, brevet of major, medal and clasp.) Served on the North West Frontier of India against the Mohmunds in 1864. (Medal.)

MILLOWAY. Charles P. Milloway. Ensign, 14th of April, 1804; half pay in 1805.

MITCHELL John Mitchell. Captain from the 19th Light Dragoons, 8th of April, 1825; major, 1st of June, 1826; half pay on the 10th of January, 1837. He had served with the 1st Foot in the Walcheren expedition, and at the siege of Flushing. He was also in the Peninsula with the 1st Foot, and was present at the battles of Busaco and Fuentes d'Onor, and at the action of Sabugal. (Medal with two clasps.)

MONEY. Gordon Lorn Campbell Money. Ensign, 8th of February, 1868; lieutenant, 28th of October, 1871; adjutant of the regiment from the 19th of December, 1879, to the 17th of August, 1880; captain, 18th of August, 1880; major, 1st of February, 1884. He served in the Nile expedition in 1884-85 with the Cameron Highlanders. (Medal and clasp.) Also served throughout the operations of the Soudan Frontier Field Force of 1885-86, as assistant-military-secretary to Sir F. Stephenson, K.C.B., and was present at the engagement at Giniss. (Mentioned in despatches, D.S.O., Fourth class of Osmanieh.)

MOORSOM. William Scarth Moorsom. Ensign, 27th of February, 1823; exchanged to the 7th Fusiliers, 1825.

MORLEY. George Lyddon Morley. Ensign, 21st of September, 1860; went to commissariat department on the 30th of June, 1865.

MORRISON. Charles Morrison. Appointed chaplain to the regiment, 22nd of June, 1858. Retired on the 7th of November, 1871. He served with the regiment in the Indian campaign of 1858-59, including the siege and capture of Lucknow. (Medal and clasp.)

MORRISON. John Whiteford Morrison. Ensign, 26th of August, 1807; lieutenant, 17th of August, 1809; appointed to the 9th Veteran battalion, 20th of October, 1820. He served with the regiment in the expedition to Sweden in 1808 with Sir John

Moore, in the expedition to Walcheren, and the siege of Flushing. He was also in the Peninsular war with the 79th, and was present at the battles of Corunna and Salamanca and at the siege of Burgos. (War medal with two clasps.)

MOSTYN. George T. B. Mostyn. Lieutenant, 2nd battalion, 1st of July, 1881. Retired in 1882.

MUNRO. William Munro. Ensign, 10th of October, 1834; lieutenant, 27th of December, 1837; captain, 14th of June, 1842. Retired in 1854.

MURRAY. Alexander Bruce Murray. Ensign, 18th of March, 1859; lieutenant, 10th of May, 1861; captain, 5th of April, 1872. Retired with the rank of major on the 29th of September, 1880.

MURRAY. Hon. Andrew David Murray. Lieutenant, 24th of December, 1884. He served with the regiment during the latter part of the Nile expedition in 1885. (Medal with clasp.) Served throughout the operations of the Soudan Frontier Field Force in 1885-86 with the Cameron Highlanders, was present at Kosheh during its investment, and at the engagement at Giniss.

MURRAY. Henry Murray. Ensign, 1st of June, 1841; lieutenant, 23rd of August, 1843; captain, 12th of December, 1851. Retired in 1857. He served with the regiment in the Eastern campaign of 1855, including the siege and fall of Sebastopol, and expedition to Kertch and Yenikale. (Medal with clasp and Turkish medal.)

MURRAY. Henry Augustus Murray. Ensign, 29th of March, 1844; lieutenant, 11th of November, 1845. Retired on the 31st of December, 1847.

MURRAY. Lord James Murray, K.C.H. Major in the 79th, from the 10th Light Dragoons, 25th of March, 1805. Retired on the 20th of February, 1806. Colonel and A.D.C. to the King, 4th of June, 1813. Created Baron Glenlyon, 17th of July, 1821. Died in 1837.

MURRAY. Sir John Murray, Bart., K.C.H. Ensign, 24th of October, 1788, in the 3rd Foot Guards; exchanged as colonel to the 79th, 11th of December, 1806; appointed to command the Royal Regiment of Malta, 23rd of February, 1808. Became full general on the 27th of May, 1825. He served in Flanders, and was present at the attack on the French lines at Famars, at the siege of Valenciennes and Dunkirk, battle of Maubeuge, actions at Cambresis and Tournay. He was present at the capture of the Cape of Good Hope. He commanded the army against Scindiah and Holkar. Also commanded the King's German Legion, under Sir John Moore, in Portugal.

MYLNE. Thomas Mylne. Ensign, 1799; lieutenant, 28th of March, 1800; captain, 24th of April, 1805; Major, 18th of June, 1815. Retired in 1821. Died at Edinburgh in 1832. He accompanied the regiment to Egypt in 1801, and was present at the battle before Alexandria. (Gold medal from Sultan Selim III.). He was present at the bombardment of Copenhagen and in the expedition to Walcheren. He served in the Peninsula and was wounded at Toulouse; was also present at the battle of Quatre Bras, where he was again severely wounded.

NAPIER. Sir Robert Napier, Bart., of Milliken. Ensign, 7th of August, 1835; lieutenant, 14th of September, 1838; captain 12th of April, 1844. Retired on the 9th of June, 1846.

NAPIER. Robert F. L. Napier, son of Sir Robert Napier. Lieutenant, 29th of November, 1876; captain, 14th of July, 1883. He served with the regiment throughout the Nile expedition of 1884-85. (Medal and clasp.) Also served throughout the operations of the Soudan Frontier Field Force in 1885-86; was present at Kosheh during its investment, and at the engagement at Giniss. (Mentioned in despatches, 5th class of the Medjidie.)

NASH. John Nash. Ensign, 18th of November, 1813; lieutenant, 19th of July, 1815; half pay, 25th of March, 1817. He served with the 79th at the battles of Quatre Bras and Waterloo. (Wounded.)

NETTLESHIP. Arthur John Nettleship. Appointed paymaster, 9th of March, 1885. He served with the Cameron Highlanders throughout the operations of the Soudan Frontier Field Force in 1885-86. (Medal.)

NEWHOUSE. Charles B. Newhouse. Ensign, 6th of April, 1825; lieutenant, 1st of August, 1826. Retired on the 25th of June, 1829.

NEWPORT. Simon George Newport. Captain from the 39th regiment, 6th of June, 1857. Died in India.

O'CONNOR. Ogle Nisbett O'Connor. Ensign, 15th of October, 1812; lieutenant, 1st of August, 1826; retired, 25th of June, 1829.

OLDHAM. Henry Hugh Oldham. Captain from the 48th regiment, 31st of October, 1871; major, 1st of July, 1881; lieutenant-colonel, half pay, 1st of July, 1886. He served with the China expeditionary force of 1860, and was present at the actions of Sinhoo and Tangku, assault and capture of the North Taku fort, and surrender of Pekin. (Medal with two clasps.) Served in the Cossyah and Jynteah campaign in 1863. (Mentioned in despatches.)

ORDE. Robert Francis Orde. Ensign, 23rd of August, 1833; he left the regiment in 1835.

ORR. Alexander Orr. Ensign, 1806; lieutenant, 16th of December, 1807; drowned, 1809, at the Isle of Wight.

PALMER. Thomas Palmer. Lieutenant, 30th of May, 1800; retired 1802. He accompanied the regiment to Egypt in 1801, and was present at the battle before Alexandria. (Gold medal from Sultan Selim III.).

PATERSON. Robert Arthur Paterson. Lieutenant, 2nd battalion, 1st of July, 1881.

PEACOCK. Samuel Peacock, M.D. Appointed surgeon, 79th Highlanders, 24th of May, 1821; retired 1824.

PERCIVAL. Philip Percival. Ensign, 16th of August, 1850; lieutenant, 6th of June, 1854; captain, 27th of March, 1855; major, 1st of April, 1870; lieutenant-colonel, 1st of October, 1877; colonel, 19th of October, 1878. He served with the 79th in the Eastern campaign of 1854-55, including the battles of Alma and Balaclava, siege of Sebastopol, assault of the 18th of June, expedition to Kertch and Yenikale. (Medal with three clasps, and Turkish medal.) He served with the regiment in the Indian campaign of 1858-59, including the siege and capture of Lucknow, attack on the fort of Rooyah, actions of Allygunge, Bareilly, and Shahjehanpore, capture of forts Bunniar and Mahomdie, passage of the Gogra at Fyzabad, capture of Rampore Kussia, and subsequent operations in Oude, across the Gogra and Raptee rivers. (Medal with clasp.)

PERSTON. David Perston, M.D. Appointed assistant surgeon, 18th of October, 1810; surgeon, 17th of February, 1825; went to the 4th Light Dragoons. He served with the regiment in the Peninsula, and was present at the action of Foz d'Aronce, at the siege of Burgos, and at the battle of Salamanca. (Silver war medal with clasp.) He was also present with the regiment at the battles of Quatre-Bras and Waterloo.

PETERS. William Bird Peters. Ensign, 21st of April, 1796; retired 1797.

PETRIE. Alexander Petrie. Lieutenant, 5th of September, 1795; captain, 26th of October, 1796; major, 28th of May, 1807; lieutenant-colonel, 11th of May, 1811; retired in 1812; died in 1844 at Bath. He served with the 79th in Holland in 1799, and was present at the battle of Egmont-op-Zee. He accompanied the regiment to Egypt in 1801, and was present at the battle before Alexandria. (Gold medal from Sultan Selim III.). He served with the 79th in the Peninsula, and was present in the retreat to Corunna, and at the battle of Fuentes d'Onor. (Gold medal.)

POTTS-CHATTO. Denis Potts-Chatto. 2nd lieutenant in the 2nd battalion, 29th of January, 1887.

POWLING. John Powling. Ensign, 29th of May, 1811; lieutenant, 15th of October, 1812; died, December, 1815, of wounds received at the battle of Waterloo.

PURVES. Patrick Purves. Lieutenant, 23rd of July, 1807; captain, 28th of October, 1810. He was killed at the battle of Toulouse, 10th of April, 1814.

PROBYN. John Langford Probyn. 2nd lieutenant, 5th of October, 1878; resigned his commission, 25th of February, 1880.

QUIN. George Quin. Ensign, 11th of December, 1858; lieutenant from the Rifle Brigade, 26th of April, 1859; retired in 1872.

RADCLIFFE. Joseph H. Francis Radcliffe. Lieutenant, 2nd battalion, 14th of February, 1885.

RAWDON. John Dawson Rawdon. Ensign, 12th of December, 1822. Transferred to Coldstream Guards 1823.

REEVE. Thomas John Reeve. Ensign, 11th of May, 1839; lieutenant, 28th of December, 1841; captain, 9th of June, 1846; retired in 1851.

REID. George Alexander Caradoc Reid, of Shandwick. Lieutenant, 20th of November, 1875; captain, 19th of September, 1881; retired in 1883. He served with the regiment throughout the Egyptian campaign of 1882, and was present at the battle of Tel-el-Kebir. (Medal with clasp, and Khedive's star.)

RIACH. Malcolm Stewart Riach. Lieutenant from the 69th regiment, 23rd of January, 1883. He served with the Cameron

Highlanders throughout the Nile expedition of 1884-85. (Medal with clasp.) Also served throughout the operations of the Soudan Frontier Field Force, 1885-86, and was present at Kosheh during its investment, at the reconnaissance on the 16th of December, and was staff officer at Kosheh during the engagement at Giniss.

RIACH. William Alexander Riach. Ensign, 27th of October, 1811; lieutenant, 17th of June, 1813; captain, 7th of April, 1825; major, 28th of June, 1838; retired, 15th of June, 1842; died at Perth in 1843. He served with the regiment in the Peninsula, and was present with the army covering the siege of Badajos, at the battle of Salamanca, occupation of Madrid, siege of Burgos, campaigns of 1811-12-13. (Silver war medal and clasp.) He also served with the regiment in the Waterloo campaign, and was severely wounded at Quatre Bras. He was present with the army of occupation in France in 1815-16-17. (Waterloo medal.)

RIDDELL. Henry James K. H. Riddell. Major from the 50th regiment, 21st of April, 1808. Exchanged to quarter-master-general's staff, 4th of February, 1810. He was present at the bombardment of Copenhagen in 1807.

RIDSDALE. George Ridsdale. Appointed surgeon, 9th of September, 1813; half pay, 1817. He was present with the regiment at the battles of Quatre Bras and Waterloo.

ROBERTSON. Alexander Robertson. Ensign, 15th of July, 1809; lieutenant, 4th of July, 1811; half pay, 1816. Died at Wick, 23rd of March, 1844. He served with the regiment in the Peninsula, and was present at the battle of the Nive.

ROBERTSON. Fulton Robertson. Ensign, 5th of January, 1809; lieutenant, 21st of February, 1811; half pay, 25th of January, 1817. He served with the regiment in the Peninsula, and was present at the battles of Busaco, Fuentes d'Onor, (severely wounded) Pyrenees, Nivelle, Nive, and Toulouse. (Silver war medal and six clasps). He was also present at the battles of Waterloo and Quatre Bras. (Medal.)

ROBERTSON. James Robertson. Ensign, 6th of January, 1814; lieutenant, 20th of July, 1815; half pay, 25th of February, 1816. He served with the regiment in the Peninsula, and was present at the battles of Corunna, Busaco, Fuentes d'Onor, and Salamanca. (Medal with four clasps.) He also served in the Waterloo campaign, and was severely wounded at Quatre Bras.

ROBERTSON. James Robertson. Ensign, 29th of February, 1841; lieutenant, 14th of April, 1843; retired, July, 1849.

ROBERTSON. Rev. James Robertson. He served as chaplain to the regiment throughout the operations of the Soudan Frontier Field Force in 1885-86, was present at Kosheh during its investment, at the reconnaissance of the 16th of December, and at the engagement at Giniss. (Mentioned in despatches. Medal.)

ROBERTSON. Thomas Gilzean Robertson. Ensign, 27th of June, 1845; retired 1846.

ROBERTSON. William Buxton Robertson. Ensign, 16th of March, 1855; lieutenant, 16th of June, 1857; went to the 25th King's Own Borderers in 1860.

ROBINSON. Samuel Robinson. Ensign, 16th of March, 1808; lieutenant, 29th of June, 1809; retired, 25th of June, 1812.

ROMILLY. Frederick Romilly. Captain from the 90th regiment, 24th of August, 1834; exchanged to the Scot Fusilier Guards, 25th of September, 1835.

ROOKE. Charles Rooke. Captain from the 3rd Foot Guards, 25th of September, 1835; retired, 3rd of June, 1838.

ROSE. William Rose. Captain, 17th of November, 1796; major, 26th of January, 1797; retired in 1799.

Ross. Allan Theophilus Ross. Captain from half pay, 29th regiment, 29th of January, 1882; placed on half pay, 5th of January, 1884.

Ross. Patrick Ross. Lieutenant, 20th of June, 1798; exchanged to 69th regiment in 1803. Killed at the storming of Java, 1811. He served with the 79th Highlanders in Egypt, and was present at the battle before Alexandria. (Severely wounded, right arm amputated. Gold medal from Sultan Selim III.).

Rowley. Henry Frederick Rowley. Ensign, 9th of April, 1861; went to the 78th Highlanders, 26th of May, 1865.

Ruse. John Ruse. Lieutenant from Cape regiment, 28th of April, 1808; he died in 1809.

Scobell. William Leaper Scobell. Ensign, 7th of December, 1826; lieutenant, 18th of May, 1832; retired, 25th of October, 1833.

Scot. Thomas Goldie Scot, M.D. Appointed assistant-surgeon, 23rd of September, 1845; surgeon, 18th of February, 1853; surgeon-major, 14th of December, 1861; retired on half pay as deputy-inspector-general, 7th of June, 1867. He served with the regiment in the Eastern campaign of 1854-55, including the battle of Alma and the siege and fall of Sebastopol. (Medal with two clasps, 5th class of the Medjidie, and Turkish medal.) Served also in the Indian campaign of 1858-59, including the siege and capture of Lucknow. (Medal and clasp.)

Scott. Alexander James Corse Scott. Ensign, 26th of January, 1866. Transferred to Bengal Staff Corps, 14th of December, 1869.

Scott. John Scott. Ensign, 27th of October, 1848.

Scott. William Scott (afterwards Sir William Scott, Bart., of Ancrum). Captain from 34th regiment, 21st of July, 1848; retired in 1854.

Scott. William Angel Scott. 2nd lieutenant from 31st regiment, 6th of December, 1879; lieutenant, 21st of July, 1880; resigned his commission, 13th of November, 1884. He served with the regiment in the Egyptian campaign of 1882. (Medal and Khedive's star.) He served in the Soudan expedition of 1884 as A.D.C. to Major-General Sir Gerald Graham, V.C., K.C.B., and was present at the actions of El-Teb and Tamaii. (Mentioned in despatches, two clasps.)

Scott-Elliot. Adam Scott-Elliot. 2nd lieutenant, 23rd of October, 1880; lieutenant, 1st of July, 1881. He served throughout the Egyptian war of 1882, and was present at the battle of Tel-el-Kebir. (Medal with clasp, and Khedive's star.) Also served throughout the Nile expedition of 1884-85. (Clasp.) Served throughout the operations of the Soudan Frontier Field Force in 1885-86, in command of the Cameron division of the camel corps, and was present at the engagement at Giniss.

Scovell. George Thomas Scovell. Ensign, 6th of June, 1854; lieutenant, 8th of October, 1854; captain, 16th of June, 1857; retired in 1868. He served with the regiment in the Indian campaign of 1858, including the siege and capture of Lucknow. (Medal with clasp.)

Sedley. Frederick Sedley. Captain from 5th Lancers, 9th of May, 1871; exchanged to 48th foot, 1st of November, 1871. He served in the China war of 1860. (Medal and two clasps.)

Sewell. William Henry Sewell, C.B. Major-general, 9th of November, 1846; colonel of 79th, 21st of March, 1854. He served on the staff in the Peninsula, and was present at the battles of Corunna, Talavera, and Busaco; sieges of Ciudad Rodrigo, Badajos, and San Sebastien; battles of Nivelle, Nive, and the sorties from Bayonne; battles of Orthes and Toulouse. (Had six horses killed under him in various actions. Medal with ten clasps.)

Shaw. James Thomas Shaw. Captain, 2nd battalion, 1st of July 1881. Retired in 1887.

SHORT. John Short, M.D. Appointed surgeon to the 79th, 25th of March, 1824; transferred to 24th regiment, 23rd of April, 1835. He had served previously in the Peninsular and American wars.

SIMPSON. William Simpson. Quarter-master, 16th of March, 1867. Retired on the 19th of April, 1878. He served in the Eastern campaign with the regiment in 1854-55, including the battles of Alma and Balaclava, expedition to Kertch and Yenikale, siege and fall of Sebastopol, and assaults of the 18th of June and the 8th of September. (Medal with three clasps, and Turkish medal.) Also in the Indian campaign of 1858-59, including the siege and capture of Lucknow. (Medal and clasp.)

SINCLAIR. Archibald Sinclair. Quarter-master, 25th of February, 1813; lieutenant in 3rd veteran battalion, 31st of August, 1815. He served with the regiment in the Peninsula.

SINCLAIR. Hon. James Sinclair. Captain from the 95th regiment, 8th of April, 1825; exchanged to 92nd Highlanders, 2nd of February, 1826.

SINCLAIR. John Sinclair. Ensign, 19th of November, 1803; lieutenant, 14th of March, 1805; captain, 4th of July, 1811. He served with the 79th Highlanders in the Peninsula, and was slightly wounded at the battle of Fuentes d'Onor. He died on the 17th of June, 1815, of wounds received at Quatre Bras.

SKENE. Charles Skene. Ensign, 12th of April, 1833; lieutenant, 6th of November, 1835; captain, 29th of January, 1841. Retired on the 4th of July, 1845.

SMITH. Astley Campbell Smith. Captain from 25th regiment, 29th of January, 1841. Retired on the 4th of July, 1845.

SMITH. George Smith. Ensign, 23rd of March, 1855; lieutenant from the 72nd regiment, 2nd of November, 1855. Retired in 1859.

SMITH. Haskett Smith. Ensign, 29th of May, 1835; lieutenant, 8th of June, 1838; captain, 14th of April, 1843. Retired on the 11th of November, 1845.

SMITH. William Haskett Smith. Ensign, 9th of February, 1870; lieutenant, 28th of October, 1871; captain, 29th of September, 1880; major, 9th of February, 1885. He served throughout the Nile expedition of 1884-85 with the Cameron Highlanders. (Medal with clasp.) Also served in the operations of the Soudan Frontier Field Force with the regiment in 1885-86, and was present at Kosheh during its investment, at the reconnaissance of the 16th of December, and at the engagement at Giniss.

SMYTH. John Stewart Smyth. Ensign, 10th of September, 1825; lieutenant, 5th of April, 1831; captain, 29th of December, 1837. Retired on the 14th of April, 1843.

SMYTHE. David Murray Smythe, younger, of Methven. Sub-lieutenant, 8th of May, 1872; lieutenant, 8th of May, 1874. Retired in 1878.

SODEN. Ambrose Soden. Appointed lieutenant, 31st of May, 1795; captain, 11th of January, 1797; superseded, 17th of September, 1803. He accompanied the regiment to Egypt in 1801, and was present at the battle before Alexandria. (Gold medal from Sultan Selim III.).

SODEN. John Smith Soden. Assistant-surgeon, 26th of June, 1800; resigned, 16th of April, 1803. He accompanied the 79th Highlanders to Egypt in 1801, and was present at the battle before Alexandria. (Gold medal from Sultan Selim III.). Also served in the expedition to Ferrol.

STEELE. Thomas Steele. Appointed captain, 3rd of September, 1795; retired in 1797.

STEPNEY. Herbert Herbert Stepney. Ensign, 29th of July, 1862; lieutenant, 5th of August, 1864; resigned his commission in 1868.

STEVENSON. Henry Halford Stevenson. Ensign, 29th of June, 1849; lieutenant, 24th of December, 1852; captain, 29th of December, 1854; brevet major, 20th of July, 1858; half pay, 23rd of October, 1860. He served with the regiment throughout the Eastern campaign of 1854-55, including the battles of Alma and Balaclava, siege and fall of Sebastopol, assaults of the 18th of June and 8th of September, expedition to Kertch and Yenikale. (Medal with three clasps, 5th class of the Medjidie, Sardinian and Turkish medals.) Served in the Indian campaign of 1858-59, including the siege and capture of Lucknow; served as brigade-major from February, 1858, to the close of the campaign. (Frequently mentioned in despatches, brevet of major, medal and clasp.)

STEWART. Charles Duncan Stewart, of Brin. Lieutenant, 2nd battalion, 8th of March, 1884.

STEWART. Francis Stewart, of Lesmurdie. Appointed major, 9th of August, 1799; lieutenant-colonel, 1st of January, 1800; half pay, 17th of February, 1800.

STEWART. P. Duncan Stewart. Lieutenant, 17th of August, 1793; captain, 1st of December, 1794. Retired in 1799.

STEWART. Robert Stewart. Ensign, 13th of July, 1855; lieutenant, 17th of June, 1859; adjutant, 18th of February, 1859; retired in 1863. He served with the regiment in the Indian campaign of 1858-59, including the siege and capture of Lucknow. (Medal and clasp.)

ST. LEGER. Henry Hungerford St. Leger, D.S.O. Major from the 71st Highlanders, February, 1881; lieutenant-colonel, 1st of July, 1881; colonel, 1st of July, 1885. Retired on the 1st of July, 1887. He served with the 80th regiment in the Indian campaign of 1858-59, and was present at the action of Gowlowlie and the capture of Calpee. (Medal and clasp.) He served throughout the Egyptian war of 1882, with the

Cameron Highlanders, and was present at the battle of Tel-el-Kebir. (Medal with clasp and Khedive's star.) Served throughout the Nile expedition of 1884-85. (Clasp.) Commanded the Cameron Highlanders throughout the operations of the Soudan Frontier Field Force in 1885-86, was commandant at Kosheh during its investment, and was present at the engagement at Giniss. (Mentioned in despatches, D.S.O.).

STOURTON. Edward G. Stourton. Lieutenant, 2nd battalion, 16th of April, 1884.

STREET. Henry Jardine Street. Ensign, 14th of November, 1845; lieutenant, 3rd of November, 1846; exchanged to 34th regiment, 21st of July, 1848.

STRONACH. Alexander Stronach. Ensign, 19th of April, 1796; Retired in 1799.

STUART. Eustace Robertson Burnett Stuart, of Crichie. Lieutenant from the 7th Fusiliers, 27th of August, 1873. Retired on the 14th of April, 1875.

STUART. John Stuart. Appointed lieutenant, 19th of November, 1795; went to 95th Rifles, 27th of August, 1800; and served with them in Egypt and in the Peninsula.

SULLIVAN. William Sullivan. Major from the 8th Garrison Battalion, 23rd of April, 1807 Retired on the 4th of October, 1810.

SUTHERLAND. George Sutherland. Ensign, 3rd of November, 1797; lieutenant, 27th of September, 1798; transferred to the 71st Highlanders, 8th of December, 1804, and died in Walcheren in 1809. He served with the 79th Highlanders in Holland in 1799, and was present at the battle of Egmont-op-Zee. He accompanied the regiment to Egypt in 1801, and was present at the battle before Alexandria. (Wounded. Gold medal from Sultan Selim III.).

SUTHERLAND. Robert Sutherland. Lieutenant from the Staff Corps Cavalry, 20th of April, 1815; half pay, 25th of February, 1816.

TAYLOR. Sir Richard C. H. Taylor, K.C.B. Ensign, 11th of December, 1835; lieutenant, 29th of March, 1839; captain, 23rd of August, 1844; major, 8th of August, 1854; lieutenant-colonel, 12th of December, 1854; colonel, 21st of May, 1858; major-general, 6th of March, 1868; lieutenant-general, 1st of October, 1877; general, 1st of April, 1883. He served with the regiment in the Eastern campaign of 1854-55, including the battles of Alma and Balaclava, and siege and fall of Sebastopol. (Medal with three clasps, 5th class of the Medjidie, Sardinian and Turkish medals.) He commanded the 79th Highlanders from February to November, 1858, in the Indian campaign, including the siege and capture of Lucknow, and commanded a brigade in Oude from November, 1858, to January, 1859. (Mentioned in despatches, C.B., brevet of colonel, medal and clasp.)

THARPE. John Tharpe. Ensign, 20th of May, 1814; lieutenant, 15th of October, 1815; half pay, 25th of January, 1816.

THOMSON. Thomas Thomson. Appointed chaplain, 17th of August, 1793. Retired in 1797.

THOMSON. William Seaman Thomson. Ensign, 31st of May, 1859; appointed to Scots Greys, 12th of June, 1860.

THOMPSON. Frederick Hacket Thompson. 2nd lieutenant, 6th of August, 1879; lieutenant, 22nd of May, 1880; captain, 20th of February, 1884. He served with the regiment throughout the Egyptian war of 1882 as transport officer, and was present at the battle of Tel-el-Kebir. (Medal with clasp and Khedive's star.) Served also throughout the operations of the Soudan Frontier Field Force in 1885-86, was present at Kosheh during its investment (wounded), and at the engagement at Giniss.

THOMPSON. John Thompson. Ensign, 31st of October, 1811; lieutenant, 18th of November, 1813; half pay, 27th of January, 1820. He served with the regiment in the Peninsula, and was slightly wounded at the battle of Nivelle; also at the battles of Quatre Bras and Waterloo.

TOWNSHEND. Lee Porcher Townshend. Ensign from the 54th regiment, 23rd of May, 1822; lieutenant, 7th of April, 1825; captain, unattached, in 1826.

TRAVERS. Sir R. Travers, C.B., K.C.M.G. Captain from the 112th regiment, 3rd of July, 1799; appointed to the 95th Rifles, 25th of August, 1800. He served with the 79th Highlanders in Holland, and was present at the battle of Egmont-op-Zee, also in the expedition to Ferrol. (Wounded in the head.) He afterwards served with great distinction, and received gold medals for Maida, Roleia, and Vimiera. He became a major-general on the 27th of May, 1825, and died in 1834 at Cork.

TURNER. Augustus Henry Turner. Ensign, 24th of May, 1861; lieutenant, 4th of July, 1865; transferred to the Bengal Staff Corps, 7th of May, 1868.

TURNER. Francis Charles Turner. Ensign, 9th of July, 1852; lieutenant, 6th of June, 1854; captain, 15th of June, 1855; exchanged to the 39th regiment in 1859. He served with the 79th Highlanders in the Eastern campaign of 1854-55, including the battles of Alma and Balaclava, siege and fall of Sebastopol, and the assault of the 8th of September. (Medal with three clasps and Turkish medal.) Also served with the regiment in the Indian campaign of 1858-59, and was present at the siege and capture of Lucknow. (Medal and clasp.)

URQUHART. Beauchamp Colclough Urquhart, younger, of Meldrum. 2nd lieutenant, 14th of January, 1880; lieutenant, 12th of February, 1881; captain, 2nd of November, 1885. He served with the regiment in the Egyptian war of 1882, from the landing at Ismailia, and was present at the battle of Tel-el-Kebir. (Medal with clasp and Khedive's star.) Also served throughout the Nile expedition of 1884-85. (Clasp.) Served with the regiment throughout the operations of the Soudan Frontier Field Force in 1885-86, was present at Kosheh during its investment and at the engagement at Giniss.

URQUHART. John Urquhart. Appointed lieutenant, 20th of Augus , 1793 ; captain-lieutenant and captain, 2nd of September, 1795. Retired in 1797.

WALBEOFFE. Thomas Wilkins Walbeoffe. Ensign, 29th of March, 1810 ; lieutenant, 13th of October, 1812 ; half pay, 25th of December, 1815.

WALKER. Arthur Walker. Ensign, 9th of March, 1855 ; lieutenant, 16th of June, 1857 ; captain, 20th of February, 1866 ; half pay, 11th of January, 1867. He served throughout the Indian campaign of 1858-59 as aide-de-camp to Brigadier-General Douglas, including the operations across the Goomtee ; siege and capture of Lucknow, and subsequent operations on the march to the relief of Azimghur. (Mentioned in despatches. Medal with clasp.)

WAUGH. Gilbert Waugh. Captain, 17th of August, 1793. Retired in 1795.

WEBB. John Wynne Webb. Ensign, 15th of March, 1808 ; lieutenant, 20th of July, 1810 ; captain, 23rd of September, 1813 ; transferred to the 3rd Veteran Battalion in 1815. Died in 1845. He served with the regiment in the expedition to Sweden under Sir John Moore ; also in the Walcheren expedition, at the siege of Flushing, defence of Cadiz, and action at Sancti Pietri. He served with the 79th in the Peninsula, and was present at the passage of the Coa ; actions of Zobral, Sabugal, Foz d'Aronce ; battles of Corunna, Busaco, Fuentes d'Onor (severely wounded), Salamanca (three times wounded) ; and at the siege of Badajos. At these two latter he was doing duty with the Portuguese troops. (Silver war medal and five clasps.)

WEBSTER. James Webster. Ensign, 2nd of April, 1847 ; lieutenant, 12th of October, 1849. Retired in 1854.

WELD. Edmund Weld. Assistant-surgeon from the Elgin Fencibles, 16th of April, 1803. Went to the 67th regiment, 19th of July, 1806

WIGHT. James Wight. Ensign, 12th of October, 1815; half pay, 25th of February, 1816.

WILLIAMSON. James Williamson. Lieutenant from the 42nd Highlanders, 25th of March, 1805; captain, 8th of June, 1809; exchanged to the 94th regiment, and was killed at Ciudad Rodrigo in 1812.

WIMBERLEY. Douglas Wimberley. Ensign, 24th of May, 1855; lieutenant, 30th of June, 1857; adjutant, 18th of June, 1858. Retired on the 12th of May, 1863. He served with the regiment in the Indian campaign of 1858-59, including the siege and capture of Lucknow. (Medal with clasp.)

WOLRIGE-GORDON. Henry Gordon Wolrige-Gordon (Esslemont.) Lieutenant, 6th of May, 1885. He served with the regiment throughout the operations of the Soudan Frontier Field Force in 1885-86. Was present at Kosheh during its investment, and at the engagement at Giniss. (Medal.)

WOLRIGE-GORDON. Walter Gordon Wolrige-Gordon (Esslemont.) Lieutenant, 2nd battalion, 1st of July, 1881; appointed to the Black Watch, 3rd of October, 1883, and served with it in Egypt and the Soudan.

WOOD. Albert Charles Wood. Ensign, 19th of March, 1859; lieutenant, 2nd of July, 1861; went to the 8th Hussars in 1864.

WOOD. David Wood, M.D. Assistant-surgeon, 3rd of June, 1805; transferred to the 57th regiment, 3rd of November, 1808.

WOOD. William Thomas Wood. Ensign, 15th of June, 1842; lieutenant, 23rd of August, 1844; exchanged to the 20th regiment in 1845.

WYVILL. Richard Augustus Wyvill. Captain, 1st of October, 1795; major in the 7th West India Regiment, 3rd of March, 1804. He accompanied the regiment to Egypt in 1801, and was present at the battle before Alexandria. (Gold medal from Sultan Selim III.).

WYATT. James Henry Wyatt. Ensign, 20th of September, 1844; lieutenant, 26th of June, 1846; captain, 3rd of August, 1855; half pay in 1855.

YOUNG. George Frederick Young. Ensign, 30th of June, 1865; transferred to the Bengal Staff Corps, 19th of February, 1870.

YOUNG. James Young. Ensign, from sergeant-major, and adjutant, 2nd of October, 1854; lieutenant, 9th of February, 1855; captain, 11th of May, 1860. Retired in 1860. He served with the regiment in the Eastern campaign of 1854-55, including the battles of Alma and Balaclava, expedition to Kertch and Yenikale, siege and fall of Sebastopol, and assaults of the 18th of June and the 8th of September. (Medal with three clasps, Knight of the Legion of Honour, and Turkish medal.) Also served in the Indian campaign of 1858, including the siege and capture of Lucknow. (Medal with clasp.)

YOUNG. John Crawford Young. Captain from the 91st regiment, 9th of October, 1817; major, 6th of September, 1833; half pay, 10th of May, 1839. He had previously served with the 91st regiment throughout the Peninsular war, being present at the battles of Roleia, Vimiera, Corunna, Nivelle, Nive, Orthes, and Toulouse. (Medal with seven clasps.)

YOUNGER. John Henderson Younger. Lieutenant, 2nd battalion, 2nd of May, 1885.

Services of the Warrant Officers.

CAMPBELL. Joseph Campbell. Joined on the 31st of July, 1857, and became sergeant-major 18th of April, 1878. Served with the regiment during the Indian Mutiny campaign of 1858. (Medal.) Was sergeant-major of the regiment throughout the Egyptian campaign of 1882, and was present at the battle of Tel-el-Kebir. (Mentioned in despatches, silver medal for distinguished conduct in the field, medal and clasp, and Khedive's star.) Is now adjutant of the Perth (Western Australia) Volunteers. Is in possession of the silver medal for long service and good conduct.

FRASER. Alexander Donald Fraser. Appointed colour-sergeant in the Highland Light Infantry Militia from the Scots Guards on the 7th of December, 1880, and became sergeant-major of the 2nd battalion Cameron Highlanders, 1st of April, 1885.

MACDONALD. James Ronald Macdonald. Became bandmaster on the 13th of September, 1872. Served with the regiment in Egypt from 1883 to 1885. Is in possession of the silver medal for long service and good conduct. Is now inspecting bandmaster of the Egyptian Army.

MCLEAN. Hugh McLean. Became warrant officer on the 1st of July, 1881, and is now sergeant-major at the depôt at Inverness. Is in possession of the silver medal for long service and good conduct.

WAKELEN. Richard B. B. Wakelen. Joined on the 21st of March, 1873, and became bandmaster 1st of November, 1885. Served with the regiment throughout the Egyptian campaign of 1882, and was present at the battle of Tel-el-Kebir. (Medal with clasp, and Khedive's star.) Also served with the Soudan Frontier Field Force in 1886.

YOUNG. William Young. Joined on the 28th of November, 1867, and became sergeant-major 13th of April, 1887. Served with the regiment throughout the Egyptian campaign of 1882, and was present at the battle of Tel-el-Kebir. (Mentioned in despatches, silver medal for distinguished conduct in the field, medal with clasp, and Khedive's star.) Also served with the regiment throughout the Nile Expedition of 1884-85. (Clasp.) Served throughout the operations of the Soudan Frontier Field Force in 1885-86, was present in Kosheh during its investment, and at the engagement at Giniss. Is in possession of the silver medal for long service and good conduct.

The following are a few of those whose honourable and distinguished services in the ranks of the 79th Cameron Highlanders have contributed so much to the credit of the Regiment, and the Committee regret that they are unable to extend the roll further.

BRAND. George Brand. Joined on the 5th of November, 1877, and became colour-sergeant 1st of January, 1884. Served with the regiment throughout the Egyptian campaign of 1882, and was present at the battle of Tel-el-Kebir. (Medal with clasp, and Khedive's star.) Also served with the regiment throughout the Nile expedition of 1884-85. (Clasp.)

BROWN. David Brown. Transferred from the Foot Guards as drum-major on the 1st of February, 1851. Served with the regiment throughout the Eastern campaign of 1854-55, including the battles of Alma and Balaclava, siege of Sebastopol, assaults of the 18th of June and the 8th of September, and the expedition to Kertch and Yenikale. (Medal with three clasps, and Turkish medal.) Also served throughout the Indian Mutiny campaign of 1858-59, including the engagement at Secundragunge, siege and capture of Lucknow, actions at Rooyah, Allygunge, Bareilly, and Shahjehanpore, capture of Mahomdie, storming of Rampore Kussia, passage of the Gogra at Fyzabad, and subsequent operations in Oude, across the Gogra and Raptee rivers. (Medal with clasp.) Discharged on the 6th of October, 1863.

BUNYAN. Thomas Bunyan. Joined in April, 1838, and became sergeant-major in October, 1854. Served as sergeant-major of the regiment throughout the Eastern campaign of 1854-55, including the battles of Alma and Balaclava, siege of Sebastopol, assaults of the 18th of June and the 8th of September, and expedition to Kertch and Yenikale. (Silver medal for distinguished conduct in the field, medal with three clasps, and Turkish medal.) Also served throughout the Indian Mutiny campaign of 1858-59, including the engagement at Secundragunge, siege and capture of Lucknow, actions of Allygunge, Rooyah, Bareilly, and Shahjehanpore, and the capture of Mahomdie. (Medal with clasp.) Discharged in June, 1859. Is now chief warder of the Tower of London.

CAMERON. John Cameron. Joined on the 10th of August, 1878, and became colour-sergeant 16th of July, 1887. Served with the regiment throughout the Egyptian campaign of 1882, and was present at the battle of Tel-el-Kebir. (Medal with clasp, and Khedive's star.) Also served with the regiment in the Nile expedition of 1884-85. (Clasp.)

CHAPMAN. Francis Chapman. Joined on the 11th of August, 1869, and became quarter-master-sergeant 1st of December, 1883. Served with the regiment throughout the Egyptian campaign of 1882, and was present at the battle of Tel-el-Kebir. (Wounded.

Medal with clasp, and Khedive's star.) Also throughout the Nile expedition of 1884-85. (Clasp.) **Served with the** regiment throughout the operations of the Soudan Frontier Field Force in 1885-86. Was present in Kosheh during its investment, and at the engagement at Giniss.

EWING. John Ewing. Joined on the 26th of May, 1879, and became colour-sergeant in July, 1886. Served with the regiment throughout the Egyptian campaign of 1882, and was present at the battle of Tel-el-Kebir. (Medal with clasp, and Khedive's star.) Also throughout the Nile expedition of 1884-85. (Clasp.) Served with the regiment throughout the operations of the Soudan Frontier Field Force in 1885-86. Was present in Kosheh during its investment, and at the engagement at Giniss.

FINLAY. Robert Finlay. Joined on the 6th of July, 1868, and became pioneer-sergeant 9th of March, 1875; canteen sergeant, 1885. Served with the 42nd Black Watch in the Ashantee campaign. (Medal.) Served with the Cameron Highlanders throughout the Egyptian war of 1882, and was present at the battle of Tel-el-Kebir. (Medal with clasp, and Khedive's star.) Also throughout the Nile expedition of 1884-85. (Clasp.) Served in the operations of the Soudan Frontier Field Force in 1885-86. Is in possession of the silver medal for long service and good conduct.

FLETCHER. John Fletcher. Joined on the 20th of April, 1811, and became sergeant in 1816. Served with the 79th in the Peninsular war, and was present at the battles of the Pyrenees, Nivelle, Nive and Toulouse. (Silver medal with four clasps.) Also throughout the campaign in Holland in 1815, being present at the battles of Quatre Bras and Waterloo. (Waterloo medal.) Discharged on the 8th of March, 1837. Died in 1872.

FLETCHER. William Forman Fletcher. Joined and became armourer-sergeant on the 9th of December, 1847. Served with the regiment throughout the Eastern campaign of 1854-55, including the battles of Alma and Balaclava, and the siege of Sebastopol. (Medal with three clasps, and Turkish medal.) Also throughout the Indian Mutiny campaign of 1858-59, including the engagement at Secundragunge, siege and capture of Lucknow, actions of Allygunge, Rooyah, Bareilly, and Shahjehanpore, capture of Mahomdie, storming of Rampore Kussia, passage of the Gogra at Fyzabad, and subsequent operations in Oude, across the Gogra and Raptee rivers. (Medal with clasp.) Died at Rawul Pindee on the 11th of April, 1864.

FLETCHER. William Fletcher (son of Armourer-Sergeant Fletcher). Became cook-sergeant on the 8th of March, 1876. Served with the regiment throughout the Egyptian campaign in 1882, and was present at the battle of Tel-el-Kebir. (Medal with clasp, and Khedive's star.) Also throughout the Nile expedition of 1884-85. (Clasp.) Served with the regiment throughout the operations of the Soudan Frontier Field Force in 1885-86. Was present in Kosheh during its investment, and at the engagement at Giniss.

GRANT. John Macgregor Grant. Served as pipe-major of the regiment throughout the Egyptian war of 1882, and was present at the battle of Tel-el-Kebir. (Mentioned in despatches, medal with clasp, and Khedive's star.) Died of cholera on Mokkattam heights in July, 1883.

GUNN. Donald Gunn. Joined the 79th in 1808, and served with the regiment throughout the Peninsular war, being present at the battles of Fuentes d'Onor, Salamanca, Pyrenees, Nivelle, Nive and Toulouse, and at the siege of Burgos. At the battle of Toulouse he was three times wounded—re-joining his company twice after his wounds had been dressed. On the third occasion he was carried off the field by his wife, Jean Gunn, whose courageous behaviour in dressing the wounds of other soldiers was especially taken notice of by the Duke of Wellington. Mrs. Gunn was with the regiment with her husband in almost every battle and engagement in which it took part. She lived to be upwards of ninety-eight years of age, and died in Edinburgh about a year ago.

GUNN. William Gunn (son of Private Donald Gunn). Became sergeant in May, 1843. Served with the regiment throughout the Eastern campaign of 1854-55, including the battles of Alma and Balaclava and the siege of Sebastopol. (Medal with three clasps, French war medal, and Turkish medal.) Was in posession of the silver medal for long service and good conduct. He was discharged in July, 1857, and died in July, 1883.

GUNN. William Gunn (son of Sergeant William Gunn). Became colour-sergeant on the 8th of July, 1879 Served with the regiment throughout the Egyptian campaign of 1882, and was present at the battle of Tel-el-Kebir. (Mentioned in despatches, medal with clasp, and Khedive's star.)

GUNN. Donald Gunn (grandson of Private Donald Gunn). Served as a sergeant in the Egyptian campaign of 1882, and was present at the battle of Tel-el-Kebir. (Dangerously wounded. Mentioned in despatches, silver medal for distinguished conduct in the field, medal with clasp, and Khedive's star.)

HEALY. Thomas Healy. Became sergeant on the 1st of March, 1881. Served with the regiment throughout the Egyptian campaign of 1882, and was present at the battle of Tel-el-Kebir. (Medal with clasp, and Khedive's star.) Also with the Egyptian army throughout the Nile expedition of 1884-85. (Clasp.) Served as sergeant-major of the 9th Soudan battalion of the Egyptian army throughout the operations of the Soudan Frontier Field Force in 1885-86. Was present in Kosheh during its investment, and at the engagement at Giniss. (Silver medal for distinguished conduct in the field.) Also at the action at Sarras in May, 1887. (Mentioned in despatches. Five times wounded.)

HENDERSON. David Henderson. Joined on the 11th of December, 1812, and served with the 79th in the Peninsula, and throughout the Waterloo campaign, being present at the battles of Quatre Bras and Waterloo.

HENDERSON. Thomas Henderson (son of Private David Henderson). Sergeant on the 20th of June, 1850; colour-sergeant, 1st of June, 1852. Served with the regiment throughout the Eastern campaign of 1854-55, including the battles of Alma and Balaclava and the siege of Sebastopol. (Medal with three clasps, and Turkish medal.) Is in possession of the silver medal for meritorious service and the silver medal for long service and good conduct. Discharged on the 20th of January, 1860. Served, after leaving the 79th, for eighteen years with the Royal Perth Militia.

HENDERSON. David Henderson (son of Colour-Sergeant Thomas Henderson). Joined on the 3rd of June, 1871, and became colour-sergeant 1st of July, 1886. Served with the regiment throughout the Egyptian campaign of 1882, and was present at the battle of Tel-el-Kebir. (Medal with clasp, and Khedive's star.) Also throughout the Nile expedition of 1884-85. (Clasp.) Served as sergeant-major of the British Camel Corps throughout the operations of the Soudan Frontier Field Force in 1885-86, and was present at the engagement at Giniss. (Mentioned in general orders.)

HEWITT. Kennedy Hewitt. Joined on the 6th of June, 1876, and became sergeant-instructor of musketry 18th of April, 1887. He served with the regiment throughout the Egyptian campaign of 1882, and was present at the battle of Tel-el-Kebir. (Wounded. Medal with clasp, and Khedive's star.)

KNIGHT. James Knight. Joined on the 14th of February, 1854, and became colour-sergeant 1st of January, 1860; quartermaster-sergeant, 15th of January, 1867; canteen steward, 16th of February, 1875. Served with the regiment throughout the Eastern campaign of 1854-55, including the battles of Alma and Balaclava, siege of Sebastopol, assaults of the 18th of June and the 8th of September, and the expedition to Kertch and Yenikale. (Medal with three clasps, and Turkish medal.) Also served throughout the Indian Mutiny campaign of 1858-59, including the engagement at Secundragunge, siege and capture of Lucknow, actions of Rooyah, Allygunge, Bareilly, and Shahjehanpore, capture of Mahomdie, storming of Rampore Kussia, passage of the Gogra at Fyzabad, and subsequent operations in Oude, across the Gogra and Raptee rivers. (Medal with clasp.) Served with the 79th in the North-west Frontier campaign in 1863. (Medal.) Served with the regiment throughout the Egyptian campaign of 1882. (Medal and Khedive's star.) Also throughout the Nile expedition of 1884-85. (Clasp.) He left the regiment in 1885. Is in possession of the silver medal for long service and good conduct. Quarter-Master-Sergeant Knight had the honour of being presented to Her Majesty the Queen at the ceremony of depositing the old colours of the 79th at Osborne House on the 22nd of April, 1873.

MACALISTER. George Norman Macalister. Joined on the 24th of November, 1881, and became colour-sergeant 21st of March, 1886. Served in the campaign in the Eastern Soudan in 1884, and was present at the actions of El Teb and Tamaii. (Medal with clasp, and Khedive's star.) Served with the regiment throughout the Nile expedition of 1884-85. (Clasp.) Also in the operations of the Soudan Frontier Field Force in 1885-86.

MACDONALD. Donald Macdonald. Joined on the 13th of November, 1866, and became orderly room sergeant 13th of April, 1887. Served with the regiment throughout the Egyptian campaign of 1882, and was present at the battle of Tel-el-Kebir. (Medal with clasp, and Khedive's star.)

MACDONALD. Colin Macdonald. Was appointed ensign and town major of Montreal, from sergeant-major, 30th of January, 1835.

MACDONALD. Alexander Macdonald. Was appointed cornet in the Land Transport Corps from sergeant, 2nd of February, 1856.

MACKENZIE. John Mackenzie. Joined on the 8th of August, 1854, and became sergeant 19th April, 1855; orderly room sergeant, 8th of October, 1858; paymaster-sergeant, 21st of February, 1870. Transferred to the Royal Perth Rifles on the 1st of July, 1875. Is now quarter-master-sergeant of the 3rd battalion Royal Highlanders. Served with the 79th throughout the Eastern campaign of 1854-55, including the siege and fall of Sebastopol and assaults of the 18th of June and the 8th of September. (Medal with clasp, and Turkish medal.) Also throughout the Indian Mutiny campaign of 1858-59, including the engagement at Secundragunge, siege and capture of Lucknow, actions of Rooyah, Allygunge, Bareilly, and Shahjehanpore, capture of Mahomdie, storming of Rampore Kussia, passage of the Gogra at Fyzabad, and subsequent operations in Oude, across the Gogra and Raptee rivers. (Thanked by Colonel Taylor, C.B., commanding the 79th, for conspicuous conduct at Lucknow. Medal with clasp.) Is in possession of the silver medal for long service and good conduct. Quarter-Master-Sergeant Mackenzie had the honour of being presented to Her Majesty the Queen at the ceremony of depositing the old colours of the 79th at Osborne House on the 22nd of April, 1873.

McCABE. John McCabe. Joined on the 14th of February, 1879, and became colour-sergeant 30th of April, 1885. Served with the regiment throughout the Egyptian campaign of 1882. (Medal and Khedive's star.) Also throughout the Nile expedition of 1884-85. (Clasp.) Served with the regiment throughout the operations of the Soudan Frontier Field Force in 1885-86. Was present in Kosheh during its investment, and at the engagement at Giniss.

McDAVID. George McDavid. Became pioneer-sergeant on the 1st of April, 1887. Served with the 91st Highlanders throughout the Zulu campaign of 1879 (medal and clasp), and with the Cameron Highlanders throughout the operations of the Soudan Frontier Field Force in 1885-86. Was present in Kosheh during its investment and at the engagement at Giniss. (Medal.)

McDonald. William Mcdonald. Joined on the 27th of October, 1876, and became pipe-major, 2nd of August, 1883. He served with the regiment throughout the Nile expedition of 1884-85 (medal with clasp) and throughout the operations of the Soudan Frontier Field Force in 1885-86. Was present in Kosheh during its investment and at the engagement at Giniss.

McIntosh. Masterton McIntosh. Joined the regiment from the Inverness Fencible Highlanders on the 1st of November, 1799. He accompanied the regiment to Egypt in 1801, and was present at the battle before Alexandria. He served with the 79th throughout the Peninsular war, being brought favourably to the notice of Lord Wellington for his bravery at the storming of Burgos. He served as sergeant-major of the regiment throughout the campaign of 1815, being present at the battles of Quatre Bras and Waterloo.

McIntosh. Donald McIntosh. Served with the 79th as a sergeant in the Peninsular war, and was promoted to a commission in the 88th regiment for his conspicuous bravery at the battle of Fuentes d'Onor.

McIntyre. Duncan McIntyre. Was appointed quarter-master in the Land Transport Corps from quarter-master-sergeant, 3rd of March, 1856.

McKenzie. Donald McKenzie. Served as a sergeant with the regiment in the Peninsula, and was recommended for a commission by Lord Wellington for his bravery at the storming of Burgos, where he was dangerously wounded.

McKenzie. John McKenzie. Served with the regiment in the Walcheren expedition in 1809. Served throughout the Peninsular war with the 79th, being present at the attack on Cadiz, battles of Busaco, Foz d'Aronce, Fuentes d'Onor, Salamanca, Pyrenees, Nivelle, Nive, and Toulouse. He was promoted to corporal for his bravery at the battle of the Pyrenees. He volunteered for the "Forlorn Hope" in the projected attack on the French position at Trocadero on the 16th of March, 1810. He again volunteered for the " Forlorn Hope " at the storming of Burgos, and was actually the first man to enter the horn-work, being lifted over the palisades by Sergeant Masterton McIntosh of the 79th. He served with the regiment throughout the campaign in Holland in 1815, being present at the battles of Quatre Bras and Waterloo. He received a bayonet wound through his left arm at the storming of Burgos, a bullet in his ancle at the battle of Toulouse, and at Waterloo he was bayoneted in the thigh and received a severe contusion on the right shoulder from a piece of a shell, which tore the wing off his jacket. He left the regiment in Canada.

McLAGGAN. Robert McLaggan. Joined on the 22nd of September, 1875, colour-sergeant, 20th of April, 1885; paymaster-sergeant, 10th of July, 1887. He served with the regiment throughout the Egyptian campaign of 1882, and was present at the battle of Tel-el-Kebir. (Medal with clasp and Khedive's star.) Also throughout the Nile expedition of 1884-85. (Clasp.) Served with the regiment throughout the operations of the Soudan Frontier Field Force in 1885-86, was present in Kosheh during its investment, and at the engagement at Giniss.

McLAREN. John McLaren. Colour-sergeant on the 9th of May, 1877. He served with the regiment throughout the Egyptian campaign of 1882, and was present at the battle of Tel-el-Kebir. (Mentioned in despatches, medal with clasp, and Khedive's star.) Also served throughout the Nile expedition of 1884-85. (Clasp.) Is in possession of the silver medal for long service and good conduct.

McMURRAY. Alexander McMurray. Joined on the 18th of February, 1876, and became drum-major, 12th of June, 1884. He served with the regiment in the Egyptian campaign of 1882, from the landing at Ismailia, and was present at the battle of Tel-el-Kebir. (Medal with clasp, and Khedive's star.) Also throughout the Nile expedition of 1884-85. (Clasp.) Served with the regiment throughout the operations of the Soudan Frontier Field Force in 1885-86, was present in Kosheh during its investment, and at the engagement at Giniss.

McNEIL. James McNeil. Joined on the 9th of February, 1875, and became colour-sergeant, 12th of July, 1882. He served with the regiment throughout the Egyptian campaign of 1882, and was present at the battle of Tel-el-Kebir. (Mentioned in despatches, medal with clasp and Khedive's star.) Also throughout the Nile expedition of 1884-85. (Clasp.) Served with the regiment throughout the operations of the Soudan Frontier Field Force in 1885-86, was present in Kosheh during its investment, at the reconnaissance on the 16th of December, and at the engagement at Giniss.

McPHERSON. Alexander McPherson. Joined on the 31st of July, 1840, and became sergeant, 31st of May, 1854. He served, attached to the light cavalry brigade, throughout the Eastern campaign of 1854-55, including the battles of Alma, Balaclava, Inkerman, and the siege and fall of Sebastopol. (Medal with four clasps and Turkish medal.) He served with the 79th throughout the Indian Mutiny campaign of 1858-59, including the engagement at Secundragunge, siege and capture of Lucknow, actions at Rooyah, Allygunge, Bareilly, and Shahjehanpore, capture of Mahomdie, storming of Rampore Kussia, passage of the Gogra at Fyzabad, and subsequent operations in Oude, across the Gogra and Raptee rivers. (Medal with clasp.) Discharged, 4th of October, 1864. Is in possession of the silver medal for long service and good conduct. Is now burgh officer for Paisley and sheriff officer for Renfrewshire.

MESSENGER. Henry C. Messenger. Appointed armourer-sergeant on the 3rd of July, 1882. Served with the regiment throughout the Nile expedition of 1884-85. (Medal and Clasp.) Also throughout the operations of the Soudan Frontier Field Force in charge of machine guns. Was present in Kosheh during its investment (slightly wounded) and at the engagement at Giniss.

MORTON. James Morton. Became colour-sergeant on the 7th of April, 1880. He served with the regiment throughout the Egyptian campaign of 1882, and was present at the battle of Tel-el-Kebir. (Medal with clasp and Khedive's star.) Also throughout the Nile expedition of 1884-85. (Clasp.) Served throughout the operations of the Soudan Frontier Field Force in 1885-86, was present in Kosheh during its investment, and at the engagement at Giniss.

NEWELL. John Newell. Became colour-sergeant on the 17th of March, 1874; afterwards quarter-master-sergeant, and now canteen steward, at the depôt at Inverness. He served with the regiment throughout the Egyptian campaign of 1882, and was present at the battle of Tel-el-Kebir. (Mentioned in despatches, medal with clasp, and Khedive's star.) Is in possession of the silver medal for long service and good conduct.

RANKIN. Robert Rankin. Joined on the 10th of March, 1854; colour-sergeant, 9th of May, 1863; sergeant-major, 16th of March, 1867. Died at Kamptee on the 17th of March, 1871. He served with the regiment throughout the Eastern campaign of 1854-55, including the battle of Balaclava, siege of Sebastopol, assaults of the 18th of June and the 8th of September, and expedition to Kertch and Yenikale. (Medal with two clasps and Turkish medal.) Also served with the 79th throughout the Indian Mutiny campaign of 1858-59, including the engagement at Secundragunge, siege and capture of Lucknow, actions of Rooyah, Allygunge, Bareilly, and Shahjehanpore, capture of Mahomdie, storming of Rampore Kussia, passage of the Gogra at Fyzabad, and subsequent operations in Oude, across the Gogra and Raptee rivers. (Medal with clasp.) Served in the North West Frontier campaign against the Mohmunds in 1863. (Entitled to a medal.)

ROBERTSON. John Robertson. Became master tailor on the 29th of October, 1876. Served with the regiment throughout the Egyptian campaign of 1882. (Medal and Khedive's star.)

Also throughout the Nile expedition of 1884-85. (Clasp.) Served with the regiment throughout the operations of the Soudan Frontier Field Force in 1885-86. Was present in Kosheh during its investment and at the engagement at Giniss.

Ross. William J. Ross. Joined on the 6th of April, 1874, and became colour-sergeant 15th of September, 1885. He served with the regiment throughout the Egyptian campaign of 1882, and was present at the battle of Tel-el-Kebir. (Medal with clasp and Khedive's star.) Served throughout the Nile expedition of 1884-85. (Clasp.) Also served with the regiment throughout the operations of the Soudan Frontier Field Force in 1885-86; was present in Kosheh during its investment, at the reconnaissance on the 16th of December, and at the engagement at Giniss.

Smith. Peter Smith. Joined on the 28th of June, 1854, and became colour-sergeant 12th of April, 1861. Served with the regiment during the Eastern campaign of 1855, and was present at the siege of Sebastopol, assaults of the 18th of June and the 8th of September, and the expedition to Kertch and Yenikale. (Medal with clasp, and Turkish medal.) Also served throughout the Indian campaign of 1858-59, including the engagement at Secundragunge, siege and capture of Lucknow, actions of Rooyah, Allygunge, Bareilly, and Shahjehanpore, capture of Mahomdie, storming of Rampore Kussia, and subsequent operations in Oude, across the Gogra and Raptee rivers. (Medal with clasp.) Is in possession of the silver medal for long service and good conduct. He was discharged on the 31st of August, 1875, and is now employed as an overseer at the Forth bridge works.

Sweeney. James Sweeney. Joined the regiment on the 2nd of November, 1869, and became paymaster-sergeant on the 9th of March, 1875; staff clerk, 6th of July, 1887. He served, attached to the Black Watch, throughout the Ashantee campaign of 1873, including the battle of Amoaful, capture and destruction of Becquah, battle of Ordahsu, and capture of Coomassie. (Medal with clasp.) Served with the Cameron Highlanders throughout the Egyptian campaign of 1882. (Medal and Khedive's star.) Served throughout the Nile expedition of 1884-85. (Clasp.) Also served with the regiment throughout the operations of the Soudan Frontier Field Force in 1885-86.

SYME. Stephen Syme. Joined the regiment on the 1st of September, 1877, from the 42nd Black Watch, and became sergeant on the 15th of May, 1883. Served with the Blach Watch throughout the Ashantee campaign of 1873, including the battle of Amoaful, capture and destruction of Becquah, battle of Ordahsu, and capture of Coomassie. (Medal and clasp.) He served with the Cameron Highlanders throughout the Egyptian campaign of 1882, and was present at the battle of Tel-el-Kebir. (Mentioned in despatches, appointed lance-sergeant for conspicuous gallantry, medal with clasp, and Khedive's star.) Served throughout the Nile expedition of 1884-85. (Clasp.) Also served with the regiment throughout the operations of the Soudan Frontier Field Force in 1885-86. Was present at Kosheh during its investment and at the engagement at Giniss.

TEMPLEMAN. Thomas Templeman. Joined in 1873; colour-sergeant, 1st of August, 1882. Is now quarter-master-sergeant at the depôt. He served with the regiment throughout the Egyptian campaign of 1882, and was present at the battle of Tel-el-Kebir. (Medal with clasp, and Khedive's star.)

APPENDIX.

Roll of officers, non-commissioned officers, and men who were killed in action or died of wounds or disease in Egypt and the Soudan, 1882-87.

Sergeant	William McPherson	Died at Ismailia
Private	Alexander Denniston	Killed at Tel-el-Kebir
,,	George Rugg	,, ,,
,,	John Hyslop	,, ,,
,,	William Simon	,, ,,
,,	George Crawford	,, ,,
,,	Patrick Kenny	,, ,,
,,	Thomas King	,, ,,
,,	Donald Cameron	,, ,,
,,	Robert Brown	,, ,,
,,	William Smith	,, ,,
,,	James Pollock	,, ,,
,,	Alexander Patterson	,, ,,
,,	William Bodel	,, ,,
Corporal	William Cattanach	Died of wounds
Private	David Murray	,, ,,
,,	Alexander Murray	,, ,,
,,	William McKenzie	,, ,,
,,	Duncan McLeod	Died at Cairo
,,	James Ireland	,, ,,
,,	William Semple	,, ,,
,,	David Urquhart	,, ,,
,,	David Thow	,, ,,
,,	Thomas McCabe	,, ,,
,,	John Reeves	,, ,,
,,	Michael Dodd	,, ,,

APPENDIX

Private	William Robertson	Died at Cairo
,,	Michael Naughton	Invalided; died on passage home
,,	William Brown	,, ,, ,
,,	James Wilson	Died at Cairo
Lance-Corporal	Robert Glen	,, ,,
Private	John Smith	Died of cholera
,,	James Cameron	, ,
,,	Thomas Dodds	,, ,,
,,	Michael Carrigan	,, ,,
,,	William Morrison	, ,,
,,	Hugh McKay	,, ,,
Pipe-Major	John Macgregor Grant	,, ,,
Private	John Grant	,, ,,
,,	Robert McRae	,, ,,
,,	John McLaggan	,, ,,
,,	James Bridge	Died at Cairo
,,	Charles Roberts	,, ,,
,,	William Gow	Invalided; died in England
,,	John Hamilton	,, ,, ,,
,,	Robert Mills	Died at Cairo
Corporal	Gregor Cattanach	Died at Assioot
Private	Donald McGillivray	Died at Alexandria
,,	Donald McKenzie	,, ,,
,,	William Hatch	Died at Korosko
Colour-Sergeant	Andrew McEwen Gray	,, ,,
,,	John Wells	,, ,,
Private	James Trimble	,, ,,
,,	Thomas Gollan	Died at Wady Halfa
,,	William Cawte	Died at Alexandria
,,	Thomas Farrington	Died of wounds
Lieutenant	William Gordon Cameron	,, ,,
Private	David McKenzie	,, ,,
,,	John Kennedy	Killed at Kosheh
,,	John McLaren	,, ,,
,,	David Hogg	,, ,,
Piper	Alexander McDonald	Died at Kosheh
Captain	Wedderburn Conway Halkett	Invalided; died in England
Private	Joseph Stevenson	Died of wounds
,,	Alexander McLeod	Died at Wady Halfa
,,	Alexander Addie	,, ,, ,,
,,	John McGregor	,, ,, ,,

APPENDIX.

Private	John Bennet	Died at Wady Halfa
Lance-Sergeant	Arthur Hartley	,, ,, ,,
Private	Charles Murray	,, ,, ,,
,,	William Davidson	,, ,, ,,
Drummer	Thomas Clelland	,, ,, ,,
Private	John Gagan	,, ,, ,,
,,	William Pridgeon	,, ,, ,,
,,	William Robinson	,, ,, ,,
,,	James McLeod	Drowned at Kostamneh, Upper Nile
,,	Henry Hall	Died at Assioot
,,	William Elliot	Killed by a fall from a train
,,	Hugh Craig	Died at Assouan
,,	James Slater	,, ,,
,,	James Kennedy	Died at Cairo
Lance-Corporal	Walter Smith	,, ,,
Sergeant	James Guthrie	,, ,,
Corporal	James Douglas	,, ,,
Private	Alexander Kelly	,, ,,
Boy	William Rolls	,, ,,
Private	James McCourt	,, ,,
,,	Peter Queen	Killed by a fall from a train at Boulac Dacroor
,,	William Maben	Died at Cairo.

A. H. SWISS, "BREMNER" PRINTING WORKS, FORE STREET, DEVONPORT.

www.ingramcontent.com/pod-product-compliance
Lightning Source LLC
Chambersburg PA
CBHW030746250426
43672CB00028B/800